Organizational Learning: Creating, Retaining and Transferring Knowledge

Organizational Learning: Creating, Retaining and Transferring Knowledge

by

Linda Argote

Graduate School of Industrial Administration
Carnegie Mellon University

Kluwer Academic Publishers
Boston/Dordrecht/London

Distributors for North, Central and South America:
Kluwer Academic Publishers
101 Philip Drive
Assinippi Park
Norwell, Massachusetts 02061 USA
Telephone (781) 871-6600
Fax (781) 871-6528
E-Mail <kluwer@wkap.com>

Distributors for all other countries:
Kluwer Academic Publishers Group
Distribution Centre
Post Office Box 322
3300 AH Dordrecht, THE NETHERLANDS
Telephone 31 78 6392 392
Fax 31 78 6546 474
E-Mail <orderdept@wkap.nl>

 Electronic Services <http://www.wkap.nl>

Library of Congress Cataloging-in-Publication Data

Argote, Linda.
  Organizational learning : creating, retaining, and transferring
  knowledge / by Linda Argote.
        p.   cm.
  Includes bibliographical references and index.
  ISBN 0-7923-8420-2
  1. Organizational learning. 2. Knowledge management. I. Title.
  HD58.82.A73   1999
    658.3'124--dc21   98-51375
                                                                  CIP

Printed on acid-free paper.

Printed in the United States of America

To Dennis and Stephen

Table of Contents

List of Figures

List of Tables

Preface

In the mid 1980s, my colleagues and I began working on the phenomenon of organizational learning curves. Several aspects of this phenomenon intrigued us. Through field work we were doing on another project, we had seen learning curve data from a firm that had several plants producing the same product. Although these plants produced the same product with similar technology, the plants had very different rates of learning. This struck us as a very interesting phenomenon. We wanted to learn more about factors explaining differences in learning rates observed across organizations. Thus, we began a research program with the overarching question: Why do some organizations learn at faster rates than others?

Another learning issue that intrigued us was organizational "forgetting." The classic learning curve assumes that knowledge is cumulative—that once an organization acquires knowledge, it persists indefinitely through time. There is, of course, considerable evidence that individuals exhibit forgetting. There was little work, however, examining whether organizations exhibited "forgetting" as well. Organizations have structures, routines and information systems that arguably serve to capture knowledge. But organizations also have features, such as member turnover, that may make it hard to retain knowledge. So it struck us as a very interesting empirical question to examine whether forgetting happened in organizations and the conditions under which it occurred.

The third major issue that excited us about organizational learning was the possibility of transferring knowledge within and across organizations. Could productivity gains acquired in one part of an organization be transferred to another so that the second unit benefited from knowledge acquired at the first? Organizations often have multiple establishments producing the same product or delivering the same service. For example, a manufacturing firm might have several plants producing the same product, a bank might have many branches delivering the same services, and a fast food franchise might have many stores providing the same menu of products. The potential for these organizations to transfer productivity gains made in one establishment to the others so that all could benefit is tremendous. My colleagues and I began a research program that examined whether knowledge transferred within and between organizations.

We have conducted this research in different production settings— for example, organizations that produce aircraft, trucks and pizza. Thus, this monograph is mainly about organizations that make things. Making things, of course, also requires generating ideas and creating knowledge. The results reported here, however, are likely to be especially relevant for organizations that produce a physical product.

The goal of this monograph is to describe and integrate the results of our research and the research of other scholars on factors explaining organizational learning curves and the persistence and transfer of productivity gains acquired through experience. The monograph is organized in six chapters.

Chapter One provides an overview of research on organizational learning curves. This chapter presents the basic framework for analyzing learning-curve data. The chapter argues that although the characteristic learning-curve pattern has been found in many organizations, there is incredible variation in the rate at which organizations learn. The chapter sets the stage for subsequent chapters that examine factors contributing to the variation observed in organizational learning rates.

Chapter Two introduces the concept of organizational "forgetting" or knowledge depreciation. Our method for assessing knowledge depreciation is presented. Results from our first study of knowledge depreciation are described in depth to illustrate how knowledge depreciation might be analyzed. Results of subsequent work on knowledge depreciation are summarized. Sources of depreciation are discussed and depreciation rates in different settings are compared and contrasted.

Chapter Three discusses the concept of organizational memory. The chapter begins with a discussion of where productivity gains associated with experience are typically embedded in organizations. This discussion is then related to theoretical discussions of organizational memory and "repositories" of organizational knowledge. Empirical evidence on the extent to which knowledge is embedded in various repositories is presented. The implications of where knowledge is embedded for its persistence and transfer are discussed.

Chapter Four argues that analyzing small groups provides understanding at a micro level of the social processes through which organizations create and combine knowledge. The chapter presents evidence on the conditions under which group members will share information they already possess as well as the conditions under which new or emergent knowledge will develop through group interaction. The chapter also describes how group members weight and combine information to arrive at a collective product.

Chapter Five describes results on knowledge transfer. The chapter describes how we assess the extent of knowledge transfer and presents the results of one of our studies in depth to illustrate the approach. The results of other studies of knowledge transfer are summarized and integrated to develop the conditions under which knowledge transfers in organizations. The chapter argues that transferring knowledge from other organizations is a powerful mechanism for improving an organization's productivity and increasing its survival prospects.

Chapter Six discusses various tensions and trade-offs in the organizational learning process. The chapter develops the implications of results presented in the volume for managing firm performance. Future directions that are likely to be particularly fruitful for research are described.

Many colleagues collaborated in the work described here. I owe tremendous thanks to these individuals who taught me a great deal: Sara Beckman, Eric Darr, Dennis Epple, Deborah Gruenfeld, Chet Insko, Dick Moreland, Ken Murphy, Joe McGrath, Charles Naquin, Rukmini Devadas Rao, Anna Romero, Diane Liang Rulke, and Nancy Yovetich. I hope that this monograph adequately reflects their many important contributions.

Several institutions provided the intellectual environment to conduct the research reported here. Much of the work was carried out at the Graduate School of Industrial Administration (GSIA) at Carnegie Mellon University. I have benefited greatly from interactions with colleagues there and in the Groups and Organizations network at Carnegie Mellon University and the University of Pittsburgh. GSIA supported my introduction of a course in Organizational Learning in 1989. I have learned much from the students in my Organizational Learning course.

The work began during a year that I was a visiting faculty member at Stanford University's Department of Industrial Engineering and Engineering Management under the auspices of the National Science Foundation's Visiting Professorship for Women program. I was fortunate to interact with many scholars at Stanford, especially Jim Jucker, Jim March and Bob Sutton, from whom I learned a great deal. And I have benefited greatly from my interactions with faculty and students at the Kellogg Graduate School of Management at Northwestern University, where I was also fortunate to teach a course on organizational learning.

Thanks are due to the agencies that provided funding for this research. The National Science Foundation (Grants Number 9009930 and 8808711) and the Center for the Management of Technology and

Information in Organizations and the Carnegie Bosch Institute for Applied Studies in International Management, both at Carnegie Mellon University, funded portions of work described here. Thanks are also due to the organizations that allowed us to study and learn from them. We greatly appreciate the time members of these organizations gave us and the data they provided us. We benefited greatly from our interactions with these organizations.

Special thanks are due to the colleagues who commented on drafts of chapters: Kathleen Carley, Dennis Epple, Paul Ingram, John Levine, Bill McEvily, Dick Moreland, Ron Ophir, Ray Reagans, Peter Roberts, and Kristin Wintersteen. Thanks are also due to Karen DeCamp, Bonnie Schultz, and especially Donna Erdner, for typing and preparing the manuscript as well as providing encouragement along the way. I would also like to thank my editors at Kluwer, Julie Kaczynski and Zachary Rolnik, for their support. This monograph is dedicated to my family, Dennis and Stephen, from whom I continue to learn.

Chapter 1

Organizational Learning Curves: An Overview

1.1 Introduction

"Learning curves" have been found in many organizations. As organizations produce more of a product, the unit cost of production typically decreases at a decreasing rate. A learning curve for the production of an advanced military jet built in the 1970s and 1980s is shown in Figure 1.1. The number of direct labor hours required to assemble each jet aircraft is plotted on the vertical axis; the cumulative number of aircraft produced is plotted on the horizontal axis. As can be seen from Figure 1.1, the number of direct labor hours required to assemble each aircraft decreased significantly as experience was gained in production, and the rate of decrease declined with rising cumulative output. This and related phenomena are referred to as learning curves, progress curves, experience curves, or learning by doing.

This learning-curve pattern has been found in many organizations. Figure 1.2 shows a learning curve for a truck assembly plant. The number of direct labor hours required to assemble each vehicle is plotted on the vertical axis; the cumulative number of trucks produced is plotted on the horizontal axis. Figure 1.2 depicts the classic learning-curve pattern: the number of labor hours required to assemble each vehicle decreased at a decreasing rate as experience was gained in production.

The unit cost of producing discrete products such as aircraft (Alchian, 1963; Asher, 1956; Wright, 1936), ships (Rapping, 1965), trucks (Epple, Argote & Murphy, 1996), and semiconductors (Gruber, 1994) have all been shown to follow a learning curve. The production of continuous products such as refined petroleum (Hirschmann, 1964) and chemicals (Lieberman, 1984) have also been found to exhibit learning. Additionally, learning curves have been found to characterize a wide range of outcomes in very different settings, including success rates of new surgical procedures (Kelsey, Mullin, Detre, Mitchell, Cowley, Gruentzig & Kent, 1984), nuclear plant operating reliability (Joskow & Rozanski, 1979), and productivity in kibbutz farming (Barkai & Levhari, 1973) and pizza production (Darr, Argote & Epple, 1995).

The productivity gains derived from organizational learning are significant. For example, during the first year of production of Liberty Ships during World War II, the average number of labor hours required to produce a ship decreased by 45%, and the average time it took to build a ship decreased by 75% (Searle & Gody, 1945). During the first year of operation of a truck assembly plant, the plant's productivity grew by approximately 190% (Epple, Argote & Devadas, 1991).

Figure 1.1
The Relationship Between Assembly Hours Per Aircraft
and Cumulative Output

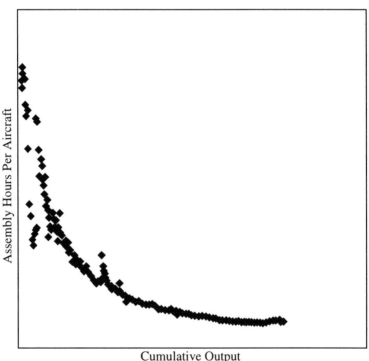

Cumulative Output

Note. Reprinted with permission from L. Argote and D. Epple, Learning curves in manufacturing, *Science*, Volume *247*, Number 4945, (February, 1990). Copyright 1990, American Association for the Advancement of Science. Units omitted to protect confidentiality of data.

Although the learning-curve pattern has been found in many organizations, organizations vary considerably in the rates at which they learn (Argote & Epple, 1990; Dutton & Thomas, 1984; Hayes & Clark, 1986). Some organizations evidence extraordinary rates of productivity growth with experience; others fail to exhibit productivity gains from learning. Understanding the contrast between organizations that evidence little or no productivity growth with experience and those that show remarkable rates of learning is an important undertaking. For organizations to compete effectively, we need to understand why some organizations show

Figure 1.2
The Relationship Between Labor Hours Per Vehicle
and Cumulative Output

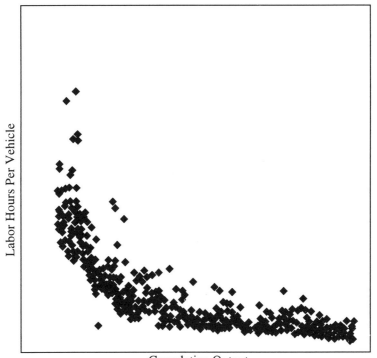

Cumulative Output

Note. Reprinted by permission from L. Argote, D. Epple and K. Murphy, An empirical investigation of the micro structure of knowledge acquisition and transfer through learning by doing, *Operations Research: Special Issue on New Directions in Manufacturing*, Volume *44*, Number 1, (January-February, 1996). Copyright 1996, The Institute of Operations Research and the Management Sciences (INFORMS), 2 Charles Street, Suite 300, Providence, RI 02904 USA. Units omitted to protect confidentiality of data.

rapid rates of learning and others fail to learn. A greater understanding of factors responsible for the variation observed in organizational learning rates is needed.

Many researchers have emphasized the importance of understanding the variation observed in organizational learning rates. Dutton and Thomas (1984), Lieberman (1984), and Lucas (1993) concluded that the dynamics underlying the learning curve need to be understood better. Similarly, Yelle (1979) indicated that a better understanding of the contributions of various factors to learning curves is needed. This monograph aims to advance knowledge about factors explaining the variation observed in organizational learning curves—to explain why some organizations are better at learning than others.

This chapter began with a discussion of the classic learning curve. It continues with a brief historical overview of the phenomenon, and recent trends in research are noted. How organizational knowledge is typically measured in the learning-curve framework is described and how learning is assessed is discussed. The chapter then presents evidence that learning rates vary tremendously across organizations. Empirical studies that assess the contribution of various factors to organizational learning curves are described. Theoretical models that aim to explain the variation observed in learning rates are presented. The chapter concludes with a discussion of learning-curve applications aimed at improving firm performance.

1.2 Historical Overview

Psychologists were the first to discover learning curves. These researchers focused on the behavior of individuals. Psychologists found that the time individuals took to perform a task and the number of errors they made decreased at a decreasing rate as experience was gained with the task (Ebbinghaus, 1885/1964; Thorndike, 1898). For example, Thurstone (1919) found that the learning-curve pattern shown in Figure 1.1 characterized the performance of students as they progressed through a typing course.

Mazur and Hastie (1978) provided a review of research on learning curves at the individual level of analysis. Researchers working in the individual psychological tradition often fit their data to an exponential rather than a power function, as is customary in organizational learning-curve analysis. There is evidence, however, that power functions may fit individual learning data better than exponential functions (Newell & Rosenbloom, 1981). Further, Delaney, Reder, Staszewski and Ritter (1998) found that the fit of power functions could be improved by plotting learning curves separately for each problem-solving strategy individuals used. When estimating learning-curve data, one should be sensitive to the choice of the appropriate functional form. Issues that arise in estimating learning rates are discussed later in this chapter and in Chapter 2.

Additionally, learning curves have been found at the group level of analysis. For example, in their studies of the effects of various communication networks on the performance of groups, Guetzkow and Simon (1955) and Leavitt (1951) found that the errors made by groups and the time groups took to complete tasks decreased at a decreasing rate as groups gained experience. Similarly, in their analysis of the effect of planning on group performance, Shure, Rogers, Larsen and Tassone (1962) found that group performance followed a learning curve.

Learning curves have also been found at the organizational (e.g., Wright, 1936) and industry levels of analysis (e.g., Sheshinski, 1967). Some researchers distinguish among learning curves, progress curves, and experience curves as a function of the level of analysis. According to Dutton and Thomas (1984), the term "learning curve" is frequently used to describe labor learning at the level of an individual employee or a production process. The term "progress curve" is often used to describe learning at the level of the firm. Experience curves are used to describe learning at the level of an industry. These distinctions, however, are not made universally in the literature. I use the term learning curve to encompass these related phenomena and specify the level of analysis of the phenomenon.

The focus of this monograph is on learning at the organizational (or organizational subunit) level of analysis. Relevant work at the group and at the interorganizational levels of analysis will be incorporated when it has implications for learning at the level of the organization. Research on group learning provides some of the micro underpinnings of organizational learning. These micro underpinnings of organizational learning are developed in Chapter 4. Research on interorganizational or population-level learning (Miner & Haunschild, 1995) provides the macro context in which organizational learning takes place and also has implications for how one organization learns from another. The implications of interorganizational learning for organizational learning and productivity are discussed in Chapter 5. Interesting tensions or trade-offs that emerge across learning at different levels of analysis are developed in Chapter 6.

An influential early documentation of a learning curve at the organizational level of analysis was published by Wright in 1936. Wright (1936) reported that the amount of labor it took to build an aircraft decreased at a decreasing rate as the total number of aircraft produced, cumulative output, increased. Dutton, Thomas and Butler (1984) noted that Rohrbach had reported that the same pattern characterized the production of aircraft in Germany in the 1920s. Alchian (1963) found that the learning-curve pattern characterized the production of a variety of aircraft.

Many studies were conducted after the publication of Wright's classic paper that investigated whether the learning-curve pattern characterized the manufacture of other products as well. Dutton, Thomas and Butler (1984) provided an excellent review and interpretation of research on organizational learning curves through the mid 1980s (see also Dutton & Thomas, 1984; and Yelle, 1979). A few of the particularly important early studies on learning are highlighted here.

One early study compared rates of learning in different types of production work. Hirsch (1952) found that improvements in unit labor costs associated with cumulative output were greater in assembly than in machining work. Hirsch's finding has been interpreted as providing evidence that learning curves are steeper in labor-intensive than in machine-intensive industries. This finding has received mixed support in subsequent studies (cf. Adler & Clark, 1991). In a similar vein, Baloff (1966, 1971) found that the tendency for learning curves to "plateau" or level off was greater in machine-intensive than in labor-intensive industries.

Although early work on learning curves focused on industries that manufactured discrete products such as planes, trains and automobiles, learning curves have also been found in continuous process industries. For example, Hirschmann (1964) found that petroleum refining followed a learning curve. His finding has important implications because it suggests that learning curves are not due solely to "labor learning" since labor played a relatively minor role in these settings but rather depend on modifications in the organization and its technology as well (see also Baloff, 1966). Dutton, Thomas and Butler (1984) described how these findings on the presence of learning curves in continuous process industries were important in contradicting the prevailing and misguided view that learning curves could be explained mainly by learning on the part of direct production workers.

Productivity, of course, has been found to depend on other factors besides cumulative output. For example, Preston and Keachie (1964) found that unit labor costs depended on the rate of output as well as on the amount of cumulative output. An organization that tries to increase its rate of production dramatically may experience productivity problems independent of learning that are reflected in high unit costs. Preston and Keachie's (1964) work showed the importance of including changes in the rate of output as well as cumulative output in assessing learning rates.

Similarly, Rapping (1965) demonstrated the importance of controlling for additional factors such as economies of scale in assessing learning rates. Rapping (1965) showed that the production of Liberty Ships during World War II followed a learning-curve pattern when inputs of labor and capital were taken into account in the analysis. Although the effects of labor and capital were significant, the effect of cumulative output remained highly significant when these additional factors were included in models of productivity. Thus, Rapping (1965) demonstrated very convincingly that productivity gains associated with cumulative output were not due to increased inputs of labor or capital or to increasing exploitation of economies of scale. Although these factors were important, evidence of learning remained strong when they were taken into account.

Much of the work on organizational learning curves between the publication of Wright's influential piece in the 1930s and the early 1980s focused on studying the phenomenon in different industries. Research during this period also focused on specifying the functional form of the relationship between the unit cost of production and cumulative output (Yelle, 1979). Although attempts were made to identify factors underlying the learning curve, empirical evidence on the importance of various factors was very limited (Dutton & Thomas, 1984).

1.3 Recent Research Trends

1.3.1 Expanded Set of Outcomes

Several important new trends have occurred in research on organizational learning curves in the 1980s and 1990s. First, researchers are expanding the set of outcome measures used as indicators of organizational performance. Research conducted before the 1980s had shown that outcomes in addition to the number of direct labor hours per unit followed a learning curve (e.g., see Greenberg, 1971; Preston & Keachie, 1964). Recent research further expands the set of outcome measures examined as a function of experience. For example, in our research, we have examined the outcome measures of quality, as measured by complaints or defects per unit (Argote, 1993), and service timeliness, as measured by the number of "late" products per unit (Argote & Darr, in press) as outcome variables. Baum and Ingram (1998) focused on the outcome of organizational survival and analyzed how organizations' survival prospects were affected by experience.

A couple of figures illustrate the wide range of outcomes that have been found to follow a learning curve. Figure 1.3 shows an example of a learning curve for quality. The figure is based on data from the production of the same advanced jet aircraft discussed earlier. Figure 1.3 plots the number of complaints made to quality assurance per aircraft as a function of cumulative output. These complaints, which are made internally to the firm, identify problems that are to be corrected before the product is shipped. As Figure 1.3 indicates, the number of quality complaints made per aircraft decreased at a decreasing rate as the organization gained experience in production. Thus, experience in production was associated with improvements in quality.

      Figure 1.4 shows an example of a learning curve for service timeliness for a very different production process—pizza production. The figure is based on one and a half years of data from a pizza store. The cumulative number of pizzas produced is plotted on the horizontal axis; the number of "late" pizzas per unit is plotted on the vertical axis. The

Figure 1.3
The Relationship Between Number of Complaints
About Quality Per Aircraft and Cumulative Output

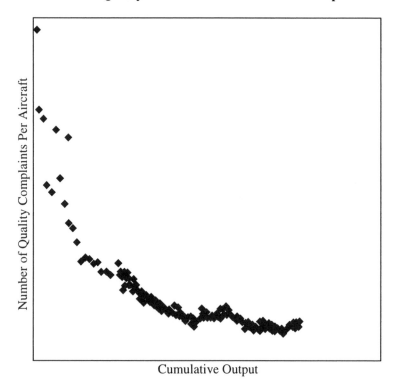

Cumulative Output

Note. Reprinted with permission from L. Argote, Group and organizational learning curves: Individual, system and , environmental components, *British Journal of Social Psychology: Special Issue on Social Processes in Small Groups*, Volume *32*, (March, 1993). Copyright 1993. Units omitted to protect confidentiality of data.

corporation's metric for assessing whether a pizza was late was adopted: if the number of minutes that elapsed from when an order was received to when the pizza was completely prepared exceeded a prespecified limit, then the pizza was coded as late. Figure 1.4 depicts the classic learning-curve pattern: the number of late pizzas per unit decreased at a decreasing rate as experience was gained in production.

Figure 1.4
The Relationship Between Proportion of Late Pizzas
and Cumulative Output

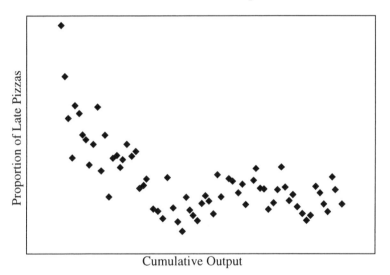

Note: Units omitted to protect confidentiality of data.

1.3.2 Understanding Productivity Differences

Another trend in recent research on organizational learning curves is a resurgence of interest in identifying factors explaining the variation observed in organizational learning rates (e.g., see Adler & Clark, 1991; Argote, Beckman & Epple, 1990; Bahk & Gort, 1993; Hayes & Clark, 1986; Ingram & Baum, 1997; Lester & McCabe, 1993; Lieberman, 1984). This work focuses on understanding why some organizations are more productive than others. Research on these productivity differences was stimulated by both practical and theoretical concerns. On the practical side, many manufacturing organizations in the United States in the 1980s experienced enormous productivity problems (Minabe, 1986). While the U.S. had once enjoyed a very large productivity advantage relative to other industrial countries, the productivity of firms in other countries caught up with and even surpassed U.S. productivity in many sectors during this period (Krugman, 1991). Understanding sources of productivity differences became a central concern.

On the theoretical side, many scholars at this time were shifting to the view that interesting performance variation occurred at the firm rather than the industry level. Resource-based and evolutionary views of the firm were gaining momentum in the fields of strategy and organizational theory (Barney, 1991; Henderson & Cockburn, 1994; Lippman & Rumelt, 1982; Montgomery, 1995; Nelson, 1991; Prahalad & Hamel, 1990; Teece, 1998; Winter, 1995). These theoretical perspectives emphasize differences across firms and aim to understand the source of the differences. Thus, research identifying factors contributing to organizational learning curves occurred against a backdrop of intense concern about productivity problems and a theoretical shift to the firm as a fundamentally important unit of analysis.

1.3.3 Organizational Forgetting

A third important new trend in research on organizational learning curves is examining the dynamics of knowledge acquisition (and loss) by firms. Research in this area examines whether organizational knowledge is cumulative and persists through time or whether it decays or depreciates (e.g., Argote, Beckman & Epple, 1990; Benkard, 1997). This stream of research occurred amidst the same currents discussed previously as motivating work on organizational productivity since differences in the ability to retain knowledge can contribute to productivity differences across organizations. Research on the dynamics of knowledge acquisition and retention also occurred against a backdrop of increased interest on the part of many scholars in applying cognitive principles to understand organizational phenomena (Walsh, 1995). Developments in computing and information systems (Stein & Zwass, 1995) also stimulated and were stimulated by work on organizational knowledge acquisition and retention since a potential benefit of these systems is their enhanced capacity for capturing and retaining knowledge.

1.3.4 Knowledge Transfer

The area of research on organizational learning curves that has exploded in recent years is work on the transfer of knowledge across organizations (e.g.,

Argote, Beckman & Epple, 1990; Baum & Ingram, 1998; Darr, Argote & Epple, 1995; Haunschild and Miner, 1997; Henderson & Cockburn, 1996; Powell, Koput & Smith-Doerr, 1996; Szulanski, 1996; Zander & Kogut, 1995). This research examines whether productivity gains acquired in one organization (or unit of an organization) transfer to another. That is, the research examines whether organizations learn from the experience of other organizations—whether one organization benefits from knowledge acquired at another. For example, research might examine whether one shift learns from another at a manufacturing plant (Epple, Argote & Murphy, 1996), whether one hotel learns from others in its chain (Baum & Ingram, 1998), or whether one biotechnology firm learns from others linked to it through a Research and Development (R&D) alliance (Powell, Koput & Smith-Doerr, 1996).

Research on knowledge transfer was shaped in part by the same concerns about productivity that shaped the trends noted previously. An organization that is able to transfer successfully a productivity improvement made at one establishment to another will be more productive than its counterparts who are ineffective at knowledge transfer. Advances in computing and in information systems also stimulated and were stimulated by interest in knowledge transfer since these systems have the potential for facilitating knowledge transfer across geographically distributed sites (e.g., Goodman & Darr, 1996).

In addition, interest in knowledge transfer was stimulated by a shift in the mode of organizing used at many firms from large integrated facilities to small, distributed sites (Galbraith, 1990). This shift enables firms to take better advantage of differences in expertise, labor costs and demand for their product around the world. For example, rather than have all product-development activities occur at one centralized site, an organization might have small teams with expertise in aspects of product development distributed around the world. Similarly, aspects of manufacturing are becoming separate and distributed rather than concentrated at one site ("Survey of manufacturing," 1998). More manufacturing is being done by multinational companies that are able to capitalize on differences in capabilities around the world. Blumenstein (1997) described how General Motors (GM) is taking advantage of such distributed expertise. Blumenstein quoted Basil Drossos, President and Managing Director of GM Argentina, as saying: "We are talking about becoming a global corporation as opposed to a multinational company; that implies that the centers of expertise may reside anywhere the best reside" (Blumstein, 1997, p. A4). Effective operation requires that this distributed expertise be coordinated—that knowledge be transferred from one expert to another and from one site to another. Thus, the successful use of this organizational form requires the ongoing transfer of knowledge.

Increased interest in organizational learning curves occurred in the context of increased interest in the more general topic of organizational learning. Many theoretical pieces have been written on the topic (see Huber, 1991, for a review). The amount of empirical work is increasing rapidly (Miner & Mezias, 1996). Numerous books and articles have appeared in the business and popular press (Garvin, 1993; Senge, 1990).

Figure 1.5
The Relationship Between Logarithm of Labor Hours Per Vehicle
and Logarithm of Cumulative Output

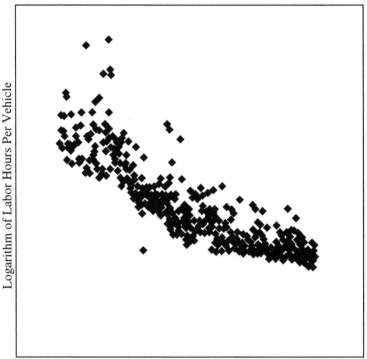

Logarithm of Cumulative Output

Research on factors affecting organizational learning curves and the persistence and transfer of productivity gains from learning has occurred in the context of increased interest in the general topic of organizational learning.

Agreement has not emerged about exactly what is meant by the concept of organizational learning.   In my view, the concept of organizational learning is likely to remain an "umbrella" concept for many related concepts (see also Easterby-Smith, 1997).   What is critical for advancing our understanding of organizational learning issues is for researchers and practitioners to be precise about the approaches they take and to develop the theoretical and practical implications that can be derived from those approaches.

This monograph aims to present and integrate research on these new trends in research on organizational learning curves.   This chapter summarizes empirical work directly aimed at assessing the contribution of particular factors to organizational learning curves. Chapter 2 describes and integrates work on the dynamics of knowledge acquisition and loss in organizations. Chapter 3 discusses organizational memory and develops the implication of where knowledge resides for organizational performance. Chapter 4 discusses the micro underpinnings of organizational learning, with particular attention to factors promoting the acquisition or creation of knowledge by groups. Research on knowledge transfer in organizations is presented in Chapter 5.   Theoretical and managerial implications of the work are developed in Chapter 6. Before these new research findings are presented, an explanation of how knowledge is measured and how learning is assessed in the learning-curve framework is required. The next section addresses these issues.

1.4 Measuring Knowledge and Assessing Learning

The classic form of an organizational learning curve is:

$$y_i = ax_i^{-b} \qquad\qquad (1.1)$$

where

y = the number of labor hours required to produce the ith unit
a = the number of labor hours required to produce the first unit
x = the cumulative number of units produced through time period i
b = the learning rate
i = a time subscript

Researchers have found that other outcomes such as defects per unit (see Figure 1.2) or accidents per unit (Greenberg, 1971) follow a learning-curve pattern. Thus, y in Equation (1.1) may represent a range of outcomes associated with the production of the xth unit.

For estimation purposes, Equation (1.1) can be rewritten in logarithmic form:

$$\ln y_i = c - b \ln x_i \qquad\qquad (1.2)$$

When converted to logarithmic scales, relationships in the form of the power function shown in Equation (1.1) become a straight line. Figure 1.5 plots the same data shown in Figure 1.2 using logarithmic (log-log) scales. That is, Figure 1.5 expresses the logarithm of direct labor hours per vehicle as a function of the logarithm of the cumulative number of vehicles produced. As can be seen from Figure 1.5, when plotted on logarithmic scales, the data more closely resemble a straight line. Analytic techniques for dealing with any curvature remaining in the data after it is converted to logarithmic scales are described later in this chapter.

The standard measure of organizational experience in the learning curve formulation is the cumulative number of units produced. This measure is computed by summing the total number of units of output produced from the start of production through the end of each time period. The cumulative number of units produced is a proxy variable for knowledge acquired through production. If unit costs change as a function of this knowledge, other variables being equal, we infer that learning has occurred. That is, if the coefficient of the cumulative output variable is significant when Equation (1.2) is estimated with appropriate control variables, organizational learning is said to occur. Thus, the basic principle underlying the learning curve is that production experience creates knowledge that improves productivity (Arrow, 1962).

Knowledge is a difficult concept to measure (Barsalou, 1992). A significant component of the knowledge acquired as organizations gain experience is tacit and difficult to assess directly (Nonaka, 1991; Polanyi, 1966). Further, the scale of many organizations and the uneven distribution of member knowledge makes it difficult to assess knowledge. For example, in a large manufacturing plant with thousands of employees it is virtually impossible to chart all the knowledge that is acquired as organizations gain experience in production. The learning-curve framework uses the cumulative number of units produced as a proxy variable for this knowledge acquired through experience.

A few studies have tried to measure the knowledge organizations acquire as they gain experience more directly. Although these studies provide only a partial picture of knowledge acquisition, they provide useful information about the content of what is being learned with experience. Many of these studies have focused at the group level rather than the organizational level of analysis and hence are discussed in Chapter 4 on the micro underpinnings of organizational learning.

Debate has occurred among researchers about whether the cumulative number of units produced at an organization is better than calendar time as a measure of experience. The cumulative output measure reflects experience at a particular organization (or unit of an organization). For example, as organizations acquire experience, members might learn who is good at what, how to structure their work better, or how to improve the layout of the production area. By contrast, the calendar time measure reflects general technological improvements in the external environment (Solow, 1957). For example, as time passes, properties of materials may improve or computing power may increase. These improvements in the general environment could translate into a reduction in a firm's unit costs. Further, these improvements may be correlated with cumulative output. Thus, it is important to control for the passage of time in analyzing learning rates. This will enable one to determine the extent to which productivity gains are due to technological improvements in the larger environment versus experience at the particular organization.

Studies of organizational learning that have included both calendar time and cumulative output as predictors of unit costs generally find that cumulative output is a better predictor of an organization's unit costs than time is (e.g., see Darr, Argote & Epple, 1995; Lieberman, 1984; Rapping, 1965). For example, Lieberman (1984) and Rapping (1965) found that time was not significant but cumulative output was when both variables were included as predictors of organizational performance. In one of our studies, we found that productivity increased significantly with the passage of time—and with increases in cumulative output (Argote, Epple, Rao & Murphy, 1997). That is, when both variables were included in the productivity models, both were significant. The magnitude of the effect of the cumulative output variable, however, was greater than the effect of calendar time. Thus, it is important to account for the passage of time since it can have a significant effect on productivity. For organizations that produce things with some degree of repetition, cumulative output is generally a more powerful predictor of productivity than simply the passage of time (see also Lieberman, 1987).

Debate has also occurred about whether organizational learning should be defined in terms of changes in knowledge or changes in behavior. This discussion is reminiscent of an earlier discussion in the psychological literature about individual learning. Certain individual learning researchers defined learning as changes in individual behavior that occurred as a result of experience (e.g., see Hilgard & Bower, 1975). Acknowledging that individuals may acquire knowledge that does not manifest itself directly in changes in behavior, other researchers defined individual learning in terms of changes in "behavior potentiality" that occurred as a result of experience (e.g., see Houston, 1986; Kimble, 1961). Still other researchers of individual learning defined learning as a change in either behavior or knowledge brought about by practice or experience (e.g., see Wingfield, 1979).

At the organizational level of analysis, Duncan and Weiss (1979) and Fiol and Lyles (1985) defined learning in terms of changes in knowledge. Huber (1991) took an approach to defining organizational learning similar to the approach Houston (1986) and Kimble (1961) used at the individual level of analysis. Huber (1991) defined organizational learning in terms of changes in the "range of potential behavior."

The organizational learning curve approach does not assume that behavior changes as a result of experience but rather examines empirically whether such behavioral change occurs as organizations acquire experience. Thus, by examining the coefficient on the cumulative output variable in Equation (1.2), one infers whether learning has occurred. If the cumulative output coefficient is significant, learning has occurred—productivity has changed as a result of experience. A positive coefficient on the cumulative output variable suggests that learning is adaptive for the organization since experience improves performance, whereas a negative coefficient suggests that learning is maladaptive since experience impairs performance. Thus, the learning curve approach allows one to assess empirically whether organizational behavior has changed as a function of experience.

Part of the success of the approach of examining the relationship between cumulative output and the unit cost of production to assess whether organizational learning has occurred hinges on one's ability to control for other factors besides cumulative output that may affect productivity. As noted previously, other factors in addition to experience have been shown to affect the rate of productivity gains in firms. For example, Rapping (1965) showed that economies of scale contributed to the productivity gains observed in the Liberty ship production program. It is important to control for these additional factors that affect productivity since failure to do so may lead to erroneous estimates of the rate at which organizations learn.

The production function[1] approach allows one to control for factors in addition to organizational experience that may affect production. For example, if economies of scale are present, as they were in the Liberty Ship production program, such that a given increase in inputs results in a more than proportionate increase in output and if the scale of operation is increased over time, productivity will rise over time because of increasing exploitation of economies of scale. If one estimates the rate of learning without controlling for the changing scale of operation, this increasing exploitation of scale economies will result in an overestimate of the amount of learning. Womer (1979) argued for the importance of integrating estimation of learning with production function estimation as a vehicle for controlling for the effects of factors other than cumulative output on productivity.

Issues that must be addressed in using a production function approach to estimating learning rates are discussed in Argote and Epple (1990). These issues include selection of functional form, choice of variables in the model, specification of the properties of factors affecting the production process, and choice of an appropriate method of estimation. An important issue that arises in estimating learning rates is choosing a flexible enough functional form to accommodate a leveling off or slowing down of the rate of learning. Even when learning curves are expressed in logarithmic form, as in Figure 1.5, there may be a slowing down of the rate of learning over time. The possibility of this leveling off or "plateau" effect is documented in Baloff (1966, 1971) and Conway and Schultz (1959). Including a quadratic function of the knowledge variable and evaluating it at values less than the value at which the function reaches a minimum can approximate a function with a positive asymptote. Thus, including a squared term for the experience variable allows for the possibility that the rate of learning plateaus or levels off.

It is also important to correct for problems that may arise if data are collected on a per period basis when several periods are required to produce each unit (Womer, 1984). For example, it may take more than one month to build a ship or assemble a plane. If it takes more than one time period to build a product, it is important to deal with this in the analysis by using measures of the fraction of product produced each time period. For example, Rapping (1965) measured the monthly productivity of shipyards by the tonnage of ships produced per month. Tonnage produced per month is the weight of all ships or portions of ships produced during a month. Thus, Rapping's measurement approach captured all the output, including fractions of ships, produced each time period.

The choice of variables to be included in the model is another issue that must be addressed. The choice of variables varies according to the production process being studied. For example, in a single plant with unchanging physical facilities, labor hours may be the only input that varies over time. Thus, in estimating productivity, one would need to include measures of labor hours but not measures of physical facilities, since these do not change. In studying multiple plants, however, it is important to include measures of capital investment and other inputs that differ across plants. Such measures would also be needed if the facilities in a given plant change over time.

When production occurs at several plants, additional variables such as cumulative output aggregated across plants may be included in addition to a plant's own cumulative output to assess whether plants benefit from the experience of other plants. This phenomenon, the transfer of knowledge across organizations, will be discussed more fully in Chapter 5. If the plant has the potential to benefit from improvements in technical knowledge in the larger environment such as developments in materials or computing power, proxies for the pace of such improvements should be included. As noted previously, one such proxy is calendar time (Solow, 1957).

It may also be necessary to control for factors such as product mix and adjustment costs associated with changing the rate of production. For example, some plants may produce a more difficult product mix. Perhaps more complex products or a wider range of models are manufactured at one plant than another. The plant with the more complex product mix may have a higher unit cost than its counterparts that is not due to deficiencies in its learning processes but rather due to the complexity of its product line. Thus, in multi-plant comparisons of learning rates, it is important to control for these differences in product mix since failure to do so will result in misleading estimates of the rate of learning. If the product mix changes over time within a plant, it would also be important to control for product mix in single plant studies.

Similarly, it is important to control for adjustment costs associated with changing the rate of output (cf. Preston & Keachie, 1964). Lockheed's production of the L-1011 is an example of a production program that evidenced wide variation in the rate of output. Lockheed experienced considerable difficulties in trying to scale up its rate of output very quickly. These difficulties could result in lowered productivity, independent of the organization's learning rate. Failure to control for adjustment costs may lead to inappropriate conclusions about the rate of learning in firms.

Learning curves are often characterized in terms of a progress ratio, p. With the learning curve in Equation 1.1, each doubling of cumulative output leads to a reduction in unit cost to a percentage, p, of its former value. An 80% progress ratio means therefore that with each doubling of cumulative output, unit costs decline to 80% of their previous value. Thus, an 80% progress ratio means that every time cumulative output doubles, costs decline by 20%. The parameter, b, in Equation 1.1 is related to the progress ratio, p, by the following expression:[2]

$$p = 2^{-b} \tag{1.3}$$

The progress ratio is the measure typically used by firms to characterize their learning rates.

1.5 Organizations Vary in Their Learning Rates

Organizations vary dramatically in the rate at which they learn. Some organizations show remarkable productivity gains with experience, whereas others evidence little or no learning. A study by Dutton and Thomas (1984) nicely illustrated the tremendous variation observed in organizational learning rates. Dutton and Thomas plotted a frequency chart or histogram (see Figure 1.6) of the progress ratios found in more than 100 different production programs in field studies of organizational learning. The field studies were conducted in a variety of industries including electronics, machine tools, papermaking, aircraft, steel and automotive. As can be seen from Figure 1.6, there was a tremendous variation in the rate at which these organizations learned. The lowest progress ratio was 55%, indicating that unit costs declined to 55% of their previous value when cumulative output doubled—an amazingly rapid rate of learning! The highest progress ratio was 107%, indicating that unit costs increased rather than decreased with each doubling of cumulative output. The modal progress ratio found in the Dutton and Thomas analysis fell at 81-82%—perhaps giving rise to the often made assumption of an "80% learning curve." Although an 80% learning curve is the most frequently observed, Figure 1.6 underscores the enormous variation in learning rates.

Although differences in product contribute to the variation observed in learning rates, the different rates of learning are not simply a function of the different products studied. Dutton and Thomas (1984) found that learning rates differed not only across different industries, processes and products but also within the same or similar processes and products. There is often more variation across organizations producing the same product than within organizations producing different products. For example, there was more variation in productivity gains across World War II shipyards that produced the same ship than there was within the shipyards that produced different ships (Searle & Gody, 1945). In a similar vein, Hayes and Clark (1986) found considerable variation in the rate of learning across plants in the same firm producing the same product.

Similarly, Chew, Bresnahan and Clark (1990) documented large differences in productivity across plants in the same firm that produced the same or similar products with similar technology. The researchers described dramatic differences in performance between the best and the worst plants in a firm. After controlling for differences in plant size, age, location and

Figure 1.6
Distribution of Progress Ratios Observed in 22 Field Studies (n=108)

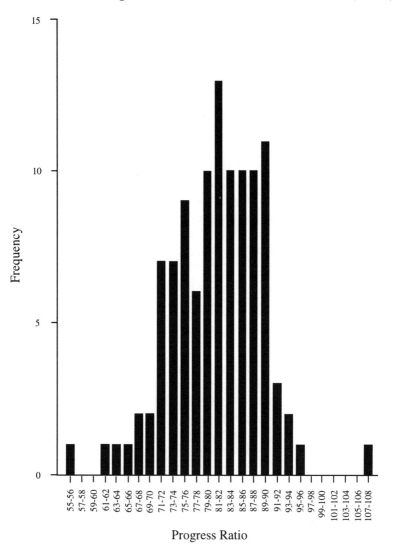

Progress Ratio

<u>Note.</u> Reprinted with permission from J. M. Dutton and A. Thomas, Treating progress functions as a managerial opportunity, *Academy of Management Review*, Volume 9, Number 2, (April, 1984). Copyright 1984.

technology, performance differences on the order of 2:1 between the best
and the worst performer remained (Chew, Bresnahan & Clark, 1990).

Different plants producing the same product that have different rates
of learning are shown in Figure 1.7. The figure is based on data from three
truck plants that assemble the same product within the same firm. The
number of direct labor hours required to assemble each truck is plotted as a
function of the cumulative number of trucks assembled.   Figure 1.7
illustrates that although unit costs decreased at a decreasing rate with

Figure 1.7
The Relationship Between Labor Hours Per Vehicle
and Cumulative Output for Three Plants

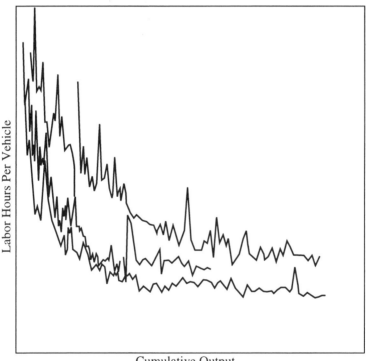

Cumulative Output

Note.   Reprinted with permission from L. Argote and D. Epple, Learning curves in
manufacturing, *Science*, Volume *247*, Number 4945, (February, 1990). Copyright 1990,
American Association for the Advancement of Science.   Units omitted to protect
confidentiality of data.

experience for each plant, the rate of the decrease differed dramatically across the three plants. There was considerable variation in the rate at which productivity grew with experience across the three plants—considerable variation in the rate at which they learned.

1.6 Sources of Variation in Learning Rates

What explains the variation in the rate at which organizations learn? Many researchers have speculated about factors explaining organizational learning curves and contributing to the variation observed in organizational learning rates. For example, Hayes and Wheelwright (1984) discussed the following factors as facilitators of organizational learning: individual learning, better selecting and training of new members, improved methods, better equipment and substitution of materials and/or capital for labor, incentives, and leadership. Joskow and Rozanski (1979) identified several factors as contributors to the productivity gains associated with experience: routinization of tasks, learning by management that leads to more efficient production control, learning by engineers who redesign the equipment and improve routing and material handling, and learning by suppliers who are able to provide a speedier and more reliable flow of material. Dutton, Thomas and Butler (1984) noted that productivity gains derived from improvements in capital goods, labor skills, materials, engineering, and managerial expertise. Lieberman (1987) indicated that the productivity gains stemmed from a variety of underlying sources, including improvements in capital equipment, improvements in product and process designs, and improved organizational and individual skills. In our interviews with managers at aerospace and truck plants regarding their perceptions of the most important determinants of organizational learning curves, the managers emphasized: improvements in the performance of individual workers; improvements in the technology, tooling and layout; improvements in the organization's structure; and better understanding of who in the organization is good at what (Argote, 1993).

Thus, a very large set of factors have been hypothesized to contribute to the productivity gains associated with increasing experience. The factors can be grouped into three general categories: increased proficiency of individuals, including managers, engineers and direct production workers; improvements in the organization's technology; and improvements in its structure, routines and methods of coordination.

As noted previously, there has been a resurgence in studies assessing the contribution of various factors to organizational learning rates. These studies aim to open up the "black box" of organizational learning curves by identifying the factors that drive the productivity gains associated with experience.   Organizational performance does not improve automatically with experience.   The variation observed in organizational learning rates clearly indicates that productivity improvements are not guaranteed to occur as experience increases.   A goal of much research on organizational learning rates is to identify the specific factors that lead to productivity improvements.

Working in this tradition, Lieberman (1984) found that investment in Research and Development appeared to accelerate the rate of learning among firms in the chemical processing industry.   Similarly, Sinclair, Klepper and Cohen (1997) found that Research and Development appeared to drive the productivity improvements observed in a chemical firm.

Hayes and Clark (1986) investigated the effect of a variety of factors on the productivity of factories.   Hayes and Clark found that reducing the work-in-process inventory, reducing the number of rejects, and decreasing the number of engineering change orders improved productivity. The researchers also found that investment in capital had a positive effect on productivity but cautioned about the importance of managing the introduction of new technology appropriately and adapting it to the organizational context.   Surprisingly, investment in training showed a consistently negative relationship to productivity in the Hayes and Clark (1986) study.   This latter finding, of course, does not imply that training necessarily hurts productivity but rather suggests that many training programs may be counterproductive or are used as a corrective device once productivity problems have appeared.   Chapter 4 discusses how new results on organizational learning can inform the design of training programs to increase their effectiveness.

Galbraith (1990) examined factors explaining the productivity of "recipient" organizations after attempts to transfer advanced manufacturing technology to them had been made.   Galbraith (1990) found that the time it took the recipient site to reach the level of productivity achieved by the donor before the transfer was greater when the organizations were geographically far apart and when the technology was complex. Conversely, the time to recover was faster when co-production occurred at the donor site, when an engineering team was relocated from the donor to the recipient site for more than one month, and when individuals involved had a financial stake in the success of the transfer. Similar to the Hayes and Clark (1986) result, training was associated with greater productivity loss. The measure of training did not reflect the appropriateness or quality of the training program.

Adler and Clark (1991) investigated the effect of two learning process variables, engineering activity (measured as the cumulative number of hours spent by direct personnel on product development changes, running experiments, or learning new specifications) and training activity (measured as the cumulative number of hours spent in training by direct personnel), on the productivity of two manufacturing departments. The researchers found that the two learning process variables had different effects in the two departments. In one department, training facilitated productivity, whereas engineering changes impaired it; in the other department, training impaired productivity, whereas engineering changes had a direct positive but (through their effect on training) an indirect negative effect on productivity. The researchers suggested that in the department where engineering changes had a negative effect on productivity, the changes were made for product performance concerns whereas in the department where engineering changes had a positive effect they were motivated by manufacturability concerns. Training had a more positive effect in the capital-intensive department where it was less disruptive to production than in the labor-intensive department where the training was seen by management as lacking discipline.

Whether organizations are specialists or generalists has been found to affect their rate of learning. Barnett, Greve and Park (1994) found that specialist banks had higher returns on average assets as a function of experience than generalist banks and that generalist banks did not exhibit performance increases as a function of experience. Similarly, in a study of the survival of hotels, Ingram and Baum (1997b) found that "geographic generalists" that operated over a large physical area were less affected by their own experience than specialists who concentrated in a smaller number of areas. Thus, generalists seem to benefit less from experience than specialists. This finding may reflect the difficulty generalist organizations have transferring knowledge across very different units and the greater likelihood that knowledge acquired in one unit will not be relevant for another.

These studies are an important first step at understanding variation observed in organizational learning rates. The studies described in this section are important because they analyze productivity in actual organizations and document performance differences across them. A challenge with the approach, however, is that the same independent or predictor variable may be implemented very differently in different organizations. For example, two firms may make the same number of engineering changes: one chooses the changes judiciously based on analyses of how to improve manufacturability of the product; the other makes the changes on an ad hoc basis. The changes at the former firm are more likely to improve productivity than those at the latter. Yet both firms would have the same value for the engineering change variable since the firms made the same number of changes. Thus, measuring organizational phenomena in such an aggregate form can mask important differences in the phenomena. These more aggregate studies of productivity are useful in suggesting that a variable may make an important contribution to productivity. The aggregate studies can be complemented by more fine-grained studies that specify the conditions under which the variable has a positive or negative effect on productivity. These more fine-grained studies are described later in this monograph (see Chapters 3-5 in particular).

In our work, we have found that differences in organizations' abilities to retain and transfer knowledge are major contributors to differences observed in organizational learning rates. For example, a firm that is consistently better at retaining knowledge will typically have a faster productivity growth rate than one where knowledge is lost. Empirical results on the acquisition and loss of knowledge are discussed in chapters on Organizational Forgetting (Chapter 2) and Organizational Memory (Chapter 3). Furthermore, a firm that is better at learning from other organizations will generally have a faster rate of productivity growth than one less adept at learning from others. Jarmin (1994) also found that firms differed in the extent to which they benefited from knowledge acquired at other firms. Empirical findings on the transfer of knowledge are presented in Chapter 5.

1.7 Theoretical Models of Organizational Learning

Several theoretical models of organizational learning curves and related phenomena have been proposed (e.g., Dorroh, Gulledge & Womer, 1994; Levy, 1965; Muth, 1986; Roberts, 1983). Muth (1986) provided an excellent review of these models and developed a new one. Muth (1986) generated the power law relationship between unit cost and experience (see Equation 1.1) by a model that involves a firm searching randomly for lower cost methods from a fixed population of technological improvements. Muth's model did not aim to explain the variation in learning rates observed across firms.

By contrast, Huberman (1996) developed a theoretical model of organizational learning that aimed at explaining the variation in learning rates observed across firms. In Huberman's model, the production process is mathematically represented by a connected graph whose nodes represent stages in the production process and whose links represent the routines connecting them. Since there are multiple ways in which products can be assembled, the goal node representing the finished product can be reached along a variety of paths. The total cost of manufacturing a product is proportional to the number of steps (or links in the graph) that are needed to reach the goal. The more steps, the greater the cost. The learning process involves finding decreasingly shorter paths from the initial state to the final product.

Learning occurs through two mechanisms in Huberman's model. First, a shortcut or new routine for going from the initial to the final node can be discovered. For example, the organization might discover a shortcut for painting a product that involves fewer procedures.

Second, the organization can improve at selecting routines (or choosing links in the graph). That is, of the many possible links leading from one node to another, the organization improves its ability to select the more efficacious links. For example, members of an organization might learn who is good at what so they know whom to go to for advice or assistance. When an issue arises in a particular domain, members of the organization go to the person with the most expertise in the domain, and thus save considerable time. These two learning mechanisms lead to a shorter path from the initial to final stage.

Huberman's model generates a power law decrease in the number of steps to assemble a product. The model also generates variation in organizational learning rates: changes in the effectiveness of the procedure for selecting routines lead to differences in the learning rates. Huberman's model also produces other empirical regularities found to characterize organizational learning such as "organizational forgetting." Thus, his model is very consistent with observed empirical regularities.

Research is needed to test whether Huberman's model corresponds to the process by which learning occurs in organizations. The correspondence of his model with known empirical regularities about organizational learning makes it attractive, and it is intuitively appealing. As organizations acquire experience, they reduce the number of steps or shorten the number of links in a production process. For example, an organization might learn that its layout is inefficient and rearrange equipment to minimize the number of steps required to produce a product. Or an organization might learn that its structure is unwieldy and shift to a structure where individuals who interact on a recurring basis are grouped together. Thus, the number of links required for them to communicate are reduced. Alternatively, members of an organization might learn who is expert about particular domains and therefore choose more effective links in the production process. Thus, in this framework, organizational learning involves building faster and more effective connections for getting work done. In my view, this is a very attractive way of conceptualizing organizational learning.

1.8 Learning Curve Applications

We turn now to a brief overview of applications for improving firm performance that are based on the learning curve. Organizations use learning curves as planning and forecasting tools. Analyses based on organizational learning curves have been used in many applications geared at improving firm performance (Dutton, Thomas & Butler, 1984). Learning curves have been used to plan and manage the internal operations of firms as well as to make strategic decisions regarding their behavior vis-à-vis other firms. For example, on the internal side, learning curves are used for planning production schedules, setting labor standards, planning for training, deciding about subcontracting, making delivery commitments, budgeting, monitoring performance, and determining manufacturing strategy (Ghemawat, 1985; Hayes & Wheelwright, 1984; Jucker, 1977; Levy, 1965). On the external or strategic side, firms use forecasts based on learning curves to predict competitor's costs (Henderson, 1984) and to decide about whether to enter a market and how to price their products.

At a more macro level, the rate and transfer of learning are also important issues for antitrust policy (Spence, 1981), trade policy (Baldwin & Krugman, 1988; Gruenspecht, 1988; Young, 1991), and market structure and performance (Dasgupta & Stiglitz, 1988; Ghemawat & Spence, 1985). Developing the implications of organizational learning and its persistence and transfer for these phenomena is an important undertaking and worthy of future research. The implications of learning for antitrust and trade policy are, however, beyond the scope of this monograph.

Dutton, Thomas and Butler (1984) vividly described the problems associated with some applications of the learning-curve concept that were too simplistic. The learning curve came into vogue as a management tool in the 1960s and 1970s (e.g., see Conley, 1970). It was promoted by consulting groups and by the United States government's requirement that defense contractors include estimates of progress rates in their proposals. Unfortunately, some of these applications treated learning as though it were automatic. Relatedly, there was also a tendency to adopt the "80 percent learning curve" as the norm. Proponents of this view believed that all production programs should achieve an 80% learning rate—that is, with each doubling of cumulative output unit costs would decline to 80% of their previous value. Indeed we have encountered a few organizations where managers were fired because their operations did not achieve an 80% learning curve. This belief in an 80% learning curve is too simplistic and neglects the many factors that affect rates of learning. The overly simplistic use of the learning curve led to some disgruntlement with it in the 1980s (Kiechel, 1981).

The 1990s have enjoyed a resurgence of interest in organizational learning. More recent analyses of learning curves are more appreciative of the many factors affecting learning than earlier treatments were. Academic interest in organizational learning has increased dramatically in recent years. The many popular books and articles on organizational learning and knowledge management reflect concern on the practitioners' side. Subsequent chapters of this monograph return to learning curve applications and develop the operational and strategic implications of new results on organizational learning for firm performance.

1.9 Conclusion

Large increases in productivity typically occur as organizations gain experience in production. Although these learning curves have been found in many organizations, organizations vary tremendously in the rates at which they learn. Some organizations show remarkable productivity gains, whereas others evidence little or no learning. Researchers are beginning to understand the variation observed in organizational learning rates. Empirical research on this important issue is underway. Research is also underway on the dynamics of knowledge acquisition, retention, and transfer in firms. Understanding sources of variation in organizational learning and its persistence and transfer is an important research agenda as well as a source of competitive advantage for firms. The remainder of this monograph is devoted to summarizing what we know about the acquisition, retention, and transfer of knowledge in organizations.

Notes

1.   The classic learning curve in Equation (1.1), $y = ax^{-b}$, can be expressed as a production function. The dependent variable in Equation (1.1) is labor hours per output ($y = h/q$). Equation (1.1) can be rewritten as $q = a^{-1}hx^{b}$. Thus, the production function implicit in the conventional learning curve has a single input, labor hours (h), and a single measure of organizational knowledge—cumulative output (x). The conventional formulation also imposes the assumption of proportionality between output and labor hours. Thus, the conventional formulation of the learning curve is a special case of the more general production function approach.

2.   The relationship between the progress ratio and the learning rate from Equation (1.1) can be derived as follows:

     Let y_1 = unit cost of producing unit x;

                y_2 = unit cost of producing unit $2x$;

     Then $y_1 = ax^{-b}$,

              $y_2 = a(2x)^{-b}$; and

              $y_2 / y_1 = 2^{-b}$.

References

Adler, P. S., & Clark, K. B. (1991). Behind the learning curve: A sketch of the learning process. *Management Science*, *37*, 267-281.

Alchian, A. (1963). Reliability of progress curves in airframe production. *Econometrica*, *31*, 679-693.

Argote, L. (1993). Group and organizational learning curves: Individual, system and environmental components. *British Journal of Social Psychology*, *32*, 31-51.

Argote, L., Beckman, S. L., & Epple, D. (1990). The persistence and transfer of learning in industrial settings. *Management Science*, *36*, 140-154.

Argote, L., & Darr, E. D. (in press). Repositories of knowledge in franchise organizations: Individual, structural and technological. In G. Dosi, R. Nelson & S. Winter (Eds.), *Nature and dynamics of organizational capabilities*.

Argote, L., & Epple, D. (1990, February 23). Learning curves in manufacturing. *Science*, *247*, 920-924.

Argote, L., Epple, D., Rao, R. D., & Murphy, K. (1997). *The acquisition and depreciation of knowledge in a manufacturing organization: Turnover and plant productivity*. Working paper, Graduate School of Industrial Administration, Carnegie Mellon University.

Arrow, K. J. (1962). The economic implications of learning by doing. *Review of Economic Studies*, *29*, 155-173.

Asher, H. (1956). *Cost-quantity relationships in the air-frame industry*. Santa Monica, CA: Rand Corporation.

Bahk, B., & Gort, M. (1993). Decomposing learning by doing in new plants. *Journal of Political Economy*, *101*, 561-582.

Baldwin, R., & Krugman, P. (1988). Industrial policy and international competition in wide-bodied jet aircraft. In R. Baldwin (Ed.), *Trade policy and empirical analysis* (pp. 45-71). Chicago: University of Chicago Press.

Baloff, N. (1966). Startups in machine intensive production systems. *Journal of Industrial Engineering*, *17*, 25-32.

Baloff, N. (1971). Extension of the learning curve–some empirical results. *Operations Research Quarterly*, *22*, 329-340.

Barkai, H., & Levhari, D. (1973). The impact of experience on kibbutz farming. *Review of Economics and Statistics*, *55*, 56-63.

Barnett, W. P., Greve, H. R., & Park, D. Y. (1994). An evolutionary model of organizational performance. *Strategic Management Journal, 15*(winter special issue),11-28.

Barney, J. B. (1991). Firm resources and sustained competitive advantage. *Journal of Management, 17*, 99-120.

Barsalou, L. W. (1992). *Cognitive psychology: An overview for cognitive scientists.* Hillsdale, NJ: Lawrence Erlbaum.

Baum, J. A. C., & Ingram, P. (1998). Survival-enhancing learning in the Manhattan hotel industry, 1898-1980. *Management Science, 44*, 996-1016.

Benkard, C. L. (1997). *Learning and forgetting: The dynamics of aircraft production.* Working paper, Yale University

Blumenstein, R. (1997, August 4). GM is building plants in developing nations to woo new markets. *The Wall Street Journal*, pp. A1, A4.

Chew, W. B., Bresnahan, T. F., & Clark, K. B. (1990). Measurement, coordination and learning in a multi-plant network. In R. S. Kaplan (Ed.), *Measures for manufacturing excellence* (pp. 129-162). Boston: Harvard Business Press.

Christian, N. M. (1997, June 5). Chrysler suppliers' cost-saving ideas likely to add $325 million to its '97 net. *The Wall Street Journal*, p. A6.

Conley, P. (1970). Experience curves as a planning tool. *IEEE Spectrum, 7*, 63-68.

Conway, R., & Schultz, J. (1959). The manufacturing progress function. Journal *of Industrial Engineering, 10*, 39-53.

Darr, E., Argote, L., & Epple, D. (1995). The acquisition, transfer and depreciation of knowledge in service organizations: Productivity in franchises. *Management Science, 41*, 1750-1762.

Delaney, P. F., Reder, L. M., Staszewski, J. J., & Ritter, F. E. (1998). The strategy-specific nature of improvement: The power law applies by strategy within task. *Psychological Science, 9*,1-7.

Dasgupta, P. & Stiglitz, J. (1988). Learning by doing, market structure and industrial and trade policies. *Oxford Economic Papers, 40*, 246-268.

Dorroh, J. R., Gulledge, T. R., & Womer, N. K. (1994). Investment in knowledge: A generalization of learning by experience. *Management Science, 40*, 947-958.

Duncan, R., & Weiss, A. (1979). Organizational learning: Implications for organizational design. *Research in Organizational Behavior, 1*, 75-123.

Dutton, J. M., & Thomas, A. (1984). Treating progress functions as a managerial opportunity. *Academy of Management Review, 9*, 235-247.

Dutton, J. M., Thomas, A., & Butler, J. E. (1984). The history of progress functions as a managerial technology. *Business History Review, 58*, 204-233.

Easterby-Smith, M. (1997). Disciplines of organizational learning: Contributions and critiques. *Human Relations, 50*, 1085-1113.

Ebbinghaus, H. (1964). *Memory: A contribution to experimental psychology.* (H. A. Ruger & C. E. Bussenius, Trans.). New York: Dover. (Original work published 1885).

Epple, D., Argote, L., & Devadas, R. (1991). Organizational learning curves: A method for investigating intra-plant transfer of knowledge acquired through learning by doing. *Organization Science, 2*, 58-70.

Epple, D., Argote, L., & Murphy, K. (1996). An empirical investigation of the micro structure of knowledge acquisition and transfer through learning by doing. *Operations Research, 44*, 77-86.

Fiol, C. M., & Lyles, M. A. (1985). Organizational learning. *Academy of Management Review, 10*, 803-813.

Galbraith, C. S. (1990). Transferring core manufacturing technologies in high technology firms. *California Management Review, 32*(4), 56-70.

Garvin, D. A. (1993). Building a learning organization. *Harvard Business Review, 71*(4), 78-91.

Ghemawat, P. (1985). Building strategy on the experience curve. *Harvard Business Review, 63*(2), 143-149.

Ghemawat, P., & Spence, A. M. (1985). Learning curve spillovers and market performance. *The Quarterly Journal of Economics, 100*(Supplement), 839-852.

Goodman, P. S., & Darr, E. (1996). Exchanging best practices through computer-aided systems. *Academy of Management Executive, 10*(2), 7-18.

Greenberg, L. (1971). Why the mine injury picture is out of focus. *Mining Engineering, 23*, 51-53.

Gruber, H. (1994). The yield factor and the learning curve in semiconductor production. *Applied Economics, 26*, 837-843.

Gruenspecht, H. (1988). Dumping and dynamic competition. *Journal of International Economics, 12*, 225-248.

Guetzkow, H., & Simon, H. A. (1955). The impact of certain communication nets upon organization and performance in task-oriented groups. *Management Science, 1*, 233-250.

Haunschild, P. R., & Miner, A. S. (1997). Modes of interorganizational imitation: The effects of outcome salience and uncertainty. *Administrative Science Quarterly, 42*, 472-500.

Hayes, R. H., & Clark, K. B. (1986). Why some factories are more productive than others. *Harvard Business Review, 64*(5), 66-73.

Hayes, R. H., & Wheelwright, S. C. (1984). *Restoring our competitive edge: Competing through manufacturing.* New York: Wiley.

Henderson, B. D. (1984). The application and misapplication of the experience curve. *The Journal of Business Strategy, 4*(3), 3-9.

Henderson, R., & Cockburn, I. (1994). Measuring competence? Exploring firm effects in pharmaceutical research. *Strategic Management Journal, 15*, 63-84.

Hilgard, E. R., & Bower, G. H. (1975). *Theories of learning* (4th ed.). Englewood Cliffs, NJ: Prentice-Hall.

Hirsch, W. Z., (1952). Manufacturing progress functions. *Review of Economics and Statistics, 34*, 143-155.

Hirschmann, W. B. (1964). Profit from the learning curve. *Harvard Business Review. 42*(1), 125-139.

Houston, J. P. (1986). *Fundamentals of learning and memory* (3rd ed.). New York: Harcourt Brace Jovanovich.

Huber, G. P. (1991). Organizational learning: The contributing processes and the literatures. *Organization Science, 2,* 88-115.

Huberman, B. A. (1996). *The dynamics of organizational learning.* Working paper, Xerox Palo Alto Research Center, Palo Alto, CA.

Ingram, P., & Baum, J. A. C. (1997). Opportunity and constraint: Organizations' learning from the operating and competitive experience of industries. *Strategic Management Journal, 18,* 75-98.

Jarmin, R. S. (1994). Learning by doing and competition in the early rayon industry. *The Rand Journal of Economics, 25,* 441-454.

Joskow, P. L., & Rozanski, G. A. (1979). The effects of learning by doing on nuclear plant operating reliability. *Review of Economics and Statistics, 61,* 161-168.

Jucker, J. V. (1977). The transfer of domestic-market production to a foreign site. *AIIE Transactions, 9,* 321-329.

Kelsey, S. F., Mullin, S. M., Detre, K. M., Mitchell, H., Cowley, M. J., Gruentzig, A. R., & Kent, K. M. (1984). Effect of investigator experience on percutaneous transluminal coronary angioplasty. *American Journal of Cardiology, 53,* 56C-64C.

Kiechel, W. (1981, October 5). The decline of the experience curve. *Fortune,* pp. 139-146.

Kimble, G. A. (1961). *Hilgard and Marquis' conditioning and learning.* New York: Appleton-Century-Crofts.

Krugman, P. A. (1991, November 8). Myths and realities of U.S. competitiveness. *Science, 254,* 811-815.

Leavitt, H. J. (1967). Some effects of certain communication patterns on group performance. *Journal of Abnormal and Social Psychology. 46,* 38-50.

Lester, R. K., & McCabe, M. J. (1993). The effect of industrial structure on learning by doing in nuclear power plant operation. *The Rand Journal of Economics, 24,* 418-438.

Lieberman, M. B. (1984). The learning curve and pricing in the chemical processing industries. *The Rand Journal of Economics, 15,* 213-228.

Lieberman, M. B. (1987). The learning curve, diffusion, and competitive strategy. *Strategic Management Journal, 8,* 441-452.

Lippman, S. A., & Rumelt, R. P. (1982). Uncertain imitability: An analysis of interfirm differences in efficiency under competition. *The Rand Journal of Economics, 13,* 418-438.

Lucas, R. E. (1993). Making a miracle. *Econometrica, 61,* 251-272.

Mazur, J. E., & Hastie, R. (1978). Learning as accumulation: A reexamination of the learning curve. *Psychological Bulletin, 85,* 1256-1274.

Minabe, S. (1986, July 18). Japanese competitiveness and Japanese management. *Science, 233,* 301-304.

Miner, A. S., & Haunschild, P. R. (1995). Population level learning. *Research in Organizational Behavior, 17,* 115-166.

Miner, A. S., & Mezias, S. J. (1996). Ugly duckling no more: Pasts and futures of organizational learning research. *Organization Science, 7,* 88-99.

Montgomery, C. A. (Ed.) (1995). *Resource-based and evolutionary theories of the firm: Towards a synthesis.* Norwell, MA: Kluwer.

Muth, J. F. (1986). Search theory and the manufacturing progress function. *Management Science, 32,* 948-962.

Nelson, R. R. (1991). Why do firms differ, and how does it matter? *Strategic Management Journal, 12,* 61-74.

Newell, A., & Rosenbloom, P. S. (1981). Mechanisms of skill acquisition and the law of practice. In J. R. Anderson (Ed.), *Cognitive skills and their acquisition* (pp. 1-55). Hillsdale, NJ: Lawrence Erlbaum.

Nonaka, I. (1991). The knowledge-creating company. *Harvard Business Review, 69*(6), 96-104.

Polanyi, M. (1966). *The tacit dimension.* Garden City, NJ: Doubleday.

Powell, W. W., Koput, K. W., & Smith-Doerr, L., (1996). Interorganziational collaboration and the locus of innovation: Networks of learning in biotechnology. *Administrative Science Quarterly, 41,* 116-145.

Prahalad, C. K., & Hamel, G. (1990). The core competence of the corporation. *Harvard Business Review, 68*(3), 79-91.

Rapping, L. (1965). Learning and World War II production functions. *Review of Economics and Statistics, 47,* 81-86.

Roberts, P. C. (1983). A theory of the learning process. *Journal of Operations Research, 34,* 71-79.

Searle, A. D., & Gody, C. S. (1945). Productivity changes in selected wartime shipbuilding programs. *Monthly Labor Review, 61,* 1132-1147.

Senge, P. M. (1990). *The fifth discipline: The art and practice of the learning organization.* New York: Currency Doubleday.

Sheshinski, E. (1967). Tests of the learning by doing hypothesis. *Review of Economics and Statistics, 49,* 568-578.

Sinclair, G., Klepper, S., & Cohen, W. (1997). *Piercing the veil of the learning curve.* Working paper, Department of Social and Decision Sciences, Carnegie Mellon University.

Solow, R. (1957). Technical change and the aggregate production function, *Review of Economics and Statistics, 39,* 312-320.

Spence, A. M. (1981). The learning curve and competition. *Bell Journal of Economics, 12,* 49-70.

Stein, E. W., & Zwass, V. (1995). Actualizing organizational memory with information systems. *Information Systems Research, 6,* 85-117.

A survey of manufacturing: Meet the global factory (1998, June 20). *The Economist,* pp. M1-M18.

Szulanski, G. (1996). Exploring internal stickiness: Impediments to the transfer of best practice within the firm. *Strategic Management Journal, 17,* 27-43.

Teece, D. J. (1998). Capturing value from knowledge assets: The new economy, markets for know-how and intangible assets. *California Management Review, 40*(3), 55-79.

Thorndike, E. L. (1898). Animal intelligence: An experimental study of the associative processes in animals. *The Psychological Review: Series of Monograph Supplements, 2,* 1-109.

Thurstone, L. L. (1919). The learning curve equation. *Psychological Monographs, 26*, 1-51.

The TriStar's trail of red ink (1980, July 28). *Business Week*, pp. 88, 90.

Walsh, J. P. (1995). Managerial and organizational cognition: Notes from a trip down memory lane. *Organization Science, 6*, 280-322.

Wingfield, A. (1979). *Human learning and memory: An introduction.* New York: Harper & Row.

Winter, S. G. (1995). Four Rs of profitability: Rents, resources, routines and replication. In. C. A. Montgomery (Ed.), *Resource based and evolutionary theories of the firm.* Norwell, MA: Kluwer.

Womer, N. K. (1979). Learning curves, production rate, and program costs. *Management Science, 25*, 312-319.

Womer, N. K. (1984). Estimating learning curves from aggregate monthly data. *Management Science, 30*, 982-992.

Wright, T. P. (1936). Factors affecting the costs of airplanes. *Journal of the Aeronautical Sciences, 3*, 122-128.

Yelle, L. E. (1979). The learning curve: Historical review and comprehensive survey. *Decision Sciences, 10*, 302-328.

Young, A. (1991). Learning by doing and the dynamic effects of international trade. *The Quarterly Journal of Economics, 106*, 369-405.

Zander, U., & Kogut, B. (1995). Knowledge and the speed of the transfer and imitation of organizational capabilities: An empirical test. *Organization Science, 6*, 76-92.

Chapter 2

Organizational Forgetting

2.1 Introduction

Do organizations forget? Or do organizations retain the knowledge they acquire as time passes? The classic learning curve assumes that organizational knowledge is cumulative and persists indefinitely through time. Yet, people leave organizations. Records are lost or misplaced. Technologies become obsolete. My colleagues and I began a research program several years ago to examine empirically whether organizational knowledge persists through time as the classic learning curve implies, or whether it evidences "forgetting" or depreciation. The results of our research program on knowledge depreciation, as well as related studies, are described in this chapter.

The chapter begins with an example of a case where unit costs did not follow the classic learning curve—Lockheed's production of the L-1011 TriStar. I suggest that this production program, which cost Lockheed billions of dollars, may have evidenced depreciation of knowledge. A method that generalizes the classic learning curve to test empirically for the possibility of knowledge depreciation is presented. Empirical results from several studies that examine whether knowledge depreciates are summarized. The results of our first study of knowledge depreciation in shipbuilding are described in detail to illustrate how we test empirically for the presence of depreciation. Rates of depreciation found in various industries are compared and contrasted. Factors affecting the rate of depreciation are discussed.

2.2 Knowledge Depreciation

Does knowledge acquired through learning by doing persist through time or does it decay or depreciate? The classic learning curve model described in Chapter 1 uses cumulative output as a proxy variable for organizational knowledge. Hence, the classic formulation implies that learning is cumulative and persists indefinitely through time. More recent research indicates, however, that this may not be true.

Several case studies reported that when production was resumed after an interruption at a manufacturing firm such as a strike, unit cost was higher than the level achieved before the interruption (Baloff, 1970; Hirsch, 1952). These case studies suggest that organizations may not retain all the knowledge they acquire indefinitely through time and that organizational "forgetting" can occur.

Organizational forgetting has important consequences for organizational performance. If forgetting occurs, organizations may not be as productive in the future as they anticipate. That is, if there is forgetting, forecasts of future production based on the classic learning curve will overestimate future production. Failure to achieve expected levels of productivity can lead to large problems for organizations. Delivery commitments may not be met. Customers may become dissatisfied. Significant financial penalties for late deliveries may be incurred. Inaccurate forecasts of future productivity make it very difficult for organizations to plan and organize their internal operations. Further, strategic analyses based on inaccurate forecasts of future productivity may be very misleading. In extreme cases, an organization's actual productivity may fall so far below its expected or forecasted productivity that the organization will not be competitive. Thus, if forgetting occurs, it is very important for the organization to allow for this forgetting in forecasts of its future productivity. Further, the organization may wish to consider strategies for minimizing forgetting. These strategies for retaining knowledge are discussed in the following chapter on organizational memory.

Theoretical papers (e.g., Batchelder, Boren, Campbell, Dei Rossi & Large, 1969; Carlson & Rowe, 1976) and simulation results have developed the theoretical implications of forgetting for forecasting, planning, and scheduling (e.g., see Smunt, 1987; Smunt & Morton, 1985; Sule, 1983). Yet empirical studies of organizational learning typically assume that there is no forgetting and use cumulative output as the measure of organizational knowledge (e.g., see the many studies in the reviews by Dutton & Thomas, 1984, and Yelle, 1979). Similarly, forecasts of future productivity based on the learning curve also do not account for forgetting. Concerns about the possibility of forgetting coupled with the absence of its consideration in empirical studies and forecasts led my colleagues and I to embark on a research program on the extent of forgetting in organizations. Such knowledge would advance our understanding of organizational learning at a theoretical level as well as lead to important information that would enable organizations to improve forecasts and perhaps increase their productivity.

My colleagues and I wanted to develop a method to test empirically whether organizational knowledge was cumulative, as the classic model implied, or whether it depreciated, as the Lockheed example suggested. We developed a method for generalizing the classic learning curve to analyze empirically whether knowledge decays or depreciates (Argote, Beckman & Epple, 1990). The conventional measure of knowledge, cumulative output, implies that there is no forgetting or depreciation: knowledge obtained from a unit of output produced in the distant past is as useful as knowledge obtained from a unit produced yesterday. My colleagues and I tested this assumption by developing a measure of knowledge that embeds the conventional measure as a special case. We introduced a parameter, lambda, that is used to create a geometric weighting of an organization's past output. Estimates of lambda equal to one correspond to the classic cumulative output measure, whereas estimates less than one imply forgetting or depreciation since output in the distant past receives less weight in predicting current productivity than recent output. We have used this approach to test empirically whether knowledge depreciates in different industries, most notably shipbuilding, automotive, and fast food.

Before turning to the empirical studies, a much publicized production program that appeared to evidence forgetting—Lockheed's production of the L-1011 TriStar—will be described. My discussion of the TriStar program is based on information publicly available in newspapers, trade publications, the company's annual reports, and the like. My intention in discussing the TriStar program is not to criticize Lockheed. Indeed the L-1011 is widely regarded as a major technological success. My intent, rather, is to demonstrate that predictions of Lockheed's productivity based on the classic learning curve were dramatically off the mark. Thus, the classic learning curve was inadequate to describe the Lockheed production program. The pattern of costs Lockheed experienced is consistent with a model in which depreciation occurred. Background information about the Lockheed case will be presented to illuminate reasons why knowledge depreciation may have occurred there. Some of the background information is described to provide context for the example; other information seems more suggestive of causes of knowledge depreciation.

2.3 A Case Example

As noted previously, analyses of organizational learning that use cumulative output as the proxy variable for organizational knowledge have been found at times to contain large errors. The L-1011 TriStar produced by Lockheed throughout the 1970s and early 1980s is an example of a production program for which predictions based on the classic learning curve formulation were dramatically off the mark.

As can be seen from Table 2.1, the number of L-1011 TriStars produced by Lockheed each year varied considerably. Applying the classic learning-curve formulation to the TriStar program led the firm to predict that unit costs would fall below price around the time Lockheed produced the fiftieth plane (Fandel, 1974). Although Reinhardt (1973) criticized Lockheed's analysis of the L-1011 program for omitting the opportunity cost of nonrecurring expenses for developing technology and facilities for the L-1011, he used the conventional cumulative output measure of organizational knowledge in his forecast of recurring production costs. Reinhardt arrived at a conclusion similar to Lockheed's: production costs would be below price at about the fiftieth plane. This prediction was borne out: Lockheed reported in 1975 that unit costs were less than the price at which each plane was being sold (Sansweet, 1975).

Table 2.1
Lockheed's Production of the L-1011 TriStar

| Year | L-1011 production | |
	Annual Units	Cumulative Units
1972	17	17
1973	39	56
1974	41	97
1975	25	122
1976	16	138
1977	6	144
1978	8	152
1979	24	176
1980	25	201
1981	18	219

Note. Reprinted with permission from L. Argote and D. Epple, Learning curves in manufacturing, *Science*, Volume *247*, Number 4945, (February, 1990). Copyright 1990, American Association for the Advancement of Science.

Cuts in production occurred in late 1975 (see Table 2.1). Costs rose to exceed price and appeared to remain above price for the rest of the production program (Harris, 1982; "Lockheed loses hope," 1980). In 1982, the L-1011 was sold for $50 to $60 million per plane. Converted to 1975 dollars, this corresponds to $29 to $35 million. By contrast, each plane sold for $20 million in 1975 before the cuts in production occurred. Thus, the unit cost of producing each plane was less than $20 million in real terms in

1975 but greater than $29 million in real terms in 1982! Clearly these data do not follow a learning curve since costs rose rather than fell with increases in cumulative output. In 1980, the Chairman of Lockheed, Ray Anderson, stated that the L-1011 would never break even if all costs incurred since 1968 were taken into account but that the company hoped to reach a point where each plane was selling for at least its current production costs (Hill, 1980). Apparently, this never happened. In December 1981, Lockheed announced that it was phasing out production of the L-1011 (Harris, 1981b), making it the last commercial aircraft Lockheed produced.

In the classic learning-curve model, unit costs decrease as a function of increasing cumulative output. Thus, according to the classic model, unit costs should have continued to fall since cumulative output of the L-1011 continued to rise. Instead, unit costs rose rather than fell with increasing experience.

Many factors contributed to the increasing costs Lockheed experienced. The L-1011 program was plagued by shortages of personnel and parts ("TriStar's trail," 1980). For example, the L-1011 production line was shut down when the company that produced its engines, Rolls Royce, went into receivership (Harris, 1981c). This shutdown delayed the delivery of the first L-1011 aircraft. During this delay in the introduction of the L-1011, McDonnell Douglas' DC-10 made significant gains in the market (Harris, 1981c).

Although personnel and parts shortages hurt every aircraft manufacturer, Lockheed appeared to suffer more than the others because of its attempt to increase production so dramatically in the late 1970s ("TriStar's trail," 1980). Lockheed went from employing 14,000 personnel to employing 25,000 in a two-year period in California. In order to accomplish this dramatic increase in personnel, Lockheed hired many workers who had no previous experience in aircraft construction and who had not finished high school ("TriStar's trail," 1980). *Business Week* concluded that these inexperienced workers hurt Lockheed's learning curve:

> Inevitably, green workers have wreaked havoc with the TriStar's 'learning curve,' dramatically boosting the man-hours required to build each airplane ("TriStar's Trail," 1980, p. 90).

Indeed Lockheed executives spent a significant amount of their time "fighting fires" on the production line ("TriStar's trail," 1980). There was a six-week strike in 1977 and a threat of one in 1980 ("TriStar's trail," 1980). Further, Lockheed's build-up in production came after Boeing had already purchased a storehouse of materials. Lockheed had to pay a premium for materials it needed ("TriStar's trail," 1980).

Another factor that may have favored a competitor of Lockheed's, McDonnell Douglas, is its shared production line between the DC-10 (a commercial product) and the KC-10 military tanker (Harris, 1981c). Thus, the DC-10 had a larger experience base from which to learn and improve than the L-1011. McDonnell Douglas' ability to transfer knowledge from the KC-10 tanker to the DC-10 may have reduced the unit cost of production of the DC-10. Further, production of the DC-10 was not characterized by the "roller coaster" production that characterized production of the L-1011 ("TriStar's trail," 1980).

In addition to these factors that seemed to disadvantage Lockheed in particular, other conditions hurt all firms producing wide-body jets. Deregulation (Harris, 1981c) and high fuel prices (Harris, 1981b) favored smaller aircraft. The market for wide-body jets, such as the L-1011, was not as large as had been anticipated.

The classic model that assumes knowledge is cumulative is too simplistic to capture the dynamics of organizational learning in firms such as Lockheed. The L-1011 is regarded as a technological—but not a financial—success (Harris, 1981a). The L-1011 data are more consistent with a model that assumes knowledge depreciates than one that assumes knowledge is cumulative.

Subsequent empirical work by Benkard (1997) confirmed that depreciation did indeed occur in the L-1011 production program. Using newly available data he obtained from Lockheed, Benkard demonstrated very convincingly that organizational forgetting explained the upturn in labor requirements observed in the Lockheed data. Given the large losses Lockheed sustained on the L-1011 program, averaging more than $15 million per year over the decade ending in 1980 ("TriStar's trail," 1980), improved strategies for estimating learning rates are clearly of great importance.

A recent discussion of Boeing's new 777 suggests that analysts are concerned about knowledge depreciation on this production program that is currently underway (Holusha, 1994). When asked about how many 777s Boeing had to sell for the plane to be profitable, Paul Nisbet, an aerospace analyst replied: "If they sell six or seven dozen a year for the next several years, they may have a return after 300 aircraft...if those sales are stretched out over 20 years, there may not be a return" (Holusha, 1994, p. F1). If cumulative output is the best predictor of current productivity (as the classic learning curve implies), these two scenarios should result in the same unit cost of production. If depreciation occurs, the latter scenario of stretching sales out over a longer period would result in higher unit cost. Thus,

Nisbet's predictions are consistent with a model that emphasizes the importance of knowledge depreciation.

2.4 Empirical Evidence

2.4.1 The Shipyard Study

Our first empirical study of knowledge depreciation was based on data from the construction of the Liberty Ship during World War II (Fisher, 1949). We learned about these data from Rapping's 1965 study, in which he found evidence of learning in the shipyards (Rapping, 1965). Rapping's study provided particularly compelling evidence of learning because he controlled for important factors such as economies of scale and technological progress associated with the passage of time in his analysis. Rapping found significant evidence of learning when these important additional factors were taken into account.

The Liberty Ship production program is particularly attractive for studying organizational learning and forgetting. The Liberty Ship was built in 16 different shipyards in the U.S.[1] All of the yards producing the Liberty Ship began production during 1941 or 1942. The yards were new yards, the Emergency Shipyards, constructed under the authority of the U.S. Maritime Commission. A central agency was responsible for purchasing raw materials and equipment, approving each yard's layout and technology, and supervising its construction (Lane, 1951). A standard design was adopted and produced with minor variation in all of the yards (Lane, 1951). The overwhelming majority of workers employed in the Emergency Shipyards had no prior experience in shipbuilding (Fisher, 1949). The yards constructed a very large number (almost 3,000) of Liberty Ships. On average, two months were required to build each Liberty Ship.

Thus, the Liberty Ship production program is ideally suited for studying organizational learning, forgetting and transfer (See Chapter 5 for a discussion of the transfer results). A large number of a single homogeneous product were produced from homogeneous raw materials in a large number of organizations by workers without prior industry experience. These features of the Liberty Ship production program control naturally for many important factors such as prior experience of workers or product characteristics that are difficult to control for statistically in most production environments. Further, the shipyards began production at different times, produced at very different scales of operation, and experienced different rates of labor turnover. Thus, there was variance on important factors that allowed us to examine whether knowledge depreciates and whether it transfers. We also explored the role of labor turnover in the acquisition and depreciation of knowledge. The following section describes in depth the method we used to assess whether knowledge depreciates. Readers less interested in the details of the estimation may wish to skip to the results or discussion sections.

2.4.1.1 Method and Sources of Data

Our general approach was to estimate production functions in which output depended on the inputs of labor, capital, organizational knowledge, and other variables. Variables used in our analysis of the shipyards data and the symbols used to designate them are listed in Table 2.2.

Table 2.2
Variables Used in the Shipyard Study

Symbol	Variable
t	Calendar time in months; $t=1$ in January, 1941
q_{it}	Tonnage (in thousands) produced in yard i in month t
H_{it}	Labor hours (in hundreds) in yard i in month t
W_{it}	Shipways used in yard i in month t
$Q_{it} = \sum_{s=0}^{t} q_{ts}$	Cumulative output in yard i through month t
$A_t = \sum_{i=1}^{13} Q_{it}$	Aggregate cumulative output through month t
K_{it}	Knowledge acquired in yard i through month t
$AK_t = \sum_{i=1}^{13} K_{it}$	Aggregate knowledge acquired through month t
S_i	Month production started in yard i
$Hire_{it}$	Number of new hires per hundred employees in yard i in month t
Sep_{it}	Number of departures per hundred employees in yard i in month t

Our primary dependent variable was tonnage of ships produced per month. Tonnage produced per month refers to the weight of all vessels or portions of vessels produced during a month. Womer (1984) demonstrated that inappropriate inferences may be drawn from empirical analyses of learning if the measure of output is based on units finished in a given month, and the period of production exceeds a month. This problem did not arise in our analysis of the shipyard data since our output measure is the tonnage actually constructed in a given month.

Independent variables included measures of labor and capital inputs. Following Rapping (1965), shipways in use is our measure of capital inputs. Shipways are the structures upon which the ships were built.

We estimated models in which output depended on the inputs of labor (labor hours), capital (shipways), and on other variables. Specifically, we estimated production functions of the following form:

$$\ln q_{it} = a_0 + \sum_{i=2}^{13} a_i D_i + \alpha \ln H_{it} + \beta \ln W_{it}$$
$$+ \gamma \ln K_{it-1} + \delta' Z_{it} + u_{it} \tag{2.1}$$

where $K_{it} = \lambda K_{it-1} + q_{it}$ (2.2)

and $u_{it} = \rho_1 u_{it-1} + \rho_2 u_{it-2} + \rho_3 u_{it-3} + \varepsilon_{it}$ (2.3)

As noted previously, Womer (1979) emphasized the importance of integrating the neoclassical production function approach and analyses of learning by doing. Because the Liberty Ship data are from several organizations that differed significantly in their scale of operation, we were able to integrate the production function approach and learning by doing. By controlling for inputs of labor and capital, we were able to separate increases in productivity due to learning from increases in productivity due to increasing exploitation of economies of scale. In addition, we controlled for calendar time in order to separate the effect of technical progress associated with the passage of time in the general environment from productivity improvements associated with increasing experience at a particular shipyard. The vector Z_{it} in Equation (2.1) varies from regression to regression and represents these other variables that may influence productivity.

Since our empirical analysis of knowledge depreciation is a new contribution, an explanation of how we measured depreciation will be developed. Our approach to measuring knowledge depreciation is formalized in Equation (2.2). Our measure of knowledge is variable K_{it} defined in Equation (2.2). Variable K_{it} is the stock of knowledge accumulated by yard i at date t. As Equation (2.2) indicates, this stock of knowledge increases with output. Equation (2.2) allows for the possibility that the stock of knowledge depreciates over time by including the parameter lambda, λ. Lambda is estimated through a scanning procedure for maximum likelihood estimation (Dhrymes, 1966; Goldfield & Quandt, 1972). If λ is estimated to be one, the accumulated stock of knowledge is simply equal to lagged cumulative output, the classic measure of learning. If λ is estimated to be less than one, however, there is evidence of depreciation since output from the distant past receives less weight than recent output.

As an example of the implications of estimates of lambda, consider a case where lambda is estimated to be 0.90. If the estimate of lambda (0.90) is substituted into Equation (2.2), output from the previous period would be weighted by 0.90, output from the period before that would be weighted by 0.81 ($\lambda^2 = 0.90^2$), output from the period before that would be weighted by 0.73 ($\lambda^3 = 0.90^3$), and so on. Thus, if lambda is estimated to be less than one, output from the distant past receives progressively less weight than recent output in predicting current productivity. Further, as lambda becomes smaller, output from the distant past receives even less weight. Thus, the smaller lambda is, the less knowledge is retained, and the more depreciation of knowledge occurs.

Our measure of knowledge computed from Equation (2.2) is substituted as a predictor variable into Equation (2.1).[2] As Equation (2.1) indicates, knowledge acquired through the end of the preceding month, K_{it-1}, appears in the production function for month t. Thus, past but not current output appears on the right-hand side of Equation (2.1).

We controlled for unmeasured yard-specific factors that may affect the productivity of the yards. In Equation (2.1), the D_i are "dummy" variables for each shipyard. These dummy variables are included to capture unmeasured yard-specific factors such as land that may affect production and are relatively constant through time.

The error u_{it} is assumed to be serially correlated as shown in Equation (2.3).[3] The serial correlation coefficients are assumed to be the same across all shipyards. The choice of a third-order autoregressive error is based on our analysis of the data. Third-order serial correlation coefficients all reached at least the .05 level of significance. This is not surprising since production of a ship required an average of two months, and longer periods were required early in the operation of the yards.[4]

2.4.1.2 Results

Our findings concerning whether knowledge depreciated in the shipyards are presented in Table 2.3. Results obtained from estimating five different models of current production are shown in Table 2.3. The dependent variable in all of these models is the logarithm of current production; the predictor variables for each model vary from column to column. The models were estimated by maximum likelihood. The coefficients of the yard-specific dummy variables are not of particular interest and are therefore not reported. A joint test of the null hypothesis that there were no yard-specific effects was rejected at a high significance level (p < .001), so important yard-specific effects were present. Yard-specific dummy variables were included in all analyses shown in Table 2.3.

Estimation was done using the following search procedure. Values of lambda, λ, in the interval [0,1] were chosen. With lambda fixed, the remaining parameters were estimated by standard procedures for estimating regression models with autocorrelated errors. Hence, for each chosen value of lambda the remaining parameters were estimated. We began with a search over values of lambda at increments of 0.05 in the interval [0, 1] to identify the subinterval in which the function reached a maximum and then located the maximum by searching that subinterval at increments of lambda of 0.01. The maximum likelihood estimates for the overall model were the value of lambda and the values of the associated coefficients that yielded the largest value of the likelihood function. This procedure is equivalent to nonlinear search procedures that vary all parameters simultaneously, but is computationally easier to implement.

The maximum likelihood estimate of the depreciation parameter, lambda, for the model shown in Column 1 of Table 2.3 was 0.75. The estimation procedure did not yield a standard error for lambda. The standard errors of the remaining coefficients were computed treating lambda as a known parameter. This may result in some understatement of the standard errors of the coefficients and a corresponding overstatement of the t-statistics. Therefore, all conclusions regarding significance of alternative measures of learning are based on likelihood ratio tests. Using the distribution of the likelihood ratio, we determined that a 93% confidence interval for lambda was approximately (0.65, 0.85). Thus, the hypothesis of no depreciation ($\lambda = 1.0$) was very strongly rejected by these data. Hence, the classic measure of learning, cumulative output, significantly overstates the persistence of learning. Depreciation of knowledge was found to occur in this production environment.

These results indicate a rapid rate of depreciation. As noted previously, the results were obtained from monthly data. A value of $\lambda = 0.75$ implies that, from a stock of knowledge available at the beginning of a year, only 3.2% ($\lambda^{12} = 0.75^{12}$) would remain one year later. Thus, if the stock of knowledge is not replenished by continuing production, it depreciates rapidly.

Third-order serial correlation coefficients all reached at least the

Table 2.3
Results Concerning the Persistence of Knowledge From the Shipyard Study

	(1)	(2)	(3)	(4)	(5)
Constant	-3.91	-3.74	-3.85	-3.83	-3.52
	(12.72)	(9.73)	(11.75)	(11.87)	(10.95)
Labor Hours	0.16	0.18	0.16	0.15	0.14
($\ln H_{it}$)	(5.14)	(5.18)	(4.60)	(4.38)	(4.09)
Shipways	1.15	1.08	1.15	1.13	1.12
($\ln W_{it-1}$)	(21.83)	(21.02)	(21.77)	(21.84)	(19.38)
Knowledge	0.65		0.71	0.71	0.67
($\ln K_{it-1}$)	(31.42)		(9.54)	(17.82)	(29.96)
λ	0.75 [a]		0.75 [a]	0.85	0.70 [a]
Cumulative output		0.44	-0.04		
($\ln Q_{it-1}$)		(15.74)	(0.72)		
Calendar Time				-0.01	
(t)				(3.33)	
New Hires					0.003
($\ln Hire_{it}$)					(0.22)
Separations					-0.019
($\ln Sep_{it}$)					(1.09)
R^2	0.9911	0.9900	0.9912	0.9912	0.905
$\ln L$	379.047	358.254	379.321	380.463	375.680
N	337	337	337	337	327

Note.   Unstandardized coefficients are reported, with associated t-statistics shown in parentheses. LnL is the natural logarithm of the likelihood function.
Reprinted by permission from L. Argote, S L. Beckman and D. Epple, The persistence and transfer of learning in industrial settings, *Management Science*, Volume 36, Number 2, (February, 1990).   Copyright 1990, The Institute of Management Sciences (currently INFORMS), 2 Charles Street, Suite 300, Providence, RI 02904 USA.

[a] Significantly different from one (p < 0.0001).

0.05 level of significance. Estimates of the other parameters were not sensitive to the order of serial correlation. For example, with either first- or second-order autocorrelation, the maximum likelihood estimate of lambda for the model in Column 1 of Table 2.3 was 0.80. Since autocorrelation coefficients up to third-order are significant, we adopted the third-order specification for the remaining analyses.

We investigated alternative models to see if a specification of the learning process that allowed for depreciation was more satisfying than one that did not. Column 2 of Table 2.3 is identical to Column 1 except that Column 2 included the classic cumulative output measure whereas Column 1 included the knowledge variable that allows for depreciation. The log of the likelihood function in Column 1 was significantly greater than the log of the likelihood function in Column 2, $\chi^2 = 41.59$, $df = 1$, $p < .0001$. The contrast of Columns 1 and 2 provides further evidence that learning depreciated and that our knowledge variable was a better measure than the conventional one, cumulative output.

Results presented in Column 3 of Table 2.3 show the effect of including the conventional measure of learning, cumulative output, and our knowledge variable in the same model. When cumulative output is included, the value of lambda that maximized the likelihood function was 0.75, as in Column 1. The conventional measure, cumulative output, had a small and statistically insignificant coefficient, whereas the knowledge variable was highly significant in this model. This is further evidence that the knowledge variable that allows for depreciation captures the effects of learning better than the conventional measure, cumulative output, does.

In Column 4, calendar time was introduced to capture the possibility that technical change associated with the passage of time rather than learning in the shipyards was responsible for productivity improvements in shipbuilding. The negative coefficient for the time variable indicates that the mere passage of time did not explain the productivity gains. When the more general translog specification of the production function (Berndt & Christensen, 1973) was used, the coefficient of the calendar time variable was smaller in magnitude and statistically insignificant. Thus, there was no evidence that the shipyards became more productive simply as a function of the passage of time.

What are the implications of depreciation for future productivity? Figure 2.1 depicts results from a simulation to illustrate the effect of depreciation on unit costs. In this simulation, input levels were held constant at the sample mean for the first 13 months of operation of a shipyard. As can be seen from Figure 2.1, during this period, unit costs declined at a decreasing rate. The levels of inputs were halved in month 14 and held constant thereafter. The reduction in input caused an immediate increase in unit costs, indicated by the vertical line at the date of the reduction. This jump in unit costs at the vertical line is due to scale economies. The subsequent increase in unit costs is due to the depreciation of knowledge. The reduction in inputs led to a reduction in output which in turn reduced the knowledge variable, K. Gains in knowledge from current production were not sufficient to offset the losses in knowledge from depreciation of the previous periods' stock. Thus, depreciation of knowledge led to an increase in the unit cost of production.

Why did knowledge depreciate? One very plausible cause for knowledge depreciation was personnel turnover. If knowledge were

Figure 2.1
The Relationship Between Unit Costs and Cumulative Output
when Inputs are Reduced to Half Their Initial Levels

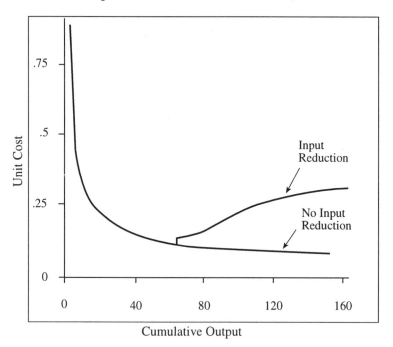

Note. Reprinted by permission from L. Argote, S L. Beckman and D. Epple, The persistence and transfer of learning in industrial settings, *Management Science*, Volume *36*, Number 2, (February, 1990). Copyright 1990, The Institute of Management Sciences (currently INFORMS), 2 Charles Street, Suite 300, Providence, RI 02904 USA.

embedded in individuals and those individuals were "separated" or departed, their turnover might hurt organizational performance. Therefore, we investigated the role of labor turnover in the productivity gains. Labor turnover was included in the model shown in Column 5 of Table 2.3. The rate of new hires and the rate of departures were included as explanatory variables. This model shown in Column 5 has fewer observations than previous runs because of missing data for the rates of hires and departures. Hence, the likelihood function values for this equation cannot be compared to those for other equations in Table 2.3. As can be seen from Column 5, these variables together did not contribute significantly to explaining changes in productivity. Additional analyses revealed that neither variable made a significant contribution when it was included separately. The estimate of the depreciation parameter in Column 5, $\lambda = 0.70$, indicates that knowledge depreciates rapidly even after the effects of labor movement were taken into account.

In summary, the results presented in Table 2.3 indicate that learning is acquired through experience in production: productivity improved markedly as the organizations gained experience in production. As discussed in Chapter 1, learning curves are often characterized in terms of a progress ratio, p. The progress ratio describes what happens to unit costs with each doubling of cumulative output. The parameter, b, in Equation (1.1) is related to the progress ratio, p, by the expression $p = 2^{-b}$. The progress ratio derived from the estimate of b in Column 2 of Table 2.3 is $2^{-.44}$%. This is a remarkable rate of productivity. With each doubling of the cumulative number of ships produced, the unit cost of production declines to 74% of its former value. This rapid rate of productivity growth is generally consistent with other analyses of productivity in the Liberty Ship production program (Searle & Gody, 1945).

The results shown in Table 2.3 also indicate that learning did not persist—knowledge acquired through production depreciated rapidly. With the exception of the model that included calendar time, estimates of lambda, the depreciation parameter, were all significantly less than one. When the model with calendar time was estimated using the more general translog specification, the depreciation parameter was significantly less than one.

We explored other potential explanations of our findings. For example, costs of changing the rate of output are often emphasized in discussions of production activities (e.g., Asher, 1956). As noted previously, Lockheed executives frequently mentioned the difficulties encountered when they increased the rate of production of the L-1011 ("Lockheed losses on TriStar," 1980). We investigated the importance of these adjustment costs in the shipbuilding program by including variables measuring the rate of change in input levels from one period to the next.

While there is evidence that adjustment costs were present in the Liberty Ship program, our results on the depreciation of knowledge were unchanged by the inclusion of the adjustment-cost variables.

We also investigated whether different results would be obtained with a more general specification of the production function. We performed additional analyses using the more general translog specification (Berndt & Christensen, 1973) that includes $(\ln H)^2$, $(\ln W)^2$ and $\ln H \ln W$ in addition to the terms appearing in the Cobb-Douglas production function shown in Table 2.3. We estimated the translog model for all of the models shown in Table 2.3. In all cases except Column 2 of Table 2.3, the additional terms introduced for the translog function were significant ($p < .05$). Estimates of lambda, the depreciation parameter, in these alternative models ranged from 0.62 to 0.80 and were all significantly less than one. Thus, the results with the more general translog model reinforced the results on knowledge depreciation.

We also allowed for the possibility that the rate of learning slowed down or leveled off. Cumulative output is the conventional measure of learning. Using cumulative output in logarithmic form, as in Equation (1.2), implies that unit costs converge to zero as cumulative output increases. It may be that cumulative output is the correct measure of learning but that unit costs converge to a positive number rather than to zero. To investigate whether the rate of learning levels off, we estimated Cobb-Douglas and translog production functions with both $\ln K$ and $(\ln K)^2$ as predictors. This quadratic function, evaluated at values of K less than the value at which the function reaches a minimum, can approximate a function with a positive asymptote—even with no depreciation of learning. The maximum likelihood estimate of lambda was significantly less than one when knowledge was included as a quadratic function. This provides further evidence that knowledge acquired through learning by doing depreciated.

We performed additional analyses to deal with the possibility that there might be simultaneity in the choice of inputs and outputs. This simultaneity might occur, for example, if shipyards that are less productive schedule more labor hours. To deal with this issue, we estimated several of the models shown in Table 2.3 using the nonlinear two-stage least-squares procedure of Amemiya (1974). As instruments, we used current and lagged values of real wages, shipyard dummy variables, time and time squared, lagged endogenous variables (output, shipways, labor hours), and current and lagged exogenous variables. The results from the nonlinear two-stage least-squares procedure were virtually identical to those obtained using ordinary least squares (see Table 2.3).

The results consistently exhibit evidence of economies of scale in shipbuilding. For example, the results in Column 1 of Table 2.3 indicate that an increase in hours and shipways of one percent would result in a 1.31 percent increase in output, other things constant. The results indicate that an increase in shipways would result in a more than proportionate increase in output, other things constant. When measures of labor hours and shipways are included in the models, the knowledge variable, K, is highly significant and the estimate of lambda, λ, that best fits the data is significantly less than one. Thus, the results indicate that when input effects and economies-of-scale effects are controlled for, strong evidence of learning and of its depreciation remains.

2.4.1.3 An Application

My colleagues and I used publicly available data to apply our findings on organizational learning and knowledge depreciation to Lockheed's production of the L-1011 (Argote, Beckman & Epple, 1990). Table 2.1 displays the yearly production of the L-1011. As Table 2.1 indicates, the rate of output of the L-1011 varied enormously over time. For a wide range of values of the depreciation parameter, Lockheed's production rates imply that the knowledge variable for the L-1011 peaked in late 1974 or early 1975 and then declined. A high level of the knowledge variable would be associated with low production costs.

Examining reports of Lockheed's cost data, we found that they are consistent with our hypothesis of depreciation. Lockheed reported in 1975 that production costs were less than the price at which each plane was sold ($20 million). Thus, production costs were low during the period when the knowledge variable was high. As can be seen from Table 2.1, cuts in production occurred in late 1975. Costs rose to exceed price and appeared to remain above price for the rest of the production program. In 1982, the L-1011 sold for between $29 and $35 million (converted to 1975 dollars for comparison with the earlier period). Thus, the unit cost of production was less than $20 million in real terms in 1975 when the knowledge variable was at its highest but greater than $29 million in real terms in 1982. These data are consistent with the hypothesis that depreciation occurred at Lockheed.

Benkard (1997) obtained detailed data from Lockheed on the production of the L-1011. Benkard demonstrated very convincingly that depreciation did indeed occur in the L-1011 production program. Indeed, the attractiveness of the model including depreciation is that it explains both the first half of production, which is consistent with the classic learning curve model, and the last half of production, in which costs rose rather than receded with increasing experience.

Benkard (1997) also investigated whether knowledge transferred completely between two different versions of the L-1011 produced by Lockheed. Although there was significant transfer across the two models, it was incomplete. That is, the second model benefited from some—but not all—of the production experience acquired on the first model. Evidence of depreciation remained—even when one allowed for incomplete knowledge transfer across the two models. This finding is very important because it suggests that the depreciation results are not due to product changes that render previous knowledge obsolete. Evidence of depreciation remained strong when incomplete knowledge transfer across the different models of the product was taken into account.

When we presented our results on depreciation along with follow-up work in aerospace, automotive and service industries to managers, the results seemed to strike a chord with them. Indeed, one manager referred to our results as documenting a phenomenon he fervently believed in and called "industrial amnesia."

2.4.1.4 Discussion of Causes of Knowledge Depreciation

What causes industrial amnesia? That is, why might knowledge depreciate? Knowledge could decay because products or processes change and thereby render old knowledge obsolete. The incomplete transfer of knowledge observed across the two models of the L-1011 by Benkard (1997) may reflect this obsolescence. Some of the knowledge acquired on the first model may not have been relevant for the second. Hence, incomplete transfer of knowledge occurred across the two models. The depreciation observed in the Lockheed case, however, was not due solely to this obsolescence. Evidence for depreciation remained strong even when incomplete transfer of knowledge across the models was taken into account. Future research aimed at assessing depreciation would benefit from allowing for incomplete transfer across models, if different models are manufactured. This would enable one to determine if depreciation occurred, while allowing for the possibility that knowledge acquired on one model may not be relevant for another.

Knowledge could also decay because organizational records are lost or become difficult to access. This phenomenon occurred at Steinway piano company. When the firm decided to put a discontinued piano back into production, Steinway discovered that it did not have any records or blueprints at its New York facility about how to produce the piano (Lenehan, 1982). Similarly, almost all of the information collected and stored before 1979 by Landsat, an earth surveillance program, is no longer accessible: the data were recorded by equipment that no longer exists or cannot be operated, and the magnetic images have "bled" over time (Marshal, 1989).

In a similar vein, the editors who restored the "Star Wars" trilogy discovered that the original prints of the film had seriously decayed (Morgenstern, 1997). The colors seemed wrong; the print looked faded. Although "Star Wars" had originally been shot on four different varieties of film stock, all of the varieties were subject to fading and various color shifts. Attempts had been made to preserve the completed negative of "Star Wars" on a pair of "protective masters." The preservation effort, however, was not successful. The negative was not cleaned properly before it was copied. The results of the copy attempt were never inspected. According to Morgenstern (1997), this problem is not unique to "Star Wars" but rather characterizes many films made as recently as the 1980s: "Many of our most cherished modern movies...are already in deep decay and could be lost to theatrical audiences forever" (p. A16). These examples illustrate that organizational knowledge can exhibit decay: having knowledge at one point in time does not guarantee that the organization will have it in the future.

Another possible cause of knowledge depreciation is member turnover. Organizational members may leave and take their knowledge with them. The shipbuilding results described previously did not indicate that turnover affected the productivity of the shipyards. There may have been conditions at the shipyards, however, that buffered them from the effects of turnover. A war was on—jobs were designed to be low in skill requirements so that inexperienced workers could be brought up to speed very quickly. Therefore, there was tremendous emphasis on standardization and formalization (Lane, 1951). Improvements made in one part of the yard were quickly codified and transmitted to others. Would organizations that place less emphasis on standardization be more affected by turnover than the highly standardized shipyards? This is a question we explored in subsequent studies. These studies of the effect of turnover on organizational learning and forgetting are discussed later in this chapter and in Chapter 3, on organizational memory.

Another question we examined in follow-up work was whether the departure of certain key people would affect organizational performance. Perhaps the departure of exceptional performers would affect organizational outcomes. Or perhaps the departure of gatekeepers (Allen, 1977) who bridge social networks or of individuals who occupy key positions in an organization's social network (Burt, 1992; Krackhardt & Hanson, 1993) would have more of an effect on organizational performance than the departure of individuals not occupying key structural positions. Whether the effect of turnover on organizational learning and forgetting depends on who turns over is a focus of our second study of knowledge depreciation. This study will now be described.

2.4.2 The Automotive Study

A major goal of our second study, which was conducted in the automotive industry, was to examine in more depth the role of labor turnover in the acquisition and depreciation of organizational knowledge. Although little empirical evidence existed about factors responsible for learning and depreciation in organizations, most discussions of organizational learning curves included individual learning as an important source of the gains in organizational productivity observed with increasing experience (Wright, 1936; Hirsch, 1952; Hayes & Wheelwright, 1984). Similarly, in their theoretical discussion of organizational learning, Walsh and Ungson (1991) pointed out that individuals can act as "retention facilities" for organizational memory. To the extent that knowledge acquired through learning by doing is embedded in individuals, their turnover would be harmful for organizational learning. Similarly, Huber (1991) and Simon (1991) suggested that turnover should be harmful for organizational memory.

2.4.2.1 Research on Consequences of Turnover

Although there has been a long tradition of research on predictors of turnover, only recently has research been devoted to determining the consequences of turnover (Dalton & Todor, 1979; Mobley, 1982; Mowday, Porter & Steers, 1982; Staw, 1980). There is little direct empirical evidence concerning the consequences of turnover for the outcome of organizational learning curves. As described previously, we did not find any evidence that the turnover of direct production workers affected the rate of learning and productivity gains in the Liberty ship production program. These results were surprising since the turnover rate in the shipyards was quite high, averaging over 10% per month.

The question then becomes: Are there conditions under which turnover affects learning and productivity gains? The automotive study analyzed whether the effect of turnover depended on who is leaving. Price (1977) suggested that the effect of turnover on organizational effectiveness depends on the performance levels of departing members. Similarly, Mowday, Porter and Steers (1982) hypothesized that characteristics of individuals leaving the organization moderate the effect of turnover on organizational performance. Boudreau and Berger (1985) developed a multivariate decision-theoretic utility model for assessing the consequences of employee movement into and out of an organization.

Empirical studies of the performance levels of departing employees have yielded mixed results. Although Price (1977) concluded that leavers are relatively more often high-performing employees than those remaining in the organization, Dalton, Krackhardt and Porter (1981), Dreher (1982), and Wells and Muchinsky (1985) all reported that the performance of employees who left an organization was significantly lower than the performance of those who remained. In their reviews of this literature, Jacovsky (1984) and McEvoy and Cascio (1987) concluded that turnover was higher among poor than among good performers. This relationship held for both voluntary and involuntary turnover but, of course, was stronger for involuntary turnover (McEvoy & Cascio, 1987).

Schwab (1991) suggested that whether it is the good or the poor performers who leave depends on several contingencies. Schwab (1991) found that the relationship between individual performance and turnover was positive for tenured faculty members and negative for untenured faculty. That is, for tenured faculty, higher performers were more likely to leave, whereas for untenured faculty the reverse was true. Schwab (1991) concluded that the relationship between individual performance and turnover depends on several contingencies, such as whether performance is externally visible, and whether there are external job opportunities. The mixed pattern of results on the relationship between individual performance and turnover suggests that it is difficult to predict a priori whether turnover is higher among good or among poor performers since the relationship depends on important contextual factors.

Nonetheless, whether it is the good or the bad performers who are leaving is likely to have important consequences for organizational outcomes (Mowday, Porter and Steers, 1982; Price, 1977). If it is the poor performers who are leaving an organization, we would not expect turnover to have a negative effect on organizational performance. Conversely, if it is the good performers who are departing, we would expect turnover to have a negative effect on performance. Thus, the performance of who is turning over should be taken into account when predicting the effect of turnover on organizational learning and productivity gains.

The automotive study examined empirically the role of turnover in organizational learning curves. We investigated whether the effect of turnover depended on the performance of who departed. We also investigated the effect of movement of employees into the plant. Our expectation was that movement of employees into the plant at moderate levels would have a positive effect on productivity. New employees may bring new ideas and new skills and be more highly motivated than employees with longer tenure (Abelson & Baysinger, 1984; Mowday, Porter & Steers, 1982; Staw, 1980). At some point, however, the cost of integrating too many new employees becomes disruptive for organizational performance. Thus, we expected a nonmontonic inverted-U shaped relationship between movement of individuals into the plant and productivity gains.

2.4.2.2 Method and Sources of Data

We collected data from a North American truck plant (Argote, Epple, Rao & Murphy, 1997). The workforce at the plant, which was unionized, numbered approximately 3,000. The technology at the plant was extremely advanced. We collected weekly data over a two-year period from the start of production at the plant. Our data include measures of the number of trucks produced, total direct labor hours worked, number of shifts worked, and movement of employees into and out of the plant.

The turnover data were disaggregated according to the various reasons employees left the plant. Based on theoretical reasons, the effects of two types of turnover were investigated: turnover of high-performing employees who left the plant because they were promoted (promotion) and turnover of employees who were discharged for poor performance (discharge). A third turnover variable included all other reasons employees departed that were not a function of performance (e.g., retired, deceased, quit, laid off, and so on). We performed sensitivity analyses which disaggregated these other types of turnover and investigated their separate effects as well.

We took the same general approach to estimation described for the shipyards study. Our general approach was to estimate production functions. Since we analyzed data from only one plant, however, there was no need to control for physical facilities since they were relatively unchanged throughout the course of the study.

The same approach to assessing depreciation was used for the automotive study as for the shipyards study. As in the previous study, if $\lambda = 1$, the accumulated stock of knowledge equaled cumulative output, the measure of knowledge in the conventional learning curve formulation. Thus, if $\lambda = 1$, there was no evidence of depreciation. If $\lambda < 1$, evidence of depreciation existed since past output received less weight than recent output in predicting current productivity.

2.4.2.3 Results

We first estimated the classic learning curve. In this analysis, the value of λ, the depreciation parameter, was constrained to equal one. Thus, this model is the conventional learning curve that assumes knowledge is cumulative and persists through time. The results from estimating this model provided strong evidence of learning at the automotive plant: production increased significantly with rising cumulative output. Results also indicated that there were constant returns to labor hours and that output went up proportionately with the number of shifts worked.

The progress ratio derived from the estimates of the learning rate in this study was 83%. Thus, each doubling of cumulative output at the plant led to a 17% reduction in unit cost. This number is generally consistent with the modal progress ratio observed by Dutton and Thomas (1984) across over 100 studies in different industries of 81-82% (see Figure 1.4).

We then estimated a model that did not constrain the depreciation parameter to equal one. The value of λ, 0.989, obtained from estimating this model, was significantly less than one. In subsequent analyses, we also included time as an explanatory variable to investigate the extent to which technical progress associated with the passage of time was responsible for productivity gains. There was evidence that the plant became more productive as time passed. The knowledge variable remained highly significant when time was included as an explanatory variable. Further, the depreciation parameter was significantly less than one in this analysis that included the time variable. Indeed, the estimated value of the depreciation parameter was lower for this model than for the previous ones.

These results may have interesting implications for organizational memory. The results suggest that there may be a relatively permanent component to organizational memory as well as a more transitory component. The permanent component, which the time variable may be picking up, may correspond to knowledge embedded in the organization's procedures and routines. This permanent or procedural component does not evidence depreciation. The more transitory component of organizational memory is reflected in the faster depreciation rate found in the model that accounts for the permanent component of organizational knowledge. This transitory component may be analogous to declarative knowledge, or knowledge of facts (cf. Singley & Anderson, 1989). Cohen and Bacdayan (1994) extended the distinction between procedural and declarative knowledge made in analyses of individual cognition to the dyadic level of analysis. In an interesting laboratory study, Cohen and Bacdayan (1994) found that procedural knowledge exhibited less forgetting than declarative knowledge. Our results from the field suggest that there may be both a permanent and a transitory component to organizational memory.

Another major focus of the automotive study was analyzing the effect of personnel movement into the plant on productivity. We found an inverted-U relationship between the number of new hires moving into the plant and the plant's productivity. Further analyses revealed that the maximum of this function was reached at 38 persons per week. Thus, increases in the number of new hires moving into the plant up to approximately 38 persons (between one and two percent of the workforce) per week were associated with increases in productivity. Beyond that point, decreases in productivity were observed.

To investigate our hypothesis that the effect of turnover depended on the performance of the departing employees, additional analyses were performed in which the turnover variable was disaggregated as a function of the reason employees departed. In these analyses, the coefficient of the variable representing employees who were promoted out of the plant as a result of their good performance was negative and significant, as predicted. Thus, the turnover of these high-performing employees negatively affected the organization's productivity. The coefficient of the variable representing employees who were discharged for poor performance was positive, consistent with the expectation that their removal would improve organizational performance. The discharge variable, however, was not consistently significant. The variable representing other types of turnover did not approach significance.

Sensitivity analyses were performed in which the types of turnover included in the "other" category were disaggregated and their effects estimated, either separately or in combination with other types of turnover. With the exception of the "lay-off" variable, these other types of turnover were not significantly related to productivity. In a few analyses, the coefficient of the lay-off variable was negative and marginally significant. In a few regressions, the positive coefficient of the discharge variable was significant. These effects, however, were not consistently significant.

Additional analyses were performed to investigate whether the rate of learning plateaued or slowed down over time. We investigated this possibility by including a quadratic term, the square of the knowledge variable. The coefficient of the square of the knowledge variable was extremely small in magnitude and did not approach statistical significance, suggesting that the rate of learning did not change in this production environment.

Since some product options may require more labor content than others, we also investigated the effect of product mix on productivity by including a variable representing different product options in the model.

The coefficient of the product mix variable was small in magnitude and statistically insignificant. Including the product mix variable did not affect the coefficients of the other variables in the model.

The results obtained from these additional analyses reinforced our previous conclusions regarding learning, depreciation, and the role of turnover in learning and its depreciation. The evidence for learning remained strong. The depreciation parameter was significantly less than one. Movement of new employees into the plant at moderate levels was consistently shown to help productivity. Turnover of high-performing employees due to promotions appeared to hurt the plant's productivity.

2.4.3 The Franchise Study

We also investigated whether knowledge depreciated in a study of fast food franchises (Darr, Argote & Epple, 1995). Since our primary goal in the franchise study was to investigate the transfer of knowledge across the various stores, this study is described in depth in Chapter 5. We also investigated whether knowledge depreciated in the study since knowledge that depreciates rapidly may be difficult to transfer.

Our analyses of learning in the fast food franchises were based on weekly data. Estimates of the depreciation parameter obtained in the fast food study ranged from 0.80 to 0.83 (Darr, Argote & Epple, 1995). This is an incredibly rapid rate of depreciation. A value of the depreciation parameter equal to 0.83 implies that roughly one half ($\lambda^4=0.84^4$) of the stock of knowledge available at the beginning of a month would remain at the end of the month. From a stock of knowledge available at the beginning of a year, a very negligible amount ($\lambda^{52}=0.84^{52}$) would remain one year later. Without continuing production to replenish the stock of knowledge, virtually all production knowledge would be lost by mid-year. The rate of depreciation found in the fast food study is the most rapid we have found.

2.5 Depreciation Rates Vary

Because the extent to which knowledge depreciated varied across the contexts we have studied, these studies provide grist to develop hypotheses about factors affecting the rate of depreciation in organizations. By far the most rapid depreciation was found in the fast food study. One important way in which the fast food franchises differed from the other organizations we have studied is their low technological sophistication. An interesting hypothesis that is consistent with our results is that more technologically sophisticated organizations exhibit less depreciation than less technologically sophisticated ones. For high technology organizations, much of their knowledge is embedded in their technology—in their layout, software and hardware. Knowledge embedded in technology may be more resistant to depreciation than knowledge embedded in other respositories.

Another interesting hypothesis worthy of further investigation concerns the role of labor turnover in knowledge depreciation. The turnover in the fast food franchises was incredibly high: the turnover rate of employees was approximately 25% per month. The shipyards had an intermediate level of turnover, averaging approximately 10% per month. The turnover rate in the automotive plant was considerably less than this, averaging between 1% and 2% each month. Thus, we found the fastest depreciation in the organizations that experienced the highest turnover. These results suggest that the average turnover rate may affect the rate of depreciation. Further research is needed to understand the conditions under which knowledge depreciates in organizations and the factors affecting the rate of depreciation.

One study that examined knowledge depreciation in a very different setting did not find evidence of decay. Ingram and Simons (1997) did not find evidence of depreciation in their analysis of the profitability of kibbutz agriculture. Ingram and Simons suggested that the persistence of knowledge observed in kibbutzim may be due to the very stable and motivated membership of these organizations. Ingram and Simons' suggestion about the importance of stable membership is consistent with the hypothesis about the role of labor turnover in knowledge depreciation.

The following chapter develops these ideas further, introducing the concept of organizational memory and describing various "retention facilities" or "repositories" for organizational knowledge. The implications of where knowledge is embedded for its persistence over time and its transfer to other organizations are developed in Chapters 3 and 5.

2.6 Implications for Practice

The results on knowledge depreciation have important implications for both operational and strategic decisions in organizations. On the operational side, depreciation has important ramifications for forecasting, planning and scheduling. If knowledge depreciates, forecasts based on the conventional learning curve will systematically overestimate future productivity. The gap between an organization's actual and predicted productivity may cause major problems for the organization, including poor relations with customers and failure to make significant gains in market share. If the gap between actual and predicted productivity is high, the organization may never reach the point where its production program is profitable (e.g., see the Lockheed case). Thus, knowledge depreciation has important implications for operational decisions in firms.

Knowledge depreciation also has important implications for the strategic behavior of firms. If knowledge depreciates, recent output is a more important predictor of current productivity than cumulative output. Thus, knowledge depreciation lessens the benefits of having a large stock of accumulated knowledge. Under conditions of knowledge depreciation, a recent entrant to an industry may not be very disadvantaged relative to firms with a large stock of cumulative output. Knowledge depreciation may explain in part how Korean semiconductor firms that started production in the 1980s, which was much later than their counterparts in the United States and Japan, achieved significant positions in world markets by the 1990s (Cho, Kim & Rhee, 1998).

2.7 Conclusion

The results of the three studies described here provide evidence that knowledge acquired through learning by doing may depreciate. Knowledge was found to depreciate to a great extent in both the shipyards and the fast food franchises. There was also evidence that knowledge depreciated in the truck assembly plant. Benkard (1997) found that depreciation of knowledge occurred in the Lockheed production program. Thus, the classic learning curve that assumes knowledge is cumulative overstates the persistence of organizational knowledge for these organizations. Results presented here suggest that recent experience is a more important predictor of current productivity than experience in the distant past.

The fastest rate of depreciation was found in the fast food franchises. Several important differences between these organizations and the other study settings were described that may explain the differences observed in their rates of knowledge depreciation. One key difference centered on the technological sophistication of the settings. Knowledge embedded in technology may be more resistant to depreciation than knowledge embedded in other repositories. Another key difference between the settings was the extent of labor turnover. High levels of turnover may make it very difficult for organizations to retain knowledge. Further research is needed to investigate the effect of these (and other) factors on knowledge depreciation.

Although we did not find evidence that turnover made a significant difference in shipbuilding, we did find evidence that turnover made a difference in the automotive plant, when who was turning over was taken into account. The departure of high-performing employees hurt the truck plant's productivity. When we presented the findings to managers at the plant, they provided an example of how individuals can make a difference even in these capital-intensive systems. The plant had been plagued by a persistent problem: the same defect (a thin scratch) appeared on all the trucks. Considerable energy was invested to isolate the source of the defect. Equipment was inspected; software was checked. It was ultimately discovered that the defect was caused by a disgruntled employee who used his watch to scratch the paint job on each truck! This example illustrates how individuals can affect organizational outcomes—even in highly capital-intensive industries.

Understanding whether knowledge depreciates is important for organizations. If depreciation occurs, failure to allow for it in forecasts of future productivity will lead to forecasts with large errors. This occurred at Lockheed. Lockheed's forecasts of future productivity systematically overshot their actual productivity by a significant amount. Lockheed lost billions of dollars on the L-1011 program, the last commercial aircraft Lockheed produced. Such overly optimistic forecasts may cause significant problems for organizations.

Notes

1. In our analysis, data from 13 of the 16 yards that produced Liberty Ships were used because data on one or more variables were missing for the other yards.
2. Data on output were available from the beginning of production in each yard, but observations on other variables typically were unavailable until the yard had been operating for a month or more. Hence, the first month of production never appears in our sample. Consequently, K_{it-1} is always greater than zero and $\ln K_{it-1}$ is always defined.
3. The error term ε_{it} in Equation (2.3) is assumed to be serially uncorrelated and uncorrelated (in large samples) with all variables other than u_{it} on the right-hand side of Equation (2.1). Furthermore, the ε_{it} are assumed to be uncorrelated across shipyards.
4. Benkard (1997) provided a more general treatment of the error structure in his analysis of knowledge depreciation.

References

Abelson, M. A., & Baysinger, B. D. (1984). Optimal and dysfunctional turnover: Toward an organizational level model. *Academy of Management Review, 9*, 331-341.

Allen, T. J. (1977). *Managing the flow of technology: Technology transfer and the dissemination of technological information within the R&D organization.* Cambridge, MA: MIT Press.

Amemiya, T. (1974). The nonlinear two-stage least-squares estimator. *Journal of Econometrics, 2*, 105-110.

Argote, L., Beckman, S. L., & Epple, D. (1990). The persistence and transfer of learning in industrial settings. *Management Science, 36*, 140-154.

Argote, L., & Epple, D. (1990, February 23). Learning curves in manufacturing. *Science, 247*, 920-924.

Argote, L., Epple, D., Rao, R. D., & Murphy, K. (1997). *The acquisition and depreciation of knowledge in a manufacturing organization: Turnover and plant productivity.* Working paper, Graduate School of Industrial Administration, Carnegie Mellon University.

Asher, H. (1956). *Cost-quantity relationships in the air-frame industry.* Santa Monica, CA: Rand Corporation.

Baloff, N. (1970). Startup management. *IEEE Transactions on Engineering Management, EM-17*, 132-141.

Batchelder, C. A., Boren, H. E., Campbell, H. G., Dei Rossi, J. A., & Large, J. P. (1969). *An introduction to equipment cost estimating.* Santa Monica, CA: Rand Corporation.

Benkard, C. L. (1997). *Learning and forgetting: The dynamics of aircraft production.* Working paper, Yale University

Berndt, E. R., & Christensen, L. R. (1973). The translog function and the substitution of equipment, structures, and labor in U.S. Manufacturing 1929-68. *Journal of Econometrics, 1*, 81-113.

Boudreau, J. W., & Berger, C. J. (1985). Decision-theoretic utility analysis applied to employee separations and acquisitions. *Journal of Applied Psychology, 70*, 581-612.

Burt, R. S. (1992). *Structural holes: The social structure of competition.* Cambridge, MA: Harvard University Press.

Carlson, J. G., & Rowe, A. J. (1976). How much does forgetting cost? *Industrial Engineering, 8*(9), 40-47.

Cho, D., Kim, D., & Rhee, D. (1998). Latecomer strategies: Evidence from the semiconductor industry in Japan and Korea. *Organization Science, 9*, 489-505.

Cohen, M. D., & Bacdayan, P. (1994). Organizational routines are stored as procedural memory: Evidence from a laboratory study. *Organization Science, 5*, 554-568.

Dalton, D. R., Krackhardt, D. M., & Porter, L. W. (1981). Functional turnover: An empirical assessment. *Journal of Applied Psychology, 66*, 715-721.

Dalton, D. R., & Todor, W. D. (1979). Turnover turned over: An expanded and positive perspective. *Academy of Management Review, 4*, 225-235.

Darr, E., Argote, L., & Epple, D. (1995). The acquisition, transfer and depreciation of knowledge in service organizations: Productivity in franchises. *Management Science, 41*, 1750-1762.

Dhrymes, P. J. (1966). On the treatment of certain recurrent nonlinearities in regression analysis. *Southern Economic Journal, 33*, 187-196.

Dreher, G. F. (1982). The role of performance in the turnover process. *Academy of Management Journal, 25*, 137-147.

Dutton, J. M., & Thomas, A. (1984). Treating progress functions as a managerial opportunity. *Academy of Management Review, 9*, 235-247.

Fandel, T. E. (1974, June 3). Lockheed is planning a writedown of $600 million on its TriStar in a complex financial restructuring. *The Wall Street Journal*, p. 3.

Fisher, G. J. (1949). A statistical summary of shipbuilding under the U.S. Maritime Commission during World War II. *Historical Reports of War Administration*, United States Maritime Commission.

Goldfeld, S. M., & Quandt, R. E. (1972). *Nonlinear methods in econometrics.* Amsterdam: North-Holland.

Harris, R. J., Jr. (1981a, May 13). Lockheed may end production of L-1011 if dearth of orders for the jet continues. *The Wall Street Journal*, p. 7.

Harris, R. J., Jr. (1981b, December 8). Lockheed plans to end output of L-1011 jet. *The Wall Street Journal*, p. 3.

Harris, R. J., Jr., (1981c, December 9). Delayed takeoff: Stalled jetliner makers may not rise steeply even if airlines do. *The Wall Street Journal*, pp. 1, 22.

Harris, R. J., Jr. (1982, April 20). All options to purchase Lockheed L-1011's apparently are canceled by air carriers. *The Wall Street Journal*, p. 8.

Hayes, R. H., & Wheelwright, S. C. (1984). *Restoring our competitive edge: Competing through manufacturing.* New York: Wiley.

Hill, C. G. (1980, July 30). Lockheed posts 2nd quarter loss of $26.6 million. *The Wall Street Journal*, p. 12.

Hirsch, W. Z., (1952). Manufacturing progress functions. *Review of Economics and Statistics, 34*, 143-155.

Holusha, J. (1994, March 27). Can Boeing's new baby fly financially? *The New York Times*, pp. F1, F6.

Huber, G. P. (1991). Organizational learning: The contributing processes and the literatures. *Organization Science, 2*, 88-115.

Ingram, P., & Simons, T. (1997). *Interorganizational relations and the performance outcomes of experience.* Working paper, Graduate School of Industrial Administration, Carnegie Mellon University.

Jacovsky, E. F. (1984). Turnover and job performance: An integrated process model. *Academy of Management Review, 9*, 74-83.

Krackhardt, D., & Hanson, J. R. (1993). Informal networks: The company behind the chart. *Harvard Business Review, 71*(4), 104-111.

Lane, F. C. (1951). *Ships for victory: A history of shipbuilding under the U.S. Maritime Commission in World War II.* Baltimore: The Johns Hopkins Press.

Lenehan, M. (1982, August). The quality of the instrument. *The Atlantic Monthly, 250*(2), 32-58

Lockheed loses hope TriStar program will show profit but sees improvement (1980, May 14). *The Wall Street Journal,* p. 24.

Lockheed losses on TriStar grew in 2nd quarter (1980, June 20). *The Wall Street Journal,* p. 19.

Marshal, E. (1989, June 6). Early data: Losing our memory. *Science, 244,* 1250.

McEvoy, G. M., & Cascio, W. F. (1987). Do good or poor performers leave? A meta analysis of the relationship between performance and turnover. *Academy of Management Journal, 30,* 744-762.

Mobley, W. H. (1982). *Employee turnover: Causes, consequences and control.* Reading, MA: Addison-Wesley.

Morgenstern, J. (1997, January 31). On film: The battle to save "Star Wars". *The Wall Street Journal,* p. A16.

Mowday, R. T., Porter, L. W., & Steers, R. M. (1982). *Employee-organization linkages: The psychology of commitment, absenteeism, and turnover.* New York: Academic Press.

Porter, M. E. (1979, October 22). Experience curve. *The Wall Street Journal,* p 30.

Price, J. L. (1977). *The study of turnover.* Iowa: The Iowa State University Press.

Rapping, L. (1965). Learning and World War II production functions. *Review of Economics and Statistics, 47,* 81-86.

Reinhardt, U. F. (1973). Break-even analysis for Lockheed's TriStar: An application of financial theory. *Journal of Finance, 28,* 821-838.

Sansweet, S. J. (1975, November 7). Lockheed net soared 108% in 3rd period but outlook for TriStar sales is dismal. *The Wall Street Journal,* p. 15.

Schwab, D. P. (1991). Contextual variables in employee performance-turnover relationships. *Academy of Management Journal, 34,* 966-975.

Searle, A. D., & Gody, C. S. (1945). Productivity changes in selected wartime shipbuilding programs. *Monthly Labor Review, 61,* 1132-1147.

Simon, H. A. (1991). Bounded rationality and organizational learning. *Organization Science, 2,* 125-134.

Singley, M. K., & Anderson, J. R. (1989). *The transfer of cognitive skill.* Cambridge, MA: Harvard University Press.

Smunt, T. L. (1987) The impact of worker forgetting on production scheduling. *International Journal of Production Research, 25,* 689-701.

Smunt, T. L., & Morton, T. L. (1985). The effect of learning on optimal lot sizes: Further developments on the single product case. *IIE Transactions, 17,* 33-37.

Staw, B. M. (1980). The consequences of turnover. *Journal of Occupational Behavior, 1,* 253-273.

Sule, D. R. (1983). Effect of learning and forgetting on economic lot size scheduling problem. *International Journal of Production Research, 21,* 771-786.

The TriStar's trail of red ink (1980, July 28). *Business Week*, pp. 88, 90.

Walsh, J. P., & Ungson, G. R. (1991). Organizational memory. *Academy of Management Review, 16*, 57-91.

Wells, D. L., & Muchinsky, P. M. (1985). Performance antecedents of voluntary and involuntary managerial turnover. *Journal of Applied Psychology, 70*, 329-336.

Womer, N. K. (1979). Learning curves, production rate, and program costs. *Management Science, 25*, 312-319.

Womer, N. K. (1984). Estimating learning curves from aggregate monthly data. *Management Science, 30*, 982-992.

Wright, T. P. (1936). Factors affecting the costs of airplanes. *Journal of the Aeronautical Sciences, 3*, 122-128.

Yelle, L. E. (1979). The learning curve: Historical review and comprehensive survey. *Decision Sciences, 10*, 302-328.

Chapter 3

Organizational Memory

3.1 Introduction

What do organizations learn as they gain experience in production? Where is this knowledge embedded within organizations? What are the consequences of where knowledge is embedded for organizational performance? This chapter begins with a discussion of what is learned as groups and organizations gain experience in production. A more general discussion of organizational memory and various "retention bins" or "repositories" of organizational knowledge follows. Examples of knowledge embedded in various repositories drawn from our studies of manufacturing and service industries are provided. Empirical evidence on the extent to which organizational knowledge is embedded in these various repositories is described. The chapter concludes with a discussion of the implications of where knowledge is embedded for important aspects of organizational functioning and effectiveness.

3.2 Sources of Productivity Gains

Many researchers have speculated about factors responsible for the productivity gains observed in organizations with increasing experience. For example, Joskow and Rosanski (1979) discussed the following factors as contributors to the productivity gains observed with increasing experience: routinization of tasks, more efficient production control, improved equipment design, and improved routing and material handling. Thus, these researchers emphasize changes in the task and technology as contributors to productivity gains associated with experience. Hayes and Wheelwright (1984) listed a broader set of factors as facilitators of organizational learning. According to Hayes and Wheelwright (1984), organizational learning curves are due to: individual learning, better selection and training, improved methods, enhanced equipment and technology, more appropriate division of labor and specialization, improved product design, substitution of capital for labor, incentives, and leadership. Similarly, Porter (1979) noted that with more experience, firms learn to make methods more productive, to design layout and workflow more efficiently, to coax more production out of machinery, to develop specialized new processes and product design modifications that improve manufacturability, and to institute better management control. In our interviews with managers at manufacturing plants about their views of the most important determinants of organizational learning curves, our respondents emphasized the following: increased proficiency of individual workers; improvements in the organization's technology, tooling, and layout; improvements in its structure, organization, and methods of coordination; and better understanding of who in the organization is good at what (Argote, 1993). Better understanding of each individual's skills enables the organization to assign tasks more appropriately so as to take better advantage of each individual's unique capabilities. Knowledge of each member's special expertise is also beneficial because members of the organization know whom to go to for help or advice about specific issues.

These myriad factors believed to affect learning can be classified into three general categories: improvements in the performance of individual employees, including direct production workers, managers, and technical support staff; improvements in the organization's structure and routines; and improvements in the organization's technology. Examples of improvements in each of these categories will now be discussed. These examples are drawn from our field studies of learning in manufacturing and service organizations.

3.2.1 Increased Individual Proficiency

Most discussions of factors responsible for organizational learning curves cite learning by individual workers as a key factor (e.g., see Hayes & Wheelwright, 1984; Yelle, 1979). A long stream of research in psychology has documented that individual performance improves as individuals acquire more experience with a task (Graham & Gagne, 1940; Thorndike, 1898; Thurstone, 1919). Reviews of the large body of research on individual learning can be found in Anzai and Simon (1979), Newell and Rosenbloom (1981), and Mazur and Hastie (1978).

Our interest is in individuals working in organized settings. What qualify as examples of improvements in individual performance that occur in ongoing groups and organizations as individuals gain experience in production? Many examples of individuals becoming more skilled at their particular tasks can be found in our study of fast food franchises. For example, pizza makers typically became more proficient at hand-tossing pizza dough and transforming it into a pizza shell as they acquired experience. Much of the knowledge about how to hand-toss pizza was tacit and therefore difficult to articulate to others (Nonaka, 1991; Polanyi, 1966). This knowledge remained primarily embedded in the individual workers who had acquired experience with the pizza-tossing task.

We also observed improvements in the performance of individual workers in manufacturing plants. At one plant we studied, a second shift was introduced almost two years after the plant had been in operation with one shift. Workers on the new shift worked side by side workers on the first shift to learn their jobs. Workers on the new shift were gradually "weaned" from their experienced counterparts until the new employees were working independently on the second shift. Through observing workers on the first shift and gaining experience with the task, workers on the new shift learned their individual jobs and became very proficient at them.

3.2.2 Modifications in Technology

Modifications in technology are another major contributor to the productivity gains observed in organizations with increasing experience. By technology, we mean equipment, including hardware and software (cf. Amber & Amber, 1962; Barley, 1986; Blau, Falbe, McKinley & Tracy, 1976) used in production. An example of modification in technology that derived from experience in production can be found in the paint shop at one of the truck assembly plants we studied. The plant experienced problems in its new highly automated paint shop. When light-colored products followed dark-colored ones, vestiges of the dark color could be found on the subsequent, light-colored product. This was clearly unacceptable. Plant managers and engineers tried various approaches to remedy the problem. The most effective solution that was developed involved dedicating particular paint booths to particular dark colors. Thus, only products of the same dark color would be processed through each booth. If any residue paint remained in the system, it would not be harmful since all the products going through the booth were the same color. While dedicating a paint booth to a particular color resulted in some loss in flexibility for the system, the lost flexibility was more than offset by the improved product quality and the reduced waste. This manufacturing example illustrates how knowledge acquired via learning by doing can lead to modifications in an organization's technology. Knowledge was embedded in the "software" and the "hardware" of the paint shop that enabled the organization to produce a higher quality, less costly product.

We also observed several examples of improvements in technology in our study of fast food franchises (Argote & Darr, in press). Technology in the context of these pizza stores includes the equipment, such as ovens, and tools used to make pizzas, as well as the physical layout of the stores. The "cheese spreader" is an example of an innovation developed through production experience that became embedded in the organization's technology. Achieving an even distribution of cheese across a pizza is a desired goal. Too much cheese decreases profit margins, whereas too little cheese decreases customer satisfaction. A manager at one of the stores we studied decided that spreading cheese by hand was not the best method. The manager believed that the problem was analogous to spreading fertilizer on a lawn and that some type of "spreader" was needed. The manager experimented with various configurations of plastic dishes and metal screens to develop a tool that would help pizza makers use a consistent amount of cheese and achieve an even distribution of the topping. The final version of the "cheese spreader" tool was a plastic cone with holes that sat on feet several inches above the pizza. A pizza maker would pour grated cheese into the cone and the cheese would fall in a consistent pattern over the pizza. This example illustrates—in a very different organizational context—how knowledge acquired via experience can be embedded in an organization's technology.

3.2.3 Elaborations in Structure and Routines

Elaborations in structure and routines made as organizations gain experience in production also contribute to organizational learning. One such elaboration we saw at a manufacturing plant involved changing the structure of the industrial engineering group. A decision was made to deploy the industrial engineering group that had previously been centralized in one area of the plant to various areas on the plant floor so that the engineers could be more responsive to production problems. Thus, the industrial engineers were shifted from a functional-type organization where they were centralized in one area to a product-type organization where they were decentralized to various areas on the plant floor. The decentralized organization enabled the engineers to respond more quickly to issues on the plant floor. In this example, knowledge about how to be more responsive was embedded in the manufacturing plant's structure.

Another example of knowledge embedded in routines occurred in a manufacturing plant we studied. The particular routine involved preparing the products (trucks) for painting: painting two-tone trucks was challenging since workers had to mask the areas of the truck that were not to be painted a particular color by taping large sheets of protective paper over the appropriate areas. As experience was gained with the task, a better method for placing the protective paper was discovered. Initially, workers masked the area of the truck that was not to be painted a particular color to protect those areas and then painted the rest of the truck the desired color (e.g., white). They then reversed the masking by placing protective paper over the area that had already been painted the desired color (e.g., white) and painted the remainder of the truck the second color (e.g., red). This process required two stages of carefully masking the truck with protective paper. A new method of masking was discovered that required only one round of masking. All of the truck was painted one background color (e.g., white). The parts of the truck that were to remain the background color were then masked and the truck was painted the second color (e.g., red). The new process saved considerable time since the trucks only had to be masked with protective paper once. The new method, which required fewer labor hours and less material to achieve the desired two-tone paint job, ultimately became embedded in a routine that all workers used.

We also observed knowledge embedded in an organization's routines in our study of fast food franchises (Argote & Darr, in press). When deep-dish pizza was introduced at the pizza stores, all stores experienced a persistent problem with the new product. The usual method of distributing pepperoni on pizzas was to distribute it evenly over the pizza before the pizza was cooked. Although this method worked for regular pizzas, it did not work well for deep-dish ones. When pepperoni was distributed evenly on deep-dish pizzas, the pieces of pepperoni would all move into the center in one "clump" as the pizza cooked and the cheese flowed. Various methods of dealing with the problem were implemented. The most successful one involved distributing the pepperoni on the pizza before it was cooked in a pattern that resembled spokes on a wheel. As the pizza was cooked, the flow of the cheese distributed the pepperoni pieces (more or less) evenly over the pizza. Thus, knowledge about how to distribute pepperoni evenly became embedded in a routine. This routine proved to be very effective at achieving an even distribution of pepperoni. The routine is now used by virtually every store in the corporation.

3.3 Repositories of Organizational Knowledge

How do these examples of sources of productivity gains relate to more theoretical discussions of organizational memory or of where knowledge is embedded in organizations? Stein (1995) defined organizational memory as the means by which knowledge from the past is brought to bear on present organizational activities.   According to Stein (1995), "memory is a persistent record not dependent on a tight coupling between sender and receiver" (p. 22).   Similarly, Walsh and Ungson (1991) defined organizational memory as stored information from an organization's past and Casey (1997) defined it as shared interpretations of the past.

Where is this knowledge from the past embedded within an organization?   Levitt and March (1988) indicated that knowledge is embedded in an organization's routines and standard operating procedures, in its products and processes, in its technologies and equipment, in its layout and structures, and in its culture and norms about how things are generally done. Similarly, Walsh and Ungson (1991) conceptualized five "retention bins" for organizational memory: individual employees, the organization's culture, its standard operating procedures and practices, roles and organizational structures, and the physical structure of the workplace. According to Starbuck (1992), in knowledge-intensive firms, knowledge is embedded in individuals, in physical capital (including hardware and software), in the organization's routines, and in its culture.

These theoretical discussions of organizational memory or retention bins share much in common. The key point on which they differ is whether or not individuals are seen as a repository for organizational knowledge. Walsh and Ungson (1991) and Starbuck (1992) took the position that they are, whereas Levitt and March (1988) argued that the memory does not become organizational until it is captured in a repository that is not dependent on the vagaries of individual membership.

Yates (1990) provided a fascinating account of the evolution of organizational memory from knowledge that resided primarily in individuals to knowledge that resided in supra-individual form. In the early 1800s, organizational memory was primarily embedded in individuals. According to Yates (1990), the growth of the railroads changed that. The changes were brought about by the need to coordinate a geographically dispersed business where lapses of coordination could result in serious accidents. For these firms, timetables and detailed operational procedures became part of their way of doing business—part of their organizational memory.

An elaboration of organizational memory occurred on a more widespread basis with the advent of scientific management at the turn of the century (Taylor, 1911). One of the principles of this movement was to capture the knowledge of individuals so that organizations would not be dependent on them or vulnerable to their turnover. Written records were elaborated; manuals were developed that described an organization's rules and procedures. Reporting systems were also established to transmit information up the hierarchy. Thus, the late 1800s and early 1900s witnessed a shift from organizational memory being embodied primarily in individuals to its embodiment in records, rules, and procedures that did not depend on individuals.

Nelson and Winter (1982) focused on routines as repositories of organizational knowledge (see March & Simon, 1958, and Cyert & March, 1963, for earlier discussions of organizational routines). Gersick and Hackman (1990) described routines at the group level of analysis. Carley (1996) provided evidence from a simulation study that the use of routines or standard operating procedures (SOPs) can enhance the accuracy of organizational decision making.

According to Nelson and Winter (1982), routines are programs or repetitive patterns of activity. In order for organizations to function effectively in routine conditions, individuals must be familiar with the procedures their jobs require and know when particular routines are appropriate. While each individual must know his or her particular job, the individual does not need to know the jobs of others or the routines that guide the organization as a whole. Indeed, the scale and complexity of many organizations make it difficult to achieve coordination through centralized information or control systems that describe all the routines used by the organization and the interrelationships among them.

Theraulaz and Bonabeau (1995) described a fascinating example of the implementation of routines in a wasp colony. The researchers noted that while individual insects possess a limited repertoire of routines, insects are collectively capable of performing complex tasks, such as nest building. Theraulaz and Bonabeau cited an early study by Grasse showing that coordination of nest building activity in termites does not depend upon interactions among the workers themselves but rather depends upon the structure of the nest. The inputs of one worker are cued by the outputs of another. Actions taken by one worker modify the nest configuration, which in turn automatically triggers new actions by other workers.

This example is similar to Nelson and Winter's discussion of routines in organizations in that individual members of the collectivity must know their own routines and the triggering conditions for them but do not need to know others' routines. The nest-building example is analogous to how work is structured on many assembly lines. Employees know their own routines. They identify which routine to implement by observing the product—either its physical condition or information cues attached to it describing its requirements. For example, an employee might observe that the next truck she is to work on requires an air conditioning system—either by observing that there already are parts of the air conditioning system installed or by reading a list of product specifications attached to the truck.

This knowledge then cues particular activities by the employee that involve installing an air conditioner. This example illustrates how an individual's activities can be cued by the product and its specification sheet. Direct interaction among individual employees may not be required.

Although these discussions of organizational memory differ concerning the exact number of repositories of knowledge, the discussions have much in common. Researchers generally agree that organizational knowledge resides in: individuals, including managers, technical support staff, and direct production workers; the organization's technology, including its layout, hardware, and software; the organization's structure, routines, and methods of coordination; and the organization's culture.

The first three factors (individuals, technology, and structure) have consistently been cited by other researchers who study manufacturing organizations as contributing to the productivity gains observed with increasing experience (e.g., Hayes & Wheelwright, 1984). These three factors were also mentioned by respondents at the organizations we studied as contributors to organizational learning curves. By contrast, culture did not emerge as being particularly important in these settings, although it may be more important in organizations that produce less tangible products. Culture is certainly a repository for some knowledge in these manufacturing organizations. In order for culture to explain the changes in productivity associated with experience, however, it would have to change as the organizations gained experience. We did not see examples of significant changes in culture in our studies and apparently neither did other researchers who study learning curves in manufacturing organizations. Thus, knowledge about productivity improvements in manufacturing organizations is primarily embedded in individuals or in the organizations' technology or structure. Empirical evidence about the extent to which knowledge is embedded in these repositories will now be presented.

3.3.1 Knowledge Embedded in Individuals

We turn now to evaluating empirical evidence on the extent to which knowledge acquired through learning by doing is embedded in individual employees. As noted previously, most discussions about factors responsible for organizational learning curves include learning by individual employees as a key factor. Similarly, most discussions of organizational memory cite individuals as a key repository of organizational knowledge. If knowledge is embedded in individuals, then their turnover should affect organizational memory.

Engeström, Brown, Engeström and Koistinen (1990) described an example of knowledge being embedded in an individual. The researchers analyzed a Urology Clinic where virtually all of the knowledge was embedded in one administrator. Few documents existed, and other individuals who were knowledgeable about the clinic had either retired or moved to a different organization. The administrator hoarded knowledge by protecting his network of personal contacts and by solving problems without explaining the rationale to his subordinates. Engeström et.al. (1990) suggested that when the administrator retired, he would take all the knowledge with him. In this example, knowledge was embedded primarily in one individual. The researchers argued that his departure would hurt the clinic's performance.

Studies of the effect of turnover provide a gauge of the extent to which knowledge is embedded in individuals. What does the evidence say about the relationship between turnover and organizational learning? As described in Chapter 2, our analysis of the effect of turnover of direct production workers in World War II shipyards did not reveal any evidence that turnover affected the productivity of the yards. The shipyards were large organizations with formalized and specialized structures. Jobs were generally designed to be low in skill requirements (Lane, 1951) so that a worker without previous experience could be brought up to speed quickly. We speculated that perhaps these conditions mitigated the effect of turnover and that one would find more of an effect of turnover for highly skilled workers or for workers who performed less structured tasks.

The Argote, Epple, Rao and Murphy (1997) study described in the previous chapter on Organizational Forgetting investigated one of these factors—whether the effect of turnover depended on the performance of departing members. We collected data that contained information on the reason employees left a manufacturing plant (e.g., whether employees were discharged for poor performance, promoted for good performance, retired, deceased, quit, "bumped" due to contractual agreements, and so on). Our results indicated that the variable representing the number of employees who were promoted out of the plant to participate in competitive apprenticeship programs on the basis of their good performance was generally negatively related to the truck plant's productivity. This study suggests that the effect of turnover on productivity depends on the performance level of departing employees: the departure of high-performing employees appeared to hurt the truck plant's productivity.

We examined whether the effect of turnover depended on how organizations were structured in another study (Devadas & Argote, 1995). Past work had suggested that how an organization was structured might moderate the effects of turnover. For example, Grusky (1961) found that managerial succession was less disruptive in large than in small firms. Grusky suggested that the greater use of written rules and hierarchies in the larger companies buffered them from the potential negative effects of managerial turnover.

To investigate whether structure affected the consequences of turnover, we simulated varying degrees of structure in the laboratory and contrasted the effect of turnover in highly structured groups to the effect in less structured groups. The central hypothesis was an interaction between turnover and work group structure—that turnover would affect the performance of groups that were high in structure less than that of groups low in structure, and that the performance of high and low structure groups would not differ when turnover did not occur. Thus, high structure was hypothesized to mitigate the effect of turnover.

The hypothesis was tested through a laboratory study in which three-person groups performed five trials of a production-type task (building origami products). The level of turnover and the structuring of activities were varied. In the no-turnover condition, the same three members worked together for the five experimental periods. In the turnover condition, one member was replaced by a new member, who had received the same training as the initial three members, at the end of each trial. In the low structure condition, group members were not given any special instructions about how to organize themselves, whereas in the high structure condition, group members were required to perform specialized roles and follow certain procedures.

Results indicated that there was a significant interaction between turnover and structure: groups in the low structure, turnover condition performed significantly more poorly than groups in the other three conditions. Videotapes of the groups performing the tasks were analyzed to shed light on the processes underlying group performance. These analyses suggested that one factor contributing to the poor performance of groups in the low structure, turnover condition was their continual need to reorganize around the skills of new members. For example, the group might organize around the idiosyncratic skills of one member who was good at a particular set of tasks (e.g., building crowns). When that person departed, not only was the group deprived of his or her individual skills, the group also found that its division of labor was obsolete since it was unlikely the new member possessed the exceptional skills of the old. This required a revision in the organization of work and assignment of tasks. Groups in the low structure, turnover condition showed more evidence of continual reorganizing than groups in any of the other conditions. The continual need to reorganize hurt their performance.

Other factors contributing to the poor performance of groups in the low structure, turnover condition included the difficulty the groups had accessing knowledge and the loss of critical knowledge when members left the group. The former occurred typically when one group member asked a question and another group member had to stop what he or she was doing to aid the person asking the question. This variable was negatively correlated with performance and its incidence was higher in the low structure, turnover condition. Knowledge was coded as "lost" when a group member asked a question that no other group member could answer. This occurred only in the low structure, turnover condition. The results of this study suggest that embedding knowledge in an organization's structure is an effective way to mitigate the effects of turnover. Groups in the high structure condition were not as adversely affected by turnover as groups in the low structure condition.

The results of this laboratory study are generally consistent with simulation results Carley (1992) obtained in her analysis of personnel turnover and organizational learning. Carley (1992) compared the effect of turnover on hierarchies and teams. A hierarchy was modeled as a three-tier organization composed of a chief executive officer, a set of assistant executive officers, and a set of analysts. Analysts made recommendations to their assistant executive officer, whom in turn forwarded his or her recommendation to the Chief Executive Officer making the final organizational decision. A team was modeled as a single-tier organization comprised of analysts. Each analyst made a decision independent of the decision of the other analysts. The final organizational decision was the decision of a majority of the analysts. Carley (1992) found that while teams learned better and faster than hierarchies, hierarchies were less affected by turnover than teams.

Argote, Insko, Yovetich and Romero (1995) analyzed whether the effect of turnover on group learning depended on the complexity of the task. We simulated varying levels of task complexity in the laboratory and contrasted the effect of turnover on groups performing complex versus simple tasks over several time periods. One theoretical argument would predict that turnover would have a more negative effect on complex than on simple tasks. Complex tasks require more distinct acts or skills (Wood, 1986). Thus, groups performing complex tasks that experience turnover would be even more disadvantaged than those performing simple tasks because the gap between the skills necessary to perform the task and those possessed by new members is greater for complex than for simple tasks. This line of reasoning leads one to predict that turnover would have a more negative effect for complex than for simple tasks.

Another theoretical argument, however, would predict that turnover would have a less negative effect on the performance of complex than of simple tasks. Several studies have found a positive effect of turnover on group or organizational performance (Guest, 1962; Wells & Pelz, 1966; Ziller, Behringer & Goodchilds, 1962; Virany, Tushman & Romanelli, 1992). These studies have all used complex tasks or studied work that involved innovation. For example, Wells and Pelz (1966) analyzed the performance of groups of scientists and engineers while Virany, Tushman and Romanelli (1992) studied executives in the computer industry. The work of scientists, engineers, and executives is more complex and more subject to innovation than, for example, work performed by direct production workers in bureaucratic organizations. Due to innovations that occur in the performance of complex tasks, knowledge of incumbents may become obsolete. Thus, their departures may not be costly since much of their knowledge may no longer be relevant for task performance. By contrast, newcomers may be more up-to-date and possess expertise relevant for the task. This theoretical argument leads one to predict that turnover would have a less negative (or even positive) effect on the performance of complex than of simple tasks.

Results indicated that group performance improved significantly as experience was gained with the task. Groups that did not experience turnover produced significantly more products than groups that experienced turnover and this difference was amplified over time. That is, the gap between the performance of groups that experienced turnover and those that did not widened over time. Groups produced more of the simple than the complex product and this difference was also amplified over time. The gap in the performance of no-turnover versus turnover groups increased over time, and the increase in the gap was greater for the simple than for the complex task. Thus, while all groups were hurt by turnover, it had less impact on the complex than on the simple task. Based on analyses of innovations generated in the experiment, we suggested that the lesser impact of turnover on the complex tasks was due to the greater frequency of innovations that occurred on the complex task. The departure of experienced group members appeared less costly on the complex tasks since some of their knowledge was no longer relevant due to technological innovations.

The effect of turnover has also been found to depend on the quality of replacements and on the extent to which turnover is anticipated. Trow (1960) investigated the effect of turnover on performance in a laboratory study that employed the common symbol task. Trow found that turnover was not disruptive when replacements had experience with the task, were at least as competent as their predecessors, and the group had previous experience with the same rate of turnover.

Although these studies of the effect of turnover have primarily focused on turnover of workers engaged in direct production activities, a few studies have examined the effect of executive turnover on organizational learning. Virany, Tushman and Romanelli (1992) examined turnover of executives as a mechanism for organizational learning and adaptation in a study of mini-computer firms. The researchers suggested that executive change facilitates learning and adaptation by changing the knowledge base and communication processes of the executive team. Their results indicated that turnover of the chief executive officer and turnover in the executive team were positively associated with organizational performance. Thus, in the turbulent mini-computer industry, executive change may have served as a means for bringing in new knowledge and relevant expertise.

Similarly, in their study of the cement industry, Tushman and Rosenkopf (1996) found that executive succession alone was positively associated with subsequent firm performance in stable contexts and negatively associated in turbulent contexts. A more complex picture emerged for executive team change. Departures of executive team members (exits) had different effects than arrivals of new members (entries). In turbulent contexts, executive team entries were more positively associated with subsequent performance, whereas executive team exits were more negatively associated with subsequent performance. The researchers suggested that when environments shift and the locus of the crisis is outside the firm, organizational performance is strengthened by bringing in new executive team expertise while retaining existing expertise. By contrast, when the source of the crisis is within the firm, executive team exits were more positively associated with organizational performance.

These results are more complex than those of the Virany, Tushman and Romanelli (1992) study in the mini-computer industry. The results suggest that turnover in the executive team may have different effects than turnover of the top executive and further that entries and exits of executive team members may have differential effects on performance. Comparing the two studies it is interesting to note that it is in the more stable cement industry that one finds some benefits of retaining existing knowledge and expertise, while in the more turbulent computer industry, turnover at the executive level was more uniformly associated with performance improvements. These results are generally consistent with the Argote, Insko, Yovetich and Romero (1995) study. Turnover is less harmful—and may even be beneficial—on complex tasks that involve change and innovation.

Taken together, these studies of turnover and organizational learning begin to suggest the conditions under which turnover is most likely to have a significant effect on organizational learning. Results indicate that turnover affects performance gains when: (1) departing members are exceptional performers (e.g., see Argote, Epple, Rao, & Murphy, 1997); and (2) when the organizations, or the positions departing members occupy, are low in structure and constraints (e.g., Devadas & Argote, 1995; Carley, 1992; Virany, Tushman & Romanelli, 1992). While turnover of high-performing direct production workers in a manufacturing plant negatively affected the plant's productivity, turnover of executives in the mini-computer industry had a positive effect on performance. The former effect may have reflected the cost of the loss of individuals who had critical knowledge embedded in them while the latter may have reflected the benefit of incorporating individuals with new knowledge into the organizations.

3.3.2 Knowledge Embedded in Organizations

We turn now to evaluating empirical evidence on the extent to which knowledge is embedded in organizations. Knowledge embedded in an organization is harder to measure and analyze than knowledge embedded in individuals since assessing the effect of individual turnover provides an indicator of the extent to which knowledge was embedded in individuals. An interesting naturally occurring experiment provided an opportunity for us to analyze the extent to which knowledge acquired thorough learning by doing became embedded in the organization versus in individual employees (Epple, Argote & Murphy, 1996). While the natural experiment did not enable us to further disentangle whether the knowledge was embedded in the organization's technology or its structure, it was informative about whether knowledge was embedded in individuals versus in the organization.

A manufacturing plant added a second shift almost two years after the first shift had been in operation (Epple, Argote & Murphy, 1996). The second shift used the same technology and was embedded in the same structure as the first shift but was composed of predominantly new employees. Thus, comparing the performance of the second to the first shift provides an indicator of the extent to which knowledge was embedded in the organization's structure and technology versus in individual workers. If the learning curve on the second shift followed the same pattern as the first shift's curve had, it suggests that knowledge is embedded primarily in individual workers since workers on each shift went through the same learning process. Alternatively, if the second shift learns faster than the first, it suggests that knowledge acquired from the start of production by the first shift was embedded in the organization and led to improvements in the performance of the second shift. To investigate this issue, we analyzed the transfer of knowledge that occurred from the period of operating with one shift to the period of operating with two shifts and the ongoing transfer of knowledge between the two shifts once they were both in operation (see Epple, Argote & Devadas, 1991, for development of the method).

Our results indicated that knowledge acquired during the period of operating with one shift carried forward quite rapidly to both shifts of the two-shift period. The second shift was composed predominantly of new employees. The second shift achieved a level of productivity in two weeks that it had taken the first shift many months to achieve. This suggests that knowledge acquired during the period of one-shift operation had been embedded in the organization's structure or technology. The second shift did not have to go through the long learning period that the first shift had. The second shift benefited from knowledge acquired by the first shift that had been embedded in the organization (i.e., its technology, structure, or layout). This knowledge improved the second shift's performance.

As noted previously, this study did not enable us to disentangle the effect of knowledge embedded in the organization's technology from knowledge embedded in its structure. Both contributed to the ability of the second shift to achieve a high level of productivity so rapidly. Our sense from observing the plant and the interviews we conducted there was that more of the action occurred on the technological than on the structural dimension. While some structural modifications were made, enormous changes occurred in the plant's layout and its technology as it gained experience in production. The studies described in the following two sections enable one to determine somewhat more clearly whether knowledge was embedded in the organization's technology or its structure.

3.3.2.1 Knowledge Embedded in Technology

Studies of technology transfer provide a more direct window on the extent to which knowledge is embedded in technology. These studies typically examine how technology developed at one site transfers to another and the conditions that facilitate or impede such transfer (e.g., Allen, 1977; Ounjian & Carne, 1987; Szulanski, 1996). Much of this work is based on surveys of the conditions that facilitate or impede the transfer of knowledge from one site to another.

A relevant study that is particularly compelling for the goals of this book is one which included productivity as the dependent measure and analyzed the effects of various factors on how long it took a "recipient" site to reach the level of productivity a "donor" site had achieved (Galbraith, 1990). Galbraith (1990) studied 32 attempts to transfer technology internally from one site to another within the same organization. The results of the Galbraith study illustrate both the difficulty of transferring technology and the savings in productivity that can occur from successful technology transfer attempts. For the 32 technology transfer attempts, the initial productivity at the recipient site after the technology was transferred averaged 34% less than what the donor site had achieved at the time of transfer. The productivity loss ranged from a low of 4% to a high of 150%. Thus, some of the recipient organizations almost instantaneously achieved a level of productivity that it had taken the donor sites months or even years to achieve whereas other recipient sites did not even approach the productivity of the donor sites after the transfer. Indeed, ten of the 32 technology transfer attempts were considered failures because they never reached the level of productivity of the donor site prior to the transfer.

The Galbraith results tell a story that is both "half-full" and "half-empty" from the perspective of knowledge embedded in technology. On the positive side, the results illustrate that some organizations can achieve remarkable productivity gains by transferring technology. These organizations are able to embed knowledge in technology and successfully transfer the knowledge to a new site. For other organizations, however, the results are less satisfying. Their attempts to embed knowledge in technology and transfer it to another site do not result in large productivity gains at the recipient organization. Factors that facilitate the successful transfer of technology will be discussed in Chapter 5 on Knowledge Transfer. Relevant to our discussion here of organizational memory, however, is that some organizations are able to embed knowledge in technology and use it to transfer knowledge effectively to a new site.

3.3.2.2 Knowledge Embedded in Structure and Routines

Researchers have also analyzed the extent to which knowledge acquired through learning by doing is embedded in routines. Cohen and Bacdayan (1994) demonstrated that knowledge acquired through task performance can be embedded in supra-individual routines. Based on empirical evidence from a laboratory study of dyads playing a card game, the researchers concluded that the behavior of the dyads was indicative of the operation of routines. In particular, the performance of the dyads became faster and more reliable over time. Different dyads evolved different routines that were stable over time (see also Weick & Gilfallen, 1971). And dyads persisted in using their idiosyncratic routines, even when more effective routines existed.

Further, Cohen and Bacdayan (1994) found that task performance slowed down significantly with the introduction of novelty in the experiment but not with an increase in time delay. The researchers argued that this pattern provided further evidence of the operation of routines. Delay should not affect routinized task performance since routines are stored as procedural memory which exhibits little decay, whereas novelty should affect routinized task performance since novelty causes subjects to switch to slower, declarative processing (Singley & Anderson, 1989).

Moorman and Miner (1998) developed propositions about the effects of procedural and declarative knowledge on organizational improvisation. Improvisation was defined as the convergence of composition and execution in time. The researchers argued that procedural memory would increase the speed but reduce the novelty of improvisational activity. By contrast, declarative memory was hypothesized to reduce the speed but increase the novelty of improvisation.

Research on "transactive memory" (Wegner, 1986; 1995) is also relevant for understanding whether knowledge is embedded in social structures versus in individuals. This research emphasizes that as social systems gain experience, members acquire knowledge about the system as well as about their individual tasks. In particular, members acquire knowledge about who is good at what, about how to coordinate and communicate effectively, and about whom to trust. This knowledge in turn improves their performance.

Let us consider an example of how a transactive memory system might work. A group of research collaborators might learn that one member of the team is particularly good at experimental design, while another excels at data analysis and a third is a very strong writer. As the group gains experience and learns who is good at what, it specializes and assigns tasks to the individual with the most skill and expertise. That is, as group members work together, they learn who has a deeper understanding of statistics and rely more on that person for dealing with statistical concerns. As group members read each other's writing, members also learn who the most gifted writer is. That person is likely to take on more of the group's writing tasks. Furthermore, as group members see the consequences of various design choices, members acquire information about who has the best instincts about the design of research studies. This knowledge of who knows what facilitates matching of tasks to individuals' skills and expertise. Individuals' meta knowledge of who knows what in the group allows them access to a much larger knowledge base than their own. Individuals learn whom to go to if they have a question or need advice. Group members also learn how to communicate and coordinate effectively with one another, perhaps by developing special terms and customs. Members also learn whom they can trust. The transactive memory system the group develops facilitates its performance.

My colleagues and I used Wegner's concept of transactive memory to investigate the effects of training methods on group performance (Liang, Moreland & Argote, 1995). In an initial study, we compared the performance of groups whose members were trained individually to that of groups whose members were trained together on a production task, assembling a radio. Groups whose members were trained together recalled more about the task and made fewer errors than groups whose members were trained apart. The superior performance of groups in the group training condition seemed to stem from the operation of a transactive memory system. Groups whose members were trained together exhibited greater specialization or memory differentiation, seemed to trust one another to a greater extent, and were better coordinated than groups whose members were trained individually. Further, the transactive memory system mediated the relationship between training and group performance (Baron & Kenny, 1986): when the degree to which the groups developed transactive memory systems was taken into account, training methods no longer mattered. Thus, the superior performance of groups who received training together was due to the operation of transactive memory systems.

A subsequent study replicated the first and included two additional conditions (see Moreland, Argote & Krishnan, 1996). One condition in which participants were trained as individuals and then given a team-building exercise was added to investigate further whether the superior performance of participants trained as a group was due to enhanced group development. The performance of participants in this individual training plus team-building condition was inferior to that of participants trained as a group, and comparable to that of participants who only received individual training. This finding enabled us to rule out the hypothesis that enhanced group development led to the superior performance of participants who were trained together. Providing groups an opportunity to interact was not sufficient to improve their performance.

Another condition was added to the second study in which participants were trained in one group and performed in another. The performance of participants who were trained in this condition was comparable to the performance of participants in the individual training condition and the individual training plus team-building condition, and inferior to that of participants who trained and performed in the same group. Thus, it is not experience in working with any group that leads to superior performance, but experience in working with particular group members that allows for the development of knowledge of who is good at what and leads to the creation of a transactive memory system. It is the transactive memory system that drives group performance.

A third study measured more directly what members of a group learned as they gained experience (Moreland, Argote & Krishnan, 1998). To assess whether group members who trained together would know more about one another than those trained apart, participants were asked to complete a questionnaire after they received training and before they took part in the second experimental session. The questionnaire measured what the members of each group knew about each other's expertise. Participants who were trained together wrote more complex analyses of each others' strengths and weaknesses. To assess the accuracy of these perceptions of each others' strengths and weaknesses, the questionnaire data were compared to objective information about performance on the radio assembly task. Results indicated that participants who were trained together had more accurate perceptions of each others' expertise than participants who were trained individually. Further, members of groups who were trained together agreed more about each others' strengths and weaknesses than members trained apart.

Another goal of the third experiment was to see if social loafing and free-riding (see Karau & Williams, 1993) affected performance in the various training conditions. Training members of a group together could lead to social loafing: some group members may not learn the task very well because they expect to be able to rely on others. During the first experimental session of this study, participants were trained either individually or in a group, as in previous studies. When they returned for the second experimental session, however, all participants were asked to perform the task *individually*. This enabled us to determine whether participants who were trained in a group learned the task as well as subjects who received individual training. Results indicated that there were no significant differences in *individual* performance between participants who were trained individually and those who were trained as a group. While further research is needed to rule out the possibility of social loafing in group training, our results suggest that individual learning occurs to about the same degree whether participants are trained individually or in a group. Thus, social loafing does not seem to be a serious problem here.

Hollingshead (1998) also compared the effect of group and individual training on group and individual performance for a different task: collective induction. Results indicated that group performance was facilitated by previous practice as a group and not by practice as individuals. Individual performance, however, was not affected by either individual or group practice. These results obtained on collective induction tasks are very similar to those already described for the radio production task.

Hollenbeck et al. (1995) also found that experience improved group performance in a study of hierarchical teams. Much (albeit not all) of the effect of experience on performance was mediated by its effect on three core variables: (1) the degree to which the team was informed about the decision; (2) the extent to which members' judgments were accurate, and (3) the degree to which the leader gave appropriate weights to group members' judgments. This last factor is similar to a dimension of transactive memory—knowing who is good at what and weighting their contributions accordingly. In a second study, Hollenbeck et al. (1995) found that teams that had an incompetent member and those low in cohesiveness performed more poorly than their counterparts. Similar to the previous results, much (but not all) of the effect of cohesion and competence on decision accuracy was mediated by the three core variables.

These laboratory studies of small groups relate to information we obtained from interviewing and observing managers at manufacturing facilities. As noted previously, when we interviewed managers about what accounts for organizational learning curve, they emphasized the importance of learning who was good at what and assigning tasks accordingly. Thus, these organizations were developing transactive memory systems— knowledge of who was good at what—and using this knowledge in task distribution and performance.

The concept of transactive memory has been extended to the organizational level and expanded to include knowledge of the capabilities of other organizations as well as knowledge of the capabilities of one's own organization. Rulke, Zaheer and Anderson (1998) developed and collected fine-grained measures of the knowledge retail food organizations possessed about their own capabilities and the capabilities of other firms. The researchers examined the relationship between these two types of knowledge (self-knowledge and knowledge of others) and objective measures of performance, such as sales per square foot. Results indicated that both types of knowledge contributed significantly to firm performance. Further, a significant interaction was found between the two knowledge variables that indicated that firms with high self-knowledge did not benefit as much from knowledge of the capabilities of others as those with low self-knowledge. The Rulke, Zaheer and Anderson (1998) study is particularly exciting because it demonstrates the importance of transactive memory in a field setting and shows the link between transactive memory and objective indicators of firm performance.

3.4 Consequences of Where Knowledge is Embedded

Although empirical work on organizational learning and memory has increased in recent years (Miner & Mezias, 1996), there is little empirical evidence about the consequences of where knowledge is embedded for aspects of organizational performance. In this section, I draw on related literature and qualitative work we have done in franchise organizations (Argote & Darr, in press) to suggest how where knowledge is embedded affects its persistence and transfer in organizations. The following sections suggest how embedding knowledge in individuals, in technology, or in structure affects its persistence over time and its transfer to other organizational units.

3.4.1 Knowledge Embedded in Individuals

Individuals provide both a sensitive and a precarious way of storing, maintaining and transferring knowledge. Individuals are capable of capturing subtle nuances that other repositories are not able to store as readily. For example, in a series of ingenuous experiments, Berry and Broadbent (1984; 1987) showed that although individuals improved their performance as they gained experience with a task, they were not able to articulate what strategies they had used to perform the task or why their performance had improved. Thus, as they gained experience with the task, individuals acquired tacit knowledge that they were not able to articulate to others. Individuals were able, however, to transfer their tacit knowledge to another similar task. When participants in the experiments performed a second task, the performance of those with previous experience on a similar task was significantly better than that of participants without any previous experience. Thus, even though participants could not articulate why their performance improved, they were able to transfer the knowledge that enabled them to improve their performance to a similar task.

These results suggest that moving personnel is a very effective way to transfer knowledge in organizations since individuals can transfer their tacit knowledge to other tasks and contexts. Thus, by transferring personnel, one transfers the tacit knowledge that individuals carry with them. Most studies of technology transfer find that moving personnel is a powerful facilitator of knowledge transfer (e.g., see Galbraith, 1990; Rothwell, 1978). A benefit of personnel movement is that it allows individuals to transfer their tacit knowledge to new contexts.

An alternative way of transferring tacit knowledge is to convert it to explicit knowledge. Nonaka (1991) described a fascinating example of how an engineer apprenticed herself to a bread maker to acquire the bread maker's tacit knowledge. Through a long period of observation of the bread maker, the engineer captured the bread maker's tacit knowledge and converted it to explicit knowledge. This explicit knowledge served as the base for Matsushita's bread-making machine.

Individuals are the most effective media for acquiring and storing tacit knowledge. They are also an effective media for transferring tacit knowledge. Individuals can apply their tacit knowledge to a new task or a new context without converting their tacit knowledge to explicit knowledge. Alternatively, through a lengthy period of observation and apprenticeship others may be able to capture an expert's tacit knowledge and convert it to explicit knowledge that others can access.

Without moving personnel or explicitly attempting to capture their knowledge, knowledge embedded in individuals will generally not transfer. Qualitative results from our study of fast food franchises illustrate how knowledge embedded in individuals generally does not transfer to new sites. In our study of fast food franchises, we observed 14 innovations at the stores (Argote & Darr, in press). Of the 14 innovations that occurred in the fast food franchises, six were embedded in individuals. For example, knowledge about how to hand toss pizza remained embedded in individual workers. Knowledge about how to prioritize pizzas so as to take advantage of cooking time differences across pizza types and sizes and, thus, make better use of the oven, also remained embedded in a few individual order-takers. Of the six innovations that were embedded in individuals, only two transferred outside the store of origin. By contrast, both of the innovations embedded in technology transferred outside the store of origin and five of the six innovations embedded in routines transferred outside the store of origin. Thus, knowledge embedded in individuals does not transfer as readily outside the organization of origin as knowledge embedded in technology or routines does.

Several pitfalls are associated with relying on individuals as a knowledge repository for organizations. Knowledge embedded in individuals may decay or depreciate faster than knowledge embedded in social systems. The results of an interesting laboratory study that compared individual and group recall suggest that knowledge embedded in groups is more stable than knowledge embedded in individuals (Weldon & Bellinger, 1997). The researchers found a tendency for groups to exhibit less forgetting than individuals. Further, the organization of group recall was more consistent over trials than the organization of individual recall. Thus, an important difference between collective and individual memories may be the relative stability of collective memories. Knowledge embedded in the group or social system seems to be more stable than knowledge embedded in individuals, even when there is no turnover of those individuals.

Another downside of relying on individuals as a knowledge repository is that individuals may not be motivated to share their knowledge. The Engeström et al. (1990) example discussed earlier in which an individual hoarded knowledge and did not share it with others is an example of this phenomenon. Many studies have shown that individuals typically do not share information that they uniquely hold (e.g., see Stasser & Titus, 1985). This line of work is discussed in depth in the next chapter.

A third downside of relying on individuals as a knowledge repository for organizations is that individuals can leave and take their knowledge with them. Conditions under which individual turnover will be especially harmful for organizations were discussed earlier in this chapter. Organizations can use a variety of strategies for capturing individual knowledge. Embedding individual knowledge in organizational structures and routines is a productive way to mitigate the effect of individual turnover (Devadas & Argote, 1995). Similarly, organizations may try to capture the knowledge of individuals and embed it in technology such as information systems and knowledge networks (cf. Moreland, in press; Stewart, 1995a, 1995b). A significant component of individual knowledge, however, such as tacit knowledge, may be less amenable to being embedded in organizational structures and technologies. For organizations with a large component of tacit knowledge, attempts to bond the individual to the organization may be more fruitful than attempts to embed the knowledge in structures and technologies. Starbuck (1992) described the strategies organizations such as law firms and consulting firms use to prevent individuals from leaving. In these organizations, where much of the knowledge is embedded in individuals, their turnover would be very harmful for the organization's performance. Hence, contracts are written and incentives are developed to motivate key individuals to remain with the firm.

A fourth disadvantage of relying on individuals to transfer knowledge is that it is hard for individuals to reach a large number of people without some degradation in the communication. Thus, for large organizations where reliability is important, it will not be efficient or effective to rely on individuals as the primary means for transferring knowledge. Individuals can be used effectively to complement other repositories, but relying solely on individuals to transfer knowledge in these settings will not be effective.

3.4.2 Knowledge Embedded in Technology

Technology is a very effective repository for retaining explicit knowledge. As noted in the discussion of organizational forgetting in Chapter 2, we observed the least depreciation of knowledge in technologically sophisticated organizations. While more research is needed to determine whether it is technological sophistication that drives these organizations' ability to retain knowledge, the depreciation rates observed across a variety of settings are consistent with the hypothesis that embedding knowledge in technology is an effective way to mitigate its depreciation. Similarly, Smunt (1987) suggested that embedding knowledge in technology is an effective way to prevent organizational forgetting. While embedding knowledge in technology does not guarantee its persistence (cf. the "Star Wars" example), it makes persistence more likely.

Embedding knowledge in technology is also an effective way of transferring knowledge to other sites. Two of the innovations we observed in our study of fast food franchises were embedded in technology. The "cheese spreader" example discussed earlier in this chapter is an example of one of these innovations. Both of the innovations embedded in technology transferred outside the store of origin. While the number of innovations embedded in technology was, of course, too small to permit firm conclusions, the results are suggestive of the effectiveness of technology as a medium for transferring knowledge.

The results of our study of knowledge transfer across shifts in a manufacturing facility also illustrate the effectiveness of technology as a mechanism for transferring organizational knowledge. The technology-transfer literature provides further evidence that embedding knowledge in technology and transferring it to another site can result in substantial savings for the recipient organization.

Interestingly, transferring knowledge by embedding it in technology is often most successful when it is accompanied by transferring a few individuals as well (e.g., see Galbraith, 1990; Rothwell, 1978). The advantages of individuals as knowledge repositories complement those of technology. Individuals capture the tacit knowledge, the subtlety, and the understanding behind the technology. By contrast, technology provides consistency and reliability and reaches a large scale.

A cost of embedding knowledge in technology is that the knowledge may become obsolete yet be more resistant to change because it is embedded in "hard" form. Abernathy and Wayne's (1974) analysis of Ford's production of the Model T suggested that Ford's investment in "hard" automation to produce the Model T made it more difficult for Ford to change to meet customer preferences and offer a more varied product line.

This example illustrates potential disadvantages of embedding knowledge in technology: increased rigidity and resistance to change. Today's technologies are generally more flexible than they were in the 1920s, so the downside potential of embedding knowledge in technology may now be somewhat less. Nonetheless, rigidity associated with embedding knowledge in hard form is an important potential cost of embedding knowledge in technology that should be considered.

3.4.3 Knowledge Embedded in Structure and Routines

Structure may be defined in this case as recurring patterns of activity (Katz & Kahn, 1978). Routines and standard operating procedures are important examples of structure. Routines are softer than technology because they are more dependent on people enacting them. While people still have to use the technology, more of the knowledge is typically embedded in the technology than in the routine. Thus, routines share many of the benefits (and costs) of embedding knowledge in technology—but to a somewhat lesser degree.

Routines are very efficient mechanisms for storing and maintaining knowledge. For example, in our study of fast food franchises, we saw an example of a very efficient and effective routine for placing pepperoni on pizza. As described previously, it was discovered that placing pepperoni in a pattern that resembled spokes on a wheel before deep-dish pizza was cooked resulted in an even distribution of pepperoni on the cooked pizza. The discovery was embodied in a routine that could be used easily by all pizza makers. Embedding the knowledge in a routine made it more resistant to employee turnover. If the individual who made the discovery of how to achieve an even distribution departed from the store, the knowledge would remain in the organization. Embedding knowledge in a routine enhances persistence.

Routines are also an effective mechanism for transferring knowledge to other organizations. The routine for placing pepperoni was discovered in a store in Southwestern Pennsylvania. The routine transferred very quickly to other stores in the same franchise. A consultant from the parent corporation who saw the routine on a visit to one of the stores was impressed by the routine's effectiveness and diffused it widely to stores throughout the corporation. The routine is now used in virtually all of the stores of the parent corporation.

Indeed, other routines we observed in the fast food franchise study also transferred outside the store of origin. Of the 14 innovations we identified in our fast food franchise study, six were embedded in routines. Of these six, five transferred outside the store of origin. And three of those transferred to stores in different franchises. Thus, embedding knowledge in a routine is an effective way to facilitate knowledge transfer.

The results of a study by Zander and Kogut (1995) are consistent with our qualitative results regarding knowledge transfer. Zander and Kogut (1995) examined factors affecting the speed of transfer of manufacturing capabilities. The researchers found that capabilities that could be codified (e.g., in documents or software) transferred more readily than capabilities not easily codified. In order to be embedded in a routine, capabilities must be codified.

A downside of relying on routines is that they may be used inappropriately. Researchers have written about the importance of "unlearning" in organizations—forgetting the old and developing a better, more appropriate routine as a way of adapting to changed circumstances (e.g., Hedberg, 1981). Unlearning is arguably an example of learning—of developing a more elaborate response repertoire that specifies the conditions under which various responses are appropriate. So rather than "forget" a routine used in the past, it would be preferable to remember the routine, the conditions under which it worked, and why it is no longer successful. Thus, lessons of the past can be applied to the present to facilitate organizational performance.

We are just beginning to understand the effect of organizational memory on organizational outcomes. An empirical study that directly examined the effect of memory on dimensions of organizational performance found that organizational memory affected the new product development process by influencing both the interpretation of new information and the performance of new product action routines (Moorman & Miner, 1997). Results indicated that higher organizational memory levels enhanced the short-term financial performance of new products, while greater memory dispersion increased both the performance and creativity of new products. Results also indicated that high memory dispersion could detract from creativity under conditions of environmental turbulence.

3.5 Conclusion

The chapter began with a discussion of examples of productivity-enhancing improvements that occurred as organizations gained experience in production. These improvements were mapped onto theoretical discussions of organizational memory. For organizations that make things, productivity improvements are generally embedded in three repositories: individual workers, an organization's technology, and its structure and routines. Empirical evidence on the effect of embedding knowledge in these three repositories was reviewed. The chapter concluded with a discussion of the implications of where knowledge was embedded for organizational performance. Individuals are capable of capturing and transferring subtle nuances and tacit knowledge. By contrast, organizational structures and technologies are less "sensitive" repositories. Knowledge embedded in organizational structures and technologies, however, is more resistant to depreciation and more readily transferred than knowledge embedded in individuals. Organizations can use the strengths of one knowledge repository to offset the weaknesses of another.

References

Abernathy, W. J., & Wayne, K. (1974). Limits of the learning curve. *Harvard Business Review, 52*(5), 109-119.

Allen, T. J. (1977). *Managing the flow of technology: Technology transfer and the dissemination of technological information within the R&D organization.* Cambridge, MA: MIT Press.

Amber, G. H., & Amber, P. S. (1962). *Anatomy of automation.* Englewood Cliffs, NJ: Prentice-Hall.

Anzai, Y., & Simon, H. A. (1979). The theory of learning by doing. *Psychological Review, 86*, 124-140.

Argote, L. (1993). Group and organizational learning curves: Individual, system and environmental components. *British Journal of Social Psychology, 32*, 31-51.

Argote, L., & Darr, E. D. (in press). Repositories of knowledge in franchise organizations: Individual, structural and technological. In G. Dosi, R. Nelson & S. Winter (Eds.), *Nature and dynamics of organizational capabilities.*

Argote, L., Epple, D., Rao, R. D., & Murphy, K. (1997). *The acquisition and depreciation of knowledge in a manufacturing organization: Turnover and plant productivity.* Working paper, Graduate School of Industrial Administration, Carnegie Mellon University.

Argote, L., Insko, C. A., Yovetich, N., & Romero, A. A. (1995). Group learning curves: The effects of turnover and task complexity on group performance. *Journal of Applied Social Psychology, 25*, 512-529.

Barley, S. (1986). Technology as an occasion for structuring: Evidence from observations of CT scanners and the social order of radiology departments. *Administrative Science Quarterly, 31*, 78-108.

Baron, R. M., & Kenny, D. A. (1986). The moderator-mediator variable distinction in social psychological research: Conceptual, strategic, and statistical considerations. *Journal of Personality and Social Psychology, 51*, 1173-1182.

Berry, D. C., & Broadbent, D. E. (1984). On the relationship between task performance and associated verbalizable knowledge. *The Quarterly Journal of Experimental Psychology, 36A,* 209-231.

Berry, D. C., & Broadbent, D. E. (1987). The combination of explicit and implicit learning processes in task control. *Psychological Research, 49,* 7-15.

Blau, P. M., Falbe, C. M., McKinley, W., & Tracy, P. K. (1976). *Technology* and organization in manufacturing. *Administrative Science Quarterly, 21,* 20-40.

Carley, K. (1992). Organizational learning and personnel turnover. *Organization Science, 3,* 20-46.

Carley, K. M. (1996). A comparison of artificial and human organization. *Journal of Economic Behavior and Organization, 896,* 1-17.

Casey, A. (1997). Collective memory in organizations. *Advances in Strategic Management, 14,* 111-146.

Cohen, M. D., & Bacdayan, P. (1994). Organizational routines are stored as procedural memory: Evidence from a laboratory study. *Organization Science, 5,* 554-568.

Cyert, R. M., & March, J. G. (1963). *A behavioral theory of the firm.* Englewood Cliffs, NJ: Prentice-Hall.

Devadas, R., & Argote, L. (1995, May). *Collective learning and forgetting: The effects of turnover and group structure.* Paper presented at Midwestern Academy of Management Meetings, Chicago.

Engeström, Y., Brown, K., Engeström, R., & Koistinen, K. (1990). Organizational forgetting: An activity theoretical perspective. In D. Middleton & D. Edwards (Eds.), *Collective remembering* (pp. 139-168). London: Sage.

Epple, D., Argote, L., & Devadas, R. (1991). Organizational learning curves: A method for investigating intra-plant transfer of knowledge acquired through learning by doing. *Organization Science, 2,* 58-70.

Epple, D., Argote, L., & Murphy, K. (1996). An empirical investigation of the micro structure of knowledge acquisition and transfer through learning by doing. *Operations Research, 44,* 77-86.

Galbraith, C. S. (1990). Transferring core manufacturing technologies in high technology firms. *California Management Review, 32*(4), 56-70.

Gersick, C., & Hackman, J. R. (1990). Habitual routines in task-performing groups. *Organizational Behavior and Human Decision Processes, 47,* 65-97.

Graham, C. H., & Gagne, R. M. (1940). The acquisition, extinction and spontaneous recovery of a conditioned operant response. *Journal of Experimental Psychology, 26,* 251-280.

Grusky, O. (1961). Corporate size, bureaucratization, and managerial succession. *American Journal of Sociology, 67,* 261-269.

Guest, R. H. (1962). Managerial succession in complex organizations. *American Journal of Sociology, 68,* 47-54.

Hayes, R. H., & Wheelwright, S. C. (1984). *Restoring our competitive edge: Competing through manufacturing.* New York: Wiley.

Hedberg, B. (1981). How organizations learn and unlearn. In P. C. Nystrom & W. H. Starbuck (Eds.), *Handbook of organizational design* (Vol. 1, pp. 8-27). London: Oxford University Press.

Hollenbeck, J. R., Ilgen, D. R., Sego, D. J., Hedlund, J., Major, D. A., & Philips, J. (1995). Multilevel theory of team decision making: Decision performance in teams incorporating distributed expertise. *Journal of Applied Psychology, 80,* 292-316.

Hollingshead, A. B. (1998). Group and individual training: The impact of practice on performance. *Small Group Research, 29,* 254-280.

Joskow, P. L., & Rozanski, G. A. (1979). The effects of learning by doing on nuclear plant operating reliability. *Review of Economics and Statistics, 61,* 161-168.

Karau, S. J., & Williams, K. D. (1993). Social loafing: A meta-analytic review and theoretical integration. *Journal of Personality and Social Psychology, 65,* 681-706.

Katz, D., & Kahn, R. L. (1978). *The social psychology of organizations* (2nd ed.). New York: Wiley.

Lane, F. C. (1951). *Ships for victory: A history of shipbuilding under the U.S. Maritime Commission in World War II.* Baltimore: The Johns Hopkins Press.

Levitt, B., & March, J. G. (1988). Organizational learning. *Annual Review of Sociology, 14,* 319-340.

Liang, D. W., Moreland, R., & Argote, L. (1995). Group versus individual training and group performance: The mediating role of transactive memory. *Personality and Social Psychology Bulletin, 21,* 384-393.

March, J. G., & Simon, H. A. (1958). *Organizations.* New York: Wiley.

Mazur, J. E., & Hastie, R. (1978). Learning as accumulation: A reexamination of the learning curve. *Psychological Bulletin, 85,* 1256-1274.

Miner, A. S., & Mezias, S. J. (1996). Ugly duckling no more: Pasts and futures of organizational learning research. *Organization Science, 7,* 88-99.

Moorman, C., & Miner, A. S. (1997). The impact of organizational memory on new product performance and creativity. *Journal of Marketing Research, 34,* 91-106.

Moorman, C. & Miner, A. S. (1998). Organizational improvisation and organizational memory. *Academy of Management Review, 23,* 698-723.

Moreland, R. L. (in press). Transactive memory: Learning who knows what in work groups and organizations. In L. Thompson, D. M. Messick & J. M. Levine (Eds.), *Shared knowledge in organizations.* Lawrence Erlbaum.

Moreland, R. L., Argote, L., & Krishnan, R. (1996). Socially shared cognition at work: Transactive memory and group performance. In J. L. Nye & Brower A. M. (Eds.), *What's so social about social cognition? Social cognition research in small groups* (pp. 57-84). Thousand Oaks, CA: Sage.

Moreland, R. L., Argote, L., & Krishnan, R. (1998). Training people to work in groups. In R. S. Tindale, L. Heath, J. Edwards, E. J. Posvac, F. B. Bryant, Y. Suarez-Balcazar, E. Henderson-King & J. Myers (Eds.), *Applications of theory and research on groups to social issues* (pp. 37-60). New York: Plenum Press.

Nelson, R. R., & Winter, S. G. (1982). *An evolutionary theory of economic change.* Boston: Belkman Press.

Newell, A., & Rosenbloom, P. S. (1981). Mechanisms of skill acquisition and the law of practice. In J. R. Anderson (Ed.), *Cognitive skills and their acquisition* (pp. 1-55). Hillsdale, NJ: Lawrence Erlbaum.

Nonaka, I. (1991). The knowledge-creating company. *Harvard Business Review,* *69*(6), 96-104.

Ounjian, M. L., & Carne, E. B. (1987). A study of the factors which affect technology transfer in a multilocation multibusiness unit corporation. *IEEE Transactions on Engineering Management, EM-34*, 194-201.

Polanyi, M. (1966). *The tacit dimension.* Garden City, NJ: Doubleday.

Porter, M. E. (1979, October 22). Experience curve. *The Wall Street Journal*, p 30.

Rothwell, R. (1978). Some problems of technology transfer into industry: Examples from the textile machinery sector. *IEEE Transactions on Engineering Management, EM-25*, 15-20.

Rulke, D., Zaheer, S., & Anderson, M. (1998, June). *Transactive knowledge and performance in the retail food industry.* Paper presented at Carnegie-Wisconsin Conference on Knowledge Transfer and Levels of Learning, Carnegie Mellon University, Pittsburgh, PA.

Singley, M. K., & Anderson, J. R. (1989). *The transfer of cognitive skill.* Cambridge, MA: Harvard University Press.

Smunt, T. L. (1987) The impact of worker forgetting on production scheduling. *International Journal of Production Research, 25*, 689-701.

Starbuck, W. H. (1992). Learning by knowledge-intensive firms. *Journal of Management Studies, 29*, 713-738.

Stasser, G., & Titus, W. (1985). Pooling of unshared information in group decision making: Biased information sampling during discussion. *Journal of Personality and Social Psychology, 48*, 1467-1478.

Stein, E. W. (1995). Organizational memory: Review of concepts and recommendations for management. *International Journal of Information Management, 15*, 17-32.

Stewart, T. A. (1995a, October 30). Mapping corporate brainpower. *Fortune*, pp. 209-201, 212.

Stewart, T. A. (1995b, November 27). Getting real about brainpower. *Fortune*, pp. 201-203.

Szulanski, G. (1996). Exploring internal stickiness: Impediments to the transfer of best practice within the firm. *Strategic Management Journal, 17*, 27-43.

Taylor, F. W. (1911). *The principles of scientific management.* New York: Harper.

Theraulaz, G., & Bonabeau, E. (1995, August 4). Coordination in distributed building. *Science, 269*, 686-688.

Thorndike, E. L. (1898). Animal intelligence: An experimental study of the associative processes in animals. *The Psychological Review: Series of Monograph Supplements, 2*, 1-109.

Thurstone, L. L. (1919). The learning curve equation. *Psychological Monographs, 26*, 1-51.

Trow, D. B. (1960). Membership succession and team performance. *Human Relations, 13*, 259-269.

Tushman, M. L., & Rosenkopf, L. (1996). Executive succession, strategic reorientation and performance growth: A longitudinal study in the U.S. cement industry. *Management Science, 42*, 939-953.

Virany, B., Tushman, M. L., & Romanelli, E. (1992). Executive succession and organization outcomes in turbulent environments: An organizational learning approach. *Organization Science, 3*, 72-91.

Walsh, J. P., & Ungson, G. R. (1991). Organizational memory. *Academy of Management Review, 16*, 57-91.

Wegner, D. M. (1986). Transactive memory: A contemporary analysis of the group mind. In B. Mullen & G. R. Goethals (Eds.), *Theories of Group Behavior* (pp. 185-205). New York: Springer-Verlag.

Wegner, D. M. (1995). A computer network model of human transactive memory. *Social Cognition, 13*, 319-339.

Weick, K. E., & Gilfallan, D. P. (1971). Fate of arbitrary traditions in a laboratory microculture. *Journal of Personality and Social Psychology, 17*, 179-191.

Weldon, M. S., & Bellinger, K. D. (1997). Collective memory: Collaborative and individual processes in remembering. *Journal of Experimental Psychology: Learning, Memory and Cognition, 23*, 1160-1175.

Wells, W. P., & Pelz, D. C. (1966). *Scientists in organizations.* New York: Wiley.

Wood, R. E. (1986). Task complexity: Definition of the construct. *Organizational Behavior and Human Decision Processes, 37*, 60-82.

Yates, J. (1990). For the record: The embodiment of organizational memory, 1850-1920. *Business and Economic History, 19*, 172-182.

Yelle, L. E. (1979). The learning curve: Historical review and comprehensive survey. *Decision Sciences, 10*, 302-328.

Zander, U., & Kogut, B. (1995). Knowledge and the speed of the transfer and imitation of organizational capabilities: An empirical test. *Organization Science, 6*, 76-92.

Ziller, R. C., Behringer, R. D., & Goodchilds, J. D. (1962). Group creativity under conditions of success or failure and variations in group stability. *Journal of Applied Psychology, 46*, 43-49.

Chapter 4

Micro Underpinnings
of Organizational Learning

4.1 Introduction

Cisco Systems, Inc. has acquired 19 firms since 1994 (Wysocki, 1997). Most of these firms are small operations that produce software with 50 to 100 employees. Cisco is paying a premium for these firms—on the order of two million dollars per employee. Why is Cisco paying so much for these firms? According to Wysocki:

> In today's economy, building work teams from scratch can be yesterday's luxury. So when you can't build fast enough, you buy....Cisco is buying new product teams on the open market because it takes too long to assemble them from the ground up (1997, p. A1).

Thus, Cisco is paying a premium for teams that have already learned how to work effectively together. These teams have learned who is good at what, which approaches to the tasks are effective, and how to coordinate their activities. Teams that have learned to work effectively together are worth much more than their individual components.

Understanding how groups or teams learn to work effectively together provides the micro foundation for understanding organizational learning because groups or teams are the building blocks of most organizations. The current chapter develops the micro underpinnings of organizational learning. The chapter focuses on group learning, since much of the learning that takes place in organizations occurs in work groups. The chapter begins with definitions of the concepts of "groups" and "group learning." A discussion of why understanding how groups learn helps us understand how organizations learn follows. Critical processes of group learning are then presented. These include how groups share, generate, evaluate and combine knowledge to arrive at a collective product. Thus, this chapter focuses primarily on the acquisition of knowledge by groups. It concludes with a discussion of limits of group learning.

4.2 Some Definitions

What is a group? In a recent review of team performance research, Guzzo and Dickson (1996) defined a group as, "made up of individuals who see themselves and who are seen by others as a social entity, who are interdependent because of the tasks they perform as members of a group, who are embedded in one or more larger social systems (e.g., an organization), and who perform tasks that affect others (such as customers or coworkers)" (pp. 308-309). Similarly, Cohen and Bailey (1997) defined a team in an organizational setting as a collection of individuals who are interdependent in their tasks, who see themselves and are seen by others as an intact social entity, and who are embedded in a larger social system.

Dimensions of definitions of groups that are particularly important are: task interdependence (what one group member does affects and is affected by another group member); social-psychological awareness (members perceive themselves as a group and are perceived by others as a group); and social embeddedness (the group exists in a larger social system). Thus, while group members may be geographically dispersed, they should have some degree of awareness of one another and some sense of belonging to a group. McGrath (1984) further noted that a distinguishing feature of groups relative to other social aggregates such as communities or organizations is the relatively small size of groups (see also Shaw, 1981, for a discussion of defining characteristics of groups). A new product development team, a self-managed work group, and a strategic planning committee are a few examples of the many groups found in organizations today.

By group learning, I mean the activities through which group members acquire, share, and combine knowledge into a collective product through experience with one another (Argote, Gruenfeld & Naquin, in press). Group learning manifests itself through changes in knowledge and in performance. For example, as groups gain experience, they may acquire information about which group members are good at which tasks, how to use a new piece of technology more effectively, or how to coordinate their activities better. This knowledge may in turn improve their performance.

Groups may "learn" without evidencing performance changes. For example, a team that develops new software may learn that consumers are not willing to pay for the capabilities built into the software (e.g., Rhodes, 1986). The team may not be given opportunities, however, to produce other software products that manifest the knowledge it acquired. Hence, there may be no apparent effect on performance of the knowledge the team acquired. Conversely, performance may change without any corresponding change in the group's knowledge. For example, a group's competitor may experience a strike or a materials shortage that disables the competitor from producing products. The dearth of competition may result in an increase in the demand for the focal group's product. This in turn may result in a decrease in the cost of producing each unit since the group has more units over which to spread its fixed costs such as equipment. In this example, although the group did not "learn" anything, its performance improved.

These examples illustrate the complexity of determining whether groups (or organizations) learn. Ideally, one would like to measure how knowledge changes as groups gain experience and the effect of changes in knowledge on performance. In some settings, however, it is hard to measure changes in knowledge. For example, in a large manufacturing plant with thousands of employees it is now virtually impossible to chart all the knowledge that is acquired as the organization gains experience in production. Further, some of the knowledge the organization acquired may be tacit and difficult to assess. Conversely, in other settings such as small groups who interact for limited periods of time, one can develop more satisfying measures of group knowledge. In these settings, however, it may be very difficult to assess the performance implications of new knowledge since they may not manifest themselves for some time and it may be difficult to attribute performance changes to the changes in knowledge that occurred.

Understanding how either group knowledge or group performance changes as a function of experience is an important undertaking. In studying group knowledge, it is important to be sensitive to the tacit nature of a significant component of the knowledge groups acquire as they gain experience. It is also important to be aware that knowledge may be distributed unevenly in groups and that it may reside in many repositories (see the discussion of knowledge repositories in Chapter 3). In studying group performance, it is imperative to control for factors in addition to changes in knowledge that may affect performance. For example, consider the scenario described earlier where a competitor temporarily stopped production and the focal group was able to sell more units of its product and, thus, had lower unit costs. The lower unit costs in this example may not have been a function of experience, a prerequisite for learning to occur, but rather a function of the changing scale of operation. Thus, in order to demonstrate that learning occurred, it is important to demonstrate that the performance gains observed are a function of experience and not a function of other factors such as the scale of production. Chapters 1 and 2 discussed how one might control for these alternative explanations to determine whether performance changes are in fact due to "learning."

4.3 Why Study Group Learning?

Research on group learning is relevant for understanding organizational learning for two reasons. First, groups are increasingly being used as a form of organizing—both in the executive suite (Ancona & Nadler, 1989) and on the factory floor (Hoerr, 1989). Understanding how groups learn helps us understand how the organizations they constitute learn (Moreland & Levine, in press).

The second reason why understanding group learning helps us understand organizational learning is that many of the social processes such as coordination, communication, and influence that go on in organizations also go on in groups—only on a smaller scale. The smaller scale of groups makes it easier to capture and understand these processes. Additional processes such as managing relationships across groups come into play in organizations. And there are issues about how well the processes "scale up" as one moves from the group to the organizational level of analysis. These complexities notwithstanding, the important information about social processes gleaned from studies of group learning helps us understand the processes of organizational learning more fully.

Research on group learning has increased dramatically in recent years. Theoretical pieces on groups as problem-solving and information-processing systems have appeared at an increasing rate (e.g., Argote, Gruenfeld & Naquin, in press; Hinsz, Tindale & Vollrath, 1997; Klimoski & Mohammed, 1994; Larson & Christensen, 1993; Levine & Moreland, 1991; Sandelands & Stablein, 1987; Wegner, 1986; Wittenbaum & Stasser, 1996). Empirical studies examining how groups recall, share, and combine information to create a collective product are also more common.

These studies of group learning have provided rigorous theoretical models and empirical evidence on the processes of group "remembering," knowledge sharing, social influence, and the like. These studies have focused primarily on internal group processes. The focus on internal processes of these studies stems in part from the methods they generally employ. In the prototypical study, a small number of individuals are brought together to form a group in the laboratory. These groups are asked to solve a problem or perform a task, usually for a short time period. This design lends itself to an analysis of internal group processes. By observing group performance or videotaping it for subsequent analysis, researchers are able to capture and analyze group processes. For example, studies have examined how group processes mediate the relationship between group goal setting and performance (Weingart, 1992) or about how processes mediate the relationship between training methods and group performance (Liang, Moreland & Argote, 1995). These studies have provided important information about the mechanism through which one variable affects another—about why variables have the effects that they do.

Another strength of laboratory studies of group learning is that researchers can design experiments to disentangle various theoretical models. The control afforded by the laboratory enables one to construct experimental conditions for which different theories would predict different outcomes. By observing the outcomes of the experiment and assessing their correspondence to various theoretical predictions, one can determine the degree of empirical support for various theories. For example, Turner, Pratkanis, Probasco and Leve (1992) tested social identity theory as an explanation of a form of flawed group decision making, "groupthink" (Janis, 1972). According to social identity theory, groupthink occurs only under certain conditions. By observing whether groupthink occurs under the conditions predicted by the theory and not under others, one can determine whether social identity is a viable explanation for groupthink. Further, because laboratory studies enjoy the benefits of random assignment to condition, researchers can more readily determine the effect of variables of interest than one can in studies that do not have the benefits of randomization.

Field research, of course, has its own strengths, especially that of external validity. When conducting field research, one can study groups that exist in an organizational and temporal context. Thus, field research enables one to analyze external group processes (how groups manage relationships with other groups and the embedding context) and to study how group processes change over time. The discussions of organizational forgetting in Chapter 2 and knowledge transfer in Chapter 5 draw primarily on field research. Laboratory and field methods each have much to offer our understanding of group and organizational learning. By incorporating information obtained from each method, one arrives at a deeper understanding of the phenomenon.

Another difference between research on group and on organizational learning is the tasks the social entities perform. Studies of group learning have typically involved cognitive tasks for which groups are asked to make a decision, solve a problem, or generate ideas. For example, groups may be asked to brainstorm new ideas or determine a preferred alternative. By contrast, research on organizational learning, especially research on organizational learning curves, is more likely to be based on production-type tasks. The organizational learning research includes studies of naturalistic groups who produce a product or deliver a service. There are exceptions, of course, to this general pattern. Nevertheless, it is important to note the general pattern because research findings reviewed in this chapter on group learning are especially relevant for groups that perform a cognitive task. Production tasks, of course, have a cognitive component. The work described here is more relevant for the cognitive than the physical component of production tasks. Further, the findings are more relevant for understanding how groups acquire knowledge than for understanding how they retain or transfer knowledge. Those issues are discussed in Chapters 3 and 5.

4.4 Processes of Group Learning

Several processes have to occur in order for groups to learn. Groups have to acquire knowledge. They can do this by eliciting or sharing knowledge that one of their members already possesses or by generating new knowledge through collaboration and interaction. Another major process of group learning involves a "weighting" or evaluating of information that has been shared or generated. This involves influence attempts on the part of those who provide information and attempts to determine the information's accuracy and appropriateness on the part of those who receive the information. The last major process of group learning is combining knowledge: once knowledge has been shared and evaluated it must be combined into a collective product. Thus, group learning involves the processes through which members (1) share, (2) generate, (3) evaluate, and (4) combine knowledge. While these processes emphasize different aspects of group learning and help us organize relevant empirical findings, there is considerable overlap and feedback among the processes. Some processes may not occur. Some may occur very explicitly, while others may be more implicit. Further, factors that affect one process may affect others. For example, factors that affect whether an individual is likely to share knowledge also affect the weight the knowledge receives once it is communicated. Findings relevant for each of these processes of group learning will now be discussed.

A major aspect of group learning is acquiring new knowledge. Groups can acquire knowledge by eliciting or sharing knowledge that their members already possess, by generating new or "emergent" knowledge, or by importing knowledge from outside the group. This last mechanism for acquiring knowledge is discussed in Chapter 5, which focuses on transferring knowledge across groups. The others are discussed in this chapter.

4.4.1 Sharing Knowledge

Individual group members possess expertise and knowledge that is relevant, to varying degrees, to the group's task or problem. Just because an individual possesses knowledge, however, does not mean that he or she will necessarily share it with the group. The individual must recall the information, perceive it as relevant, and be motivated to share it. This section discusses the sharing of information in groups. Beginning with an example of a distributed group that did not share a particular piece of knowledge critical to the design of a computer, a discussion of how groups compare to individuals on particular knowledge-sharing tasks follows. The next part of the section is devoted to reviewing what we know about factors affecting information sharing in groups. The section concludes with a discussion of the effect of group composition on knowledge sharing in groups.

4.4.1.1 A Case Example

A case study of a new product development team illustrates the importance of knowledge sharing in groups and the negative consequences that can result from the failure to share critical knowledge (Olivera & Argote, in press). The task of the product development team was to design a new computer. A critical feature of the new computer was that it should have a small "footprint" so that it did not occupy too much desk space and would thus be attractive to customers such as banks and hospitals where desk surfaces were very limited. Aspects of the design of the computer were assigned to various subgroups. The subgroup that was responsible for designing the power supply missed the critical design feature that the computer should be small in size. The subgroup designed a power supply to sit next to the computer on the desk surface and thereby defeated the design feature of a small footprint. The problem with the power supply did not become apparent until all the subgroups designing the computer met the night before the computer was to be introduced at a computer fair. By then, it was too late to make fundamental changes in the system. The product was shipped with the power supply that was inconsistent with a key design feature.

This example illustrates how the failure to share knowledge can have negative consequences for a group. The lack of knowledge sharing compromised a critical design feature of the computer. Prospective sales for the computer did not materialize. After a year or so of disappointing demand, production of the computer was discontinued. While several factors contributed to the computer's disappointing sales, the incongruency between the power supply and desired design features was cited as a contributor.

Knowledge sharing in this example was complicated by the distributed nature of the design team. Sub-components of the system were designed by geographically distributed teams. We have argued for the importance of having these teams interact face-to-face for at least some time to provide more opportunities to share tacit and taken-for-granted knowledge (see Olivera & Argote, in press). While face-to-face groups provide more opportunity for knowledge sharing, knowledge sharing does not happen automatically in these groups either. The next sections of this chapter describe the conditions that enhance knowledge sharing in groups. The first of these sections examines group remembering—whether groups are better (or worse) than individuals at recalling information to which group members were exposed. The second section examines whether group members share information that they uniquely hold. The remaining section examines the effect of group composition on knowledge sharing.

4.4.1.2 Group Remembering

Research on group or collaborative remembering examines how groups remember or recall information. Information generated from this research would be especially relevant, for example, for groups who are required to recall information to which they were previously exposed. For example, members of a jury deliberating on a verdict might try to reconstruct what they heard in the courtroom. Or members of a work team might try to recall the training they received on a new piece of technology.

The general finding of research on group or collaborative remembering is that although groups typically do not perform as well as their "best" member, they perform better than individuals, on average, on memory recognition tasks (Clark & Stephenson, 1989; Hartwick, Sheppard and Davis, 1982; Hinsz, 1990). Hinsz (1990) identified several processes that contributed to the superior recall of groups. First, groups have access to a wider pool of information than individuals. Second, groups make fewer errors than individuals. Third, groups are better than individuals at determining what they could and could not recognize correctly. These latter two benefits seem to depend on groups being required to reach agreement or consensus (Weldon & Bellinger, 1997).

A recent study replicated the findings that group or collaborative remembering was superior to individual remembering (Weldon & Bellinger, 1997). Further, the researchers found that when groups were compared to the best individuals, groups performed significantly better than the best individuals on recall of random items but not of organized stories. When the performance of a collaborative group was compared to the performance of a nominal group formed by pooling the non-redundant responses of the same number of individuals working alone as were in the groups, however, nominal groups recalled more than collaborative groups. Thus, although collaborative groups recalled more than even the best-performing individuals, collaborative groups did not achieve their maximum potential. Further, previous experience in a group consistently improved subsequent individual performance and improved group performance for meaningful tasks.

In these studies of collaborative remembering, group members are typically exposed to information together and then asked to recall it. Often, however, group members possess information that they acquired individually that may or may not overlap with information other group members possess. Through training and past experiences, some group members may acquire information that others do not possess. The next section examines the conditions under which individual members share information that they may uniquely possess.

4.4.1.3 Factors Affecting Knowledge Sharing

Information sharing in groups often takes place in the context of a meeting or face-to-face discussion. Stasser and his colleagues have conducted an important stream of research on the conditions under which group members share their knowledge in these discussions. The basic finding of this line of research is that group members are more likely to share ideas that members already have in common than to discuss unshared ideas that are unique to individual members (see Wittenbaum & Stasser, 1996, for a review). For example, if a group meets to evaluate a candidate for a job, the group is more likely to focus on information all members share than to surface information about the candidate that only one member possesses. This tendency to focus on already shared information is unfortunate from the perspective of group performance since it suggests that groups may not realize a major benefit of having multiple members—pooling their different information and viewpoints.

One explanation of why groups do not discuss unshared information is provided by Stasser and his colleagues. Stasser and Titus (1985, 1987) proposed an information-sampling model that predicts that the probability that a piece of information will be mentioned during group discussion increases as the number of members who already possess the information increases. Thus, "shared information" is said to have a sampling advantage over unshared information since it is more likely to be mentioned and discussed. Gigone and Hastie (1993) provided a different interpretation for the tendency of groups to be more influenced by shared than unshared information. They argued that the greater influence of shared information derives from its effect on group member pre-discussion preferences rather than its effect on what is mentioned during group discussion.

A "hidden profile" approach was developed by Stasser (1988) to evaluate the effectiveness of a group in integrating information. Information is distributed in a hidden profile such that group members have different pieces of information, yet if all the information is pooled together a superior solution can be achieved. Stasser and Titus (1987) found that groups with small amounts of information to remember and a high percentage of unshared information recalled more unshared information in group discussion. The latter finding suggests that diverse groups whose members possess different information may be more likely to discuss uniquely held information than groups composed of similar members because members of diverse groups are likely to have less information in common.

Many factors affect whether groups share information and discover the hidden profile (see Argote, Gruenfeld & Naquin, in press, for a review). Knowledge of how information is distributed among group members affects the retrieval and integration of information. A group's awareness of the distribution of expertise within the group increases the likelihood that unshared knowledge uniquely held by members will be shared (Stasser, Stewart & Wittenbaum, 1995, and Stewart & Stasser 1995). Further, expert roles within a group validate the credibility of uniquely held information. Group members are more likely to accept and remember information contributed by a recognized expert (Stewart & Stasser, 1995). This finding also relates to the "weighting" or evaluation process of group learning discussed later in this chapter. Information provided by a recognized expert receives more weight in determining the group output than information provided by someone not perceived as having special expertise.

Leadership can also affect the sharing of unshared information. Larson, Christensen, Abbot and Franz (1996) found that medical residents who had more experience and expertise as well as higher status repeated *both* more shared and unshared information than interns or medical students who focused more on shared information that all members possessed. This finding is consistent with results previously described on the effect of expert roles on information sharing because medical residents have more expertise than interns or medical students.

Group size also affects the sampling advantage of shared over unshared information. Stasser, Taylor, and Hanna (1989) found that larger groups were more likely to focus only on shared information than smaller groups were. In a related vein, studies of social loafing have found that the extent of social loafing increased with increases in group size (Karau & Williams, 1993). Thus, members of large groups contributed less information per person than members of small groups. Similarly, members of large groups contributed fewer pieces of unique information than members of small groups.

The nature of the task has also been found to affect information sharing in groups. The extent to which a task has an answer that can be shown to be correct, such as solving a math problem, affects group information sharing. Stasser and Stewart (1992) found that the perception of a demonstrably correct answer promoted the sharing of unshared information. Conversely, the lack of a demonstrable answer promoted consensus building and inhibited the sharing of information members uniquely possess.

The temporal phase of a discussion may also affect the mix of shared versus unshared information that is discussed. Larson, Foster-Fishman and Keys (1994) argued that the sampling advantage of shared information would dissipate as discussion developed because the pool of shared items would be depleted and only unshared items would remain. Consistent with their predictions, the researchers found sharing of unshared information increased over time (at least for groups who did not receive any special training). This finding suggests that the tendency for groups to focus on shared rather than unshared information may be more characteristic of short than of long meetings.

The sharing of unshared information may also be affected by the extent to which subjects have experience with the task and the training they receive. Wittenbaum (1996) found that while inexperienced group members mentioned more shared than unshared information, experienced members repeated more unshared than shared information. Thus, experience with the task increased the amount of unshared information that surfaced in group discussion. Similarly, Larson, Foster-Fishman and Keys (1994) found that group decision training increased the amount of *both* shared and unshared information discussed. While discussion in untrained groups focused first on shared and then on unshared information, discussion in trained groups was more balanced over time.

This line of research suggests the conditions under which information will be shared in a group discussion. Information is most likely to be shared when: group members are not overloaded with information; diversity of views exists in the group (i.e., the percentage of "shared" information is low); some group members are recognized for having special expertise; leaders are present in the group; groups are small in size; tasks are seen as having some answers that are better than others; group members are given experience or training with the task; and group meetings last long enough to get past the initial tendency to focus on information members hold in common.

Although some of these factors may be beyond the control of an organization, others are more amenable to organizational design choices. For example, groups can be kept reasonably small in size (cf. Steiner, 1972) with some diversity in membership and relevant expertise. Information loads can be managed to some degree to prevent excessive overload (cf. Kahn, Wolfe, Quinn, Snoek & Rosenthal, 1964). Admonitions to "focus" factories on a more limited range of product options (Hayes & Wheelright, 1984; Skinner, 1974) or to focus product development efforts on a smaller number of new offerings (Hayes, Wheelright & Clark, 1988) are consistent with the recommendation to manage information loads in organizations. Groups can also be given appropriate training and experience working together.

Although most problems and challenges in organizations do not have one right solution in the sense of a math problem, certain solutions are usually better than others. Promoting finding the best solution rather than voting or other more political solutions is likely to lead to higher quality decisions for organizations. Attempts on the part of organizations to rely on data and find the best solution are consistent with this recommendation. For example, Dout Ivestor, the new Chief Executive Officer of the Coca-Cola Company is described as the most demanding, data-driven CEO in the world (Morris, 1998). Ivester reduced the amount of time it took to gather data from Coke's operations around the world from two and a half months to less than five days (Morris, 1998). This has enabled Coke to respond almost instantaneously to changes in competitors' moves or customers' preferences.

Let us return to the example of the computer discussed previously to determine whether these factors that have been found to increase information sharing in groups existed in that case. Group members were clearly perceived as having special expertise. This factor favored the sharing of information in the computer design group.

Most of the characteristics of the group, however, were not conducive to sharing information. For example, when one took into account all the individuals involved in designing sub-systems for the computer, the group was large in size. The failure to share information did not occur on a decision for which some solutions were perceived as technically better than others; rather it surfaced at the level of the overall design of the system. The decision to have a small footprint was a design choice made on the basis of judgments about sales opportunities rather than dictated by technical exigencies. Thus, at this level the task was not perceived as having a "correct" answer.

The point on which the computer design team most clearly diverged from the conditions that promote the sharing of unshared information in groups is the team's experience working together. The subgroup that designed the power system did not meet the other group members face-to-face until the night before the computer was to be unveiled at a computer fair! Thus, the group did not have much opportunity to develop common understandings and shared conceptions of the task. What one subgroup took for granted as a key feature of the task was not transmitted to another subgroup. Face-to-face opportunities to interact with and observe one another are better mechanisms for transferring tacit knowledge and taken-for-granted understandings than the electronic media often relied on so heavily to coordinate geographically dispersed teams (cf. Nonaka, 1991).

4.4.1.4 Group Composition

Another issue to consider in the acquisition of knowledge by groups is their composition, especially the diversity or heterogeneity of their membership. As noted previously, results of a study by Stasser and Titus (1987) suggest that diverse groups whose members possess different information due to variation in their backgrounds, training, or experiences may be more likely to share their unshared information than homogeneous groups composed of similar members. Considerable research has been conducted regarding the effect of group composition (especially the heterogeneity of group membership) on dimensions of group performance (see Jackson, May & Whitney, 1995; Moreland & Levine, 1992; Shaw, 1981; and Williams & O'Reilly, 1998, for reviews).

Research on group composition has yielded contradictory findings. In a review of the literature concerning the effect of group composition on group performance, Bettenhausen (1991) concluded that most studies have found that homogeneous groups composed of similar members performed better than groups composed of dissimilar members. For example, Ophir, Ingram and Argote (1998) found that homogeneous kibbutzim composed of similar members learned more from their experience than their counterparts composed of more heterogeneous members. By contrast, in their review, Jackson, May and Whitney (1995) emphasized the beneficial effects of group member heterogeneity for group decision quality. Jackson, May and Whitney (1995) concluded that heterogeneous groups were more innovative and creative than homogeneous groups (e.g., see the Bantel & Jackson, 1989, empirical study).

After carefully reviewing 40 years of empirical findings on the effects of group heterogeneity or diversity, Williams and O'Reilly (1998) concluded that diversity is more likely to have negative than positive effects on group performance. An exception to this pattern was found for the effects of functional diversity or diversity in backgrounds: functional diversity generally had a positive effect on group performance. Williams and O'Reilly (1998) emphasized that a critical issue in managing diversity is balancing the benefits of the increased information diverse members provide with the costs associated with communicating in diverse groups.

The computer design example discussed previously illustrates the difficulties heterogeneous groups composed of members with different "thought worlds" (Dougherty, 1992) can have working together. The design team for the computer consisted of members from different functional areas. Members of these different functions tend to have different values, preferences, and orientations (Dearborn & Simon, 1958; Lawrence & Lorsch, 1967). In the computer case, designers had specified that a key feature of the computer was to be its silent operation. Given this specification, the product planners did not want a fan to be installed on the computer since the fan would generate noise that conflicted with the desire for silent operation. Further, the product planners had conducted many tests that indicated that the computer would not overheat without a fan. Thus, planners felt strongly that a fan was not needed on this particular model. By contrast, manufacturing engineers were adamant that a fan was needed to prevent overheating. Manufacturing is the department that is responsible for any equipment that is returned due to malfunctioning. If a computer overheated, manufacturing would bear the cost of its repair. Manufacturing was not persuaded by the results of tests indicating that the computer would not overheat without a fan, but the department finally agreed to ship computers without fans as long as space was provided to install fans if they were needed!

None of the machines has ever been returned because of overheating. Unfortunately, costs were associated with the compromise of leaving room for a fan. The extra space required by leaving room for the fan compromised the design feature of a small size computer. This example illustrates the difficulties members of different functional areas can have when they work together. A degree of agreement is necessary for effective task performance (cf. Argote, 1989).

The disparate research findings and examples about the effects of member heterogeneity can be reconciled in part by considering the particular dimension of heterogeneity focused on, the performance measured used, the nature of the task, and the time span of the study (see Argote & McGrath, 1993). Concerning the dimension of heterogeneity, Williams and

O'Reilly (1998) found different effects for different dimensions of diversity. As noted previously, functional diversity generally had more positive effects on performance than other dimensions of diversity.

The performance measure used also matters. For example, Hambrick, Cho and Chen (1996) found that heterogeneous top management teams were more likely to launch a greater number of initiatives but were slower in responding to competitors' initiatives than homogeneous teams. In their review of the literature, Williams and O'Reilly (1998) concluded that heterogeneous groups were generally more creative but had more difficulty implementing ideas than homogeneous groups.

Heterogeneous groups seem most beneficial on creative tasks that involve innovation while homogeneous groups are more beneficial for tasks requiring considerable coordination. For example, Eisenhardt and Tabrizi (1995) found that team member heterogeneity (in terms of functional background) fostered product innovation in the computer industry. Similarly, Moorman and Miner (1997) found that heterogeneity of views among product development team members enhanced new product creativity during turbulent periods of changes in technology or customer preferences. By contrast, Murnighan and Conlon (1991) found that string quartets whose members were homogeneous (with respect to gender, age, and skill backgrounds) performed better than those composed of heterogeneous members. The studies finding a positive effect of heterogeneity examined tasks that involved creativity: product innovation. By contrast, the study finding a negative effect of heterogeneity examined a task where precise coordination of interdependent activities was critical: the performance of a string quartet.

The point in time at which the effects of heterogeneity are assessed is also likely to make a difference in determining its consequences. Watson, Kumar and Michaelson (1993) found that although the performance of homogeneous groups was initially superior to that of heterogeneous groups, the performance of culturally heterogeneous groups improved at a faster rate than that of homogeneous groups. At the conclusion of the several month-long study, the heterogeneous groups were more effective than the homogeneous groups at identifying problems and generating solutions. The overall performance of the heterogeneous and homogeneous groups was roughly the same at the end of the study. Thus, while it may take heterogeneous groups longer to work through process difficulties (Steiner, 1972) and develop effective task performance strategies, with experience, the performance of heterogeneous groups can equal (or exceed in certain dimensions) the performance of homogeneous groups.

Much of the advantage of heterogeneous groups stems from the diverse pool of information their members have access to and share in group discussion. Heterogeneous groups, however, are also better than homogeneous groups at developing new knowledge. Their advantage along this dimension will be discussed in the following section.

4.4.2 Generating New Knowledge

In addition to acquiring knowledge by sharing knowledge that members already possess, groups also acquire knowledge by generating new or "emergent" knowledge. The term "emergent" refers to knowledge that no individual group member possessed before group discussion, but comes out or "emerges" in the discussion. For example, one group member might make a comment that stimulates another to form a new idea. Or two members might present conflicting views that lead a third member to develop another alternative that reconciles the differing viewpoints. Thus, new or emergent knowledge that no member possessed before the discussion can develop through group discussion and interaction (cf. Kogut & Zander, 1992). The development of emergent knowledge is particularly important for groups engaged in tasks that involve creativity and innovation. Past work on the generation of emergent knowledge has generally focused on procedural changes that increase the likelihood of new knowledge emerging or compositional effects on the generation of new knowledge. Each of these approaches will now be discussed.

4.4.2.1 Procedural Approaches to Knowledge Generation

Brainstorming is a popular procedural technique designed to increase the number of new ideas generated by groups. Brainstorming involves encouraging group members to come up with as many ideas as possible, forbidding members from criticizing each others' ideas, and fostering members' building on ideas to generate new ones (Osborn, 1957). Thus, this technique involves sharing knowledge which group members already possess (see previous section) as well as generating new knowledge through group discussion.

      While brainstorming is intuitively appealing, the evidence on its effectiveness at generating new ideas is disappointing. Compared to individuals who work alone, groups who use brainstorming generate fewer non-overlapping ideas per person (see Mullen, Johnson & Salas, 1991, for a review). That is, four individuals working alone would generate more unique ideas in total than a four-person brainstorming group would. Further, productivity losses in brainstorming groups are greatest when: (a) the group is large in size, (b) an authority figure is present, (c) group members vocalize their ideas (rather than write them down), and (d) the result is compared with individuals who perform truly alone rather than individuals who perform in the presence of others (Mullen, Johnson & Salas, 1991).

Several mechanisms have been proposed to explain why brainstorming groups do not realize their "potential" productivity. Mullen, Johnson and Salas (1991) organized these mechanisms into three categories: (1) procedural mechanisms such as production blocking whereby idea generation is "blocked" while group members wait for their turns to talk (e.g., Stroebe & Diehl, 1994); (2) social-psychological mechanisms such as social influence processes whereby group members attempt to match their performance to that of other group members (Paulus & Dzindolet, 1993); and (3) "economic" mechanisms such as social loafing (Latane, Williams & Harkins, 1979) that represent an intentional decrease in effort on the part of group members. Mullen, Johnson and Salas (1991) concluded that research findings provide the most support for social-psychological mechanisms, moderate support for procedural mechanisms, and little support for economic mechanisms as explanations of the failure of brainstorming groups.

Sutton and Hargadon (1996) challenged research documenting the disappointing performance of brainstorming groups by noting that there may be many benefits to brainstorming besides idea generation. Based on evidence from a qualitative study of a product design firm that used brainstorming, Sutton and Hargadon (1996) concluded that brainstorming had many benefits for the firm such as supporting the organization's collective memory, providing skill variety for designers, and impressing clients.

Their study suggested that while using brainstorming to generate more ideas may be misguided, there may be other benefits to using brainstorming in organizations. Further, the conclusion described previously that it is primarily social-psychological mechanisms that explain the poorer performance of brainstorming groups (relative to individuals working alone) suggests that knowledge of these processes can be used to design conditions that minimize productivity losses. For example, having brainstorming groups consist of members who know each other rather than strangers (and this seems likely in real organizations in contrast to laboratory studies) may minimize productivity losses by reducing evaluation apprehension and the like. Providing brainstorming groups with high external standards or comparison norms may also increase their performance (cf. Paulus & Dzindolet, 1993). Further, there is evidence that the gap in output of brainstorming groups and the pooled output of the same number of noninteracting individuals decreases over time to the point where the productivity of brainstorming groups may even surpass that of noninteracting individuals (Paulus & Dzindolet, 1993).

Taken together, these arguments suggest that one-shot laboratory studies of brainstorming groups of strangers may significantly overstate the losses in productivity brainstorming groups experience. When brainstorming groups are composed of individuals who know each other and are given time to work through social-psychological processes such as evaluation apprehension, their productivity may approach and even surpass individuals. These are the conditions one is more likely to find in ongoing organizations rather than in laboratory studies. This may explain the apparent popularity of brainstorming in organizations.

4.4.2.2 Compositional Approaches to Knowledge Generation

Having individuals with different views in a group often leads to conflict that can create new knowledge. For example, Nemeth and her colleagues have examined the effect of conflict on the stimulation of divergent thinking in groups (Nemeth, 1992). "Divergent thinking" refers to the process of considering an issue from multiple perspectives (see Argote, Gruenfeld & Naquin, in press, for a review). Divergent thinking is stimulated by the presentation of minority views during group discussion. When presented with a variety of tasks, groups that considered alternative solutions presented by a minority were found to outperform groups that lacked a minority view. Such groups formulated more appropriate solutions after experimenting with a variety of strategies, and they produced more creative and original arguments than groups lacking minority input (Nemeth & Kwan, 1987; Nemeth & Wachtler, 1983). The divergent thinking exemplified by these groups is a result of their presentation and consideration of unusual alternatives without the pressure to accept them (Nemeth, 1986). Groups with a minority influence therefore have advantages in generating new knowledge over groups without minorities. These advantages apply to subsequent tasks (Smith, Tindale & Dugoni, 1996).

Similarly, the presence of conflict coupled with the absence of pressure to conform has been found to increase "integrative complexity" in groups. Dimensions of integrative complexity are: (1) a group's ability to identify and differentiate between multiple dimensions of an issue, and (2) a group's ability to identify and integrate connections among those dimensions (Gruenfeld & Hollingshead, 1993). A group with high integrative complexity perceives and accepts multiple viewpoints and the trade-offs associated with them. A group with low integrative complexity, for example, might believe that full participation is unconditionally productive in making group decisions; conversely, a group with high integrative complexity might foresee certain instances where full participation would not improve the projected outcome.

Examining Supreme Court decisions, Gruenfeld (1995b) found that majority opinions written on behalf of a non-unanimous court exhibited greater integrative complexity than those written on behalf of a minority or unanimous court. Furthermore, assigning subjects to majority factions in non-unanimous laboratory groups fostered an increase in integrative complexity, whereas assigning subjects to minority factions and unanimous groups fostered a decrease in integrative complexity (Gruenfeld, 1995a).

Groups display an increase in integrative complexity as members gain experience working together. During a semester-long course involving a variety of tasks, group essays initially exhibited similar integrative complexity to the average individual essay, but significantly lower integrative complexity than that exhibited by the best individual essay (Gruenfeld & Hollingshead, 1993). With experience in collaboration, however, the level of group integrative complexity increased: during the second half of the semester, group complexity was significantly higher than average individual complexity and even comparable to that of the best individual. The Gruenfeld and Hollingshead (1993) study therefore contests the assertion that groups do not perform as well as their "best" members (e.g., see Hill, 1982), suggesting that, with experience working together, groups' integrative complexity may evolve to the level of their best members.

Do groups that are high in integrative complexity perform better than groups that are not? Gruenfeld and Hollingshead (1993) found that the relationship between group integrative complexity and task performance depended on the nature of the task. High levels of group integrative complexity were associated with superior performance on conceptual synthesis and problem-solving tasks, whereas low levels of integrative complexity were marginally associated with superior performance on mixed-motive negotiation tasks. No significant relationships were found between group integrative complexity and performance on judgmental decision-making tasks. These results suggest that integrative complexity is beneficial for tasks where group members are interdependent and coordination is required. Groups high in integrative complexity performed better on tasks that involved coordinated efforts to identify a single, optimal solution. By contrast, groups low in integrative complexity performed slightly better on negotiation tasks in which members' interests were not compatible.

Taken together, these findings suggest the conditions under which new or emergent knowledge is likely to develop in groups as a result of their interaction. Emergent knowledge is most likely to develop when: there is some diversity of opinion among group members; group norms favor learning rather than finding the "best" or the "fastest" solution; and groups have time to learn to interact effectively and develop appropriate task performance strategies. These are the conditions under which groups are most likely to create new knowledge. It is interesting to note that a couple of the conditions that promote the generation of new knowledge, such as diversity and experience, also promote the sharing of knowledge discussed previously.

4.4.3 Evaluating Knowledge

Once groups have acquired knowledge (either by sharing it among members or by generating it themselves), they must evaluate it. Past research has shown that groups are better than individuals at evaluating one type of knowledge—knowledge embedded in hypotheses. Research on "collective induction" examines how groups perform on inductive tasks, which involve the search for rules and principles (Laughlin & Hollingshead, 1995). For example, a maintenance team in a factory might try to determine the conditions under which a machine breakdown occurs; a hospital emergency service unit might try to diagnose a patient's condition; a team of medical researchers might try to specify the conditions under which a new drug has desired effects. The two basic processes of induction are hypothesis generation and hypothesis evaluation (see Laughlin & Hollingshead, 1995, for a fuller discussion). Hypothesis generation is the development of a tentative explanation or hypothesis for the observed phenomenon. Hypothesis evaluation is the testing of that hypothesis against data. Although groups are not better than individuals at generating hypotheses, they are better able than individuals to recognize a correct hypothesis once it is proposed (e.g., Laughlin & Futoran, 1985; Laughlin & Shippy, 1983). This superiority in the ability to evaluate hypotheses proposed by group members leads groups to be better than individuals on inductive tasks.

How do groups evaluate hypotheses or other information provided by their members? In order to evaluate hypotheses and other information, groups need to determine whether the information provided by a member is accurate or appropriate and whether it should figure in their final output. This involves both implicit and explicit judgments of the expertise, status and role of the individual offering the information as well as political considerations of the implications of accepting it. Research on perceptions of expertise and on minority influence is relevant for understanding how groups evaluate the contributions of their members.

4.4.3.1 Perceptions of Expertise

Research discussed previously on expertise and knowledge sharing is relevant for determining the weight information receives in group judgment. Factors that affect whether an individual is likely to volunteer information also affect whether the information is likely to be accepted and acted upon. As noted previously, expertise can provide validation of information. Stewart and Stasser (1995) found that group members were more likely to accept and remember information contributed by a recognized expert.

This finding has important implications for real groups that exist in naturalistic settings. These groups, such as task forces or problem-solving teams, are often brought together precisely because members have different expertise. For example, a task force of members from different departments might be put together to solve a problem that cuts across the departments, such as being more responsive to customers or reducing cycle time. Also, a strategic planning committee might be composed of members with different functional expertise because high-level strategic problems do not fall neatly into one functional area but rather require input from many different ones. Stasser, Stewart and Wittenbaum's (1995) results suggest that the differential in expertise that exists in these naturalistic groups increases the likelihood that information will be shared in them. Further, Stasser and Stewart's (1992) results suggest that information contributed by an expert is more likely to be recognized and accepted than information contributed by someone not perceived as having expertise.

Will these perceptions of expertise that group members develop be accurate? Empirical evidence on the ability of group members to identify the best performer in the group is somewhat mixed (see Littlepage, Robison & Reddington, 1997, for a recent review). Although Miner (1984) found that groups identified their best performer only slightly better than random chance, Yetton and Bottger (1982) found that groups performed significantly better than chance in identifying their best performers. Henry (1995) found that groups identified their best member significantly more frequently than would be predicted by chance alone. In Henry's (1995) study, groups were still not able, however, to identify their most accurate member most of the time. Henry, Strickland, Yorges and Ladd (1996) found that groups that were given outcome feedback were better at identifying their best member than groups that were not provided any feedback.   The benefit of feedback occurred even though the same individual was rarely the most accurate across tasks.

Perceptions of the expertise of others have generally been found to become more accurate with increasing experience. Hollenbeck et al. (1995) found that as teams gained experience working together, their leaders became better at appropriately weighting group members' judgments in arriving at the group decision. That is, through experience with the task, leaders learned about the competence of team members and about which members could be relied upon for accurate judgments. Similarly, Moreland, Argote and Krishnan (1998) found evidence that experience working together improved the complexity and accuracy of group members' judgments about each others' expertise. In a similar vein, Littlepage, Robison and Reddington (1997) found that experience working together improved members' ability to recognize expertise when it transfers to new performance situations.

Will having accurate perceptions of expertise improve group performance? Libby, Trotman and Zimmer (1987) found that both variation in individual performance and the ability of groups to recognize expertise were associated with more accurate group performance. Liang, Moreland and Argote (1995) and Moreland, Argote and Krishnan (1996) found that knowledge of who was good at what in a group improved subsequent group performance. By contrast, Henry, Strickland, Yorges and Ladd (1996) found that while outcome feedback improved the ability of groups to identify who was best at a task, this ability did not improve group performance. The researchers suggested that participants in their laboratory study may have been more concerned with maintaining positive group relations by incorporating everyone's input than with increasing group accuracy by relying on the best member. It is also important to note that the task used in the study (estimating different items) was deliberately chosen so that the same individual would not be the most proficient at the task or even at a certain type of item in the task. While this design choice was well-suited to the researchers' purpose of determining how subjects utilized cues, the design made the task less representative of the types of tasks real groups encounter. Real groups are likely to experience more stability in who is good at which subtask. Littlepage, Robison and Reddington (1997) found that group performance was predicted by the recognition of the expertise of group members. In general, the evidence seems to suggest that accurate perceptions of expertise improve group performance.

It is interesting to return at this point to our earlier discussion of factors explaining organizational learning curves. An important factor identified by members of organizations we interviewed was learning who is good at what—that is, learning the expertise of organizational members.

This knowledge enables organizations to match tasks with the most qualified people. Knowledge of who is good at what also speeds problem solving since members know whom to ask for assistance or needed information. Many organizations such as consulting firms are investing considerable resources in developing databases or knowledge networks that catalog the expertise and past work products of their members (Moreland, in press; Stewart, 1995a and 1995b) and make this knowledge available to the entire organization. While definitive work has not been done on the effectiveness of these databases, their development suggests that firms view the knowledge of who knows what as important to firm success. The experimental evidence on expertise described in this section supports the evidence obtained from our interviews in the field and the practice of developing databases about employee expertise. Knowing who is good at what appears to be an important contributor to group and organizational performance.

4.4.3.2 Influence of Minorities

Minority influence is an important factor in understanding the way in which groups weight information provided by their members (see Argote, Gruenfeld & Naquin, in press; Levine & Thompson, 1996, for recent reviews). A small percentage of group members may have minority viewpoints that conflict with the majority opinion. Research on minority influence reveals factors that might affect their ability to persuade the group to accept their alternative ideas. In other words, the study of minority influence allows for examination of the conditions under which minority views might be heavily weighted in a group's decision. The overall influence of minorities is directly related to the previously discussed work concerning minority contributions to divergent thinking (e.g., see Nemeth, 1992).

A group's acceptance of minority views or accomodation of them into the final judgment may be affected by the minority's characteristics or the characteristics of the particular task the group faces. One specific characteristic which is very important in the minority's ability to influence the group is credibility (Wood, Lundgren, Ouelette, Busceme & Blackstone, 1994). Several factors may determine a minority's credibility, including consistency of opinion (Moscovici, Lage & Naffrechoux, 1969), flexibility (Mugny, 1982), and gradual distancing from the majority view (Levine, Saxe & Harris, 1976).

Credibility may also be gained if the minority demonstrates concerns for the welfare of the group rather than for individual purposes.

That is, a minority is more influential if he or she advocates outcomes that are not guided by his or her personal interests (Eagly, Wood & Chaiken, 1978). Also, support from other group members may bolster a minority's credibility (Penrod & Hastie, 1980).

Characteristics of the group's task or problem may also affect a minority's ability to influence other members. "Demonstrably correct" suggestions, or those which seem to be logical answers, will be more readily acceptable to the group than those which do not seem as obviously appropriate for the problem (Laughlin, 1988). Furthermore, when the group's objective is to learn rather than to perform, members may be more open to minority ideas (Smith, Tindale & Dugoni, 1996).

These findings help to identify specific conditions when individually proposed information might significantly influence the final group decision or product. The primary factors allowing information to be heavily weighted are: the level of expertise of the information's contributor; the extent to which the contributor is perceived to be concerned primarily with the group's welfare rather than his or her personal interests; the consistency of the contributor's opinion while being flexible and open to other input; the degree of support from other group members; and whether the information is conceived to be an appropriate, logical solution to the problem at hand. Individuals who possess these characteristics or craft arguments characterized by these features will be more influential in group discussions than those lacking such characteristics.

4.4.4 Combining Knowledge

Once group members have shared information and determined (either implicitly or explicitly) how much weight to place on various bits of information, it must be combined into a collective product. Several lines of research are relevant for understanding how groups combine information: descriptive work on group social decision schemes, normative work on social decision themes, models of persuasive argumentation, and models of participation in decisions.

4.4.4.1 Social Decision Schemes

A social decision scheme is a rule or procedure that converts individual preferences into a group product (Davis, 1973). Thus, a social decision scheme describes the social processes by which a group makes a decision. These processes can be explicit or implicit. Examples of social decision schemes include: "truth wins," in which a single correct member proposes a response that is then accepted by the group; "truth supported wins," in which one member proposes and another supports a correct response that the group then accepts; majority, in which the group decision is the alternative preferred by the majority of members; and equiprobability, in which the collective group decision is equally likely among the proposed alternatives regardless of the number of members favoring them.

The extent to which the task is perceived as having a demonstrably correct answer is a critical factor that affects the decision scheme groups employ (Laughlin & Ellis, 1986). Tasks can be classified upon a continuum from intellective to judgmental tasks. Intellective tasks have a demonstrably correct answer, such as a solution to a math problem. Judgmental tasks, such as selecting a job candidate, do not have demonstrably correct answers. Taken together, the results of several studies suggest that the number of group members necessary and sufficient for a collective group decision decreases as the demonstrability of the "answer" increases (Laughlin & Ellis, 1986).

For intellective tasks with an obvious demonstrably correct answer, a "truth wins" social decision scheme best characterizes the decision process groups use (Lorge & Solomon, 1955; Laughlin & Ellis, 1986). For intellective tasks with non-obvious demonstrably correct answers, such as tests of knowledge, a "truth supported wins" social decision scheme best describes the decision process typically employed (e.g., see Laughlin & Adamopoulos, 1980). For collective induction tasks in which answers are neither demonstrably correct or demonstrably incorrect, a combination of majority and truth-supported wins characterizes the group decision process (Laughlin & Futuran, 1985; Laughlin & Shippy, 1983). For judgmental tasks without a demonstrably correct answer, a majority or equiprobability social decision scheme characterizes how groups make their decisions (e.g., see Davis, 1980, 1982; and Penrod & Hastie, 1979, for reviews).

Einhorn, Hogarth and Klempner (1977) also analyzed how individual inputs are combined into a group output. Rather than describing the decision scheme groups actually used, the researchers analyzed whether using different decision schemes or models theoretically affected the quality of group judgment. Four models that characterize how groups form judgments were contrasted. The four models involved: (1) randomly picking an individual's judgment as the group's judgment (random model); (2) taking the mean of the judgments of individual group members as the group's judgment (mean model); (3) using the judgment of the "best" group member, whom the group is able to identify with certainty (best member model); and (4) using the judgment of the best member, whom the group identifies with some probability (the proportion model). The researchers examined the four models under varying conditions of group size and individual member bias.

Theoretical results indicated that the random model generally led to the poorest decision accuracy while the best member model consistently led to the highest decision accuracy. The proportional model and the mean model were intermediate in accuracy. For low levels of bias, the mean model performed better than the proportional model, while the reverse was true for high levels of bias. As bias increased, the best member model improved relative to the other three models. As group size increased, the accuracy of group judgment increased. The increase in accuracy observed with increasing group size was particularly pronounced for the best member model and for the mean and proportional models under low levels of bias.

These results represent the theoretical baseline that could be achieved under various conditions of decision model, group size and member bias. Thus, the results do not tell us the actual performance of groups but rather tell us the ideal level that could be achieved under various conditions. If one knows the best member with certainty, relying on the best member's judgment is clearly the best strategy. Under conditions of uncertainty about the best member, forming a mean of members' judgments is the best strategy when individual judgments are not very biased. For high levels of bias, relying on the person believed to be the best member is more effective than averaging the judgments of all group members. It is interesting to note that the importance of knowing who is best at what figures so prominently in this and other discussions of group learning and performance.

4.4.4.2 Persuasive Arguments

Another perspective on how groups combine knowledge to arrive at a collective decision can be found in "persuasive arguments" theory (Burnstein & Vinokur, 1977). This theory has received considerable support as an explanation of the risky shift or group polarization phenomenon (for reviews of the risky shift and related phenomena, see Cartwright, 1973; Dion, Baron & Miller, 1970; Myers & Lamm, 1976). According to persuasive arguments theory, the greatest choice shifts found after group discussion occur when: (1) the preponderance of arguments in the "population" of arguments favors one alternative; and (2) the probability that a given individual group member possesses the arguments is low. Group discussion exposes individuals to new arguments. Since there are many more arguments in favor of one alternative than the others, individuals' preferences shift to that alternative during group discussion.

In order for persuasive arguments to effect a choice shift, individual group members must possess only a small subset of the arguments in favor of an alternative at the start of group interactions. This is one of the conditions that Stasser and Titus (1987) found increased the sharing of unshared information in groups. When the percentage of shared information is low, individuals were more likely to share "unshared" information. When they share their unshared information and when most of the information favors a particular alternative, individuals are exposed to a large number of arguments in favor of the alternative through group discussion. In the persuasive arguments theory, it is the balance of the arguments that determines the group outcome. The alternative with more arguments in its favor is accepted.

The studies of group decision making reviewed in this section are largely laboratory studies where groups are convened for the purpose of forming a judgment or making a decision. Hence, the social decision schemes used by these groups may be more explicit and perhaps more collective than one finds in ongoing groups in organized settings. For those groups, the decision may be made by a formal leader who may or may not consult with group members. The influence processes described in the previous section are likely to come into play to affect whom a leader or manager consults and whether their opinion is incorporated in the final decision. Political factors also influence how knowledge is combined (Pfeffer, 1981).

4.4.4.3 Participation

Aspects of work on leadership and participation are also relevant for understanding the social decision schemes used in naturalistic groups. Vroom and Yetton's model of decision making specifies when a leader should make a decision him or herself and when a leader should encourage participation of subordinates (Vroom & Jago, 1988; Vroom & Yetton, 1973). According to the model, there is a continuum of decision-making styles ranging from autocratic, in which a manager makes the decision him or herself, to highly participative, in which the group makes the decision.

The model is stated in the form of a decision tree that specifies the conditions under which an effective decision, characterized by high quality, subordinate acceptance, and timeliness, will be made. Conditions that determine the extent to which decisions should be made participatively include the technical quality requirements of the decision, the importance of subordinate commitment to the decision, whether the leader or subordinate have adequate information to make the decision, how structured the decision is, and the extent to which subordinates share the organization's goals. For example, according to the model, autocratic decisions should be made when the technical quality of the decision is high, when managers have adequate information to make the decision, and when subordinates are likely to be committed to the decision, even if the manager makes it alone. By contrast, decisions should be made in a highly participative style when the importance of subordinate commitment is high and subordinates are not likely to be committed unless they were involved in the decision. The Vroom and Yetton (1973) model of decision making has generally been supported in empirical studies (Cotton, Vollrath, Froggart, Lengnick-Hall & Jennings, 1988).

The Vroom and Yetton model is consistent at a very general level with work on social decision schemes. Both types of models specify that when the decision facing the group is of the "right answer" type and an individual has the requisite expertise to provide the answer, the decision is likely to be made by the expert. For decisions that do not have right answers (and in the Vroom and Yetton model, for decisions for which group member acceptance is key), the decision will be made by a larger number of group members.

4.5 Limits of Group Learning

The general pattern found on a variety of tasks is one of groups being superior to individuals (certainly the "average" individual, and sometimes even the "best" individual—see Reagan-Cirincione, 1994; Weldon & Bellinger, 1997) and of groups improving with experience. Groups are better than individuals on recall (Hinsz, 1990) and induction tasks (Laughlin & Hollingshead, 1995). Groups become better at sharing information (Wittenbaum, 1996) and developing more complex understandings of phenomena (Gruenfeld & Hollingshead, 1993) as they gain experience. With experience, groups also become better at identifying expertise and who knows what and who can be counted on in the group (Liang, Moreland, & Argote, 1995) and at recognizing and accepting the correct solution proposed by a group member (Laughlin & Hollingshead, 1995). Group performance improves as groups gain experience (Argote, Insko, Yovetich & Romero, 1995; Goodman & Leyden, 1991; Guetzkow & Simon, 1955; Shure, Rogers, Larsen & Tassone, 1962).

Although the general pattern is one of group superiority to individuals, there are important examples where groups make very poor decisions. Janis (1972) vividly described examples of fundamentally flawed group decisions with disastrous consequences and attributed the flaws to the groupthink phenomenon. Controversy has swirled around the groupthink phenomenon, the conditions under which it occurs and whether it leads to defective outcomes (see Aldag & Fuller, 1993, for a recent review).

Several of the conditions hypothesized to lead to groupthink arguably prevent groups from learning. For example, a leader who actively promotes his or her opinions might prevent others from speaking up or voicing their views. Similarly, a lack of norms about the importance of incorporating all members' inputs in decisions could discourage members from sharing information they possess. Thus, groupthink may block the learning processes that generally occur in groups as members gain experience working together. In a related vein, Argyris (1992) demonstrated how the defensive routines organizations invoke to avoid embarrassment or threat can prevent organizational learning (see also Argyris & Schon, 1978).

There is some (albeit sparse) evidence that experience can reduce the tendency of groups to engage in the groupthink phenomenon. For example, Janis (1972) described how the same group of policy makers that made very poor decisions in the Bay of Pigs fiasco functioned much more effectively in the Cuban Missile Crisis. By contrast, Kim (1997) found that groups with both experience on a similar task (task experience) and experience working together (team experience) performed more poorly than their counterparts lacking both types of experience. The poor performance of groups with both task and team experience was due in part to their tendency to focus on information that members held in common rather than discuss unique information that different members possessed. Thus, in this laboratory study, experience led to a narrower set of information being considered and to poorer performance.

Katz (1982) found a non-monotonic inverted U-shaped relationship between group "longevity" (the average amount of time group members had worked together) and the performance of Research and Development (R&D) groups. Performance initially increased and then decreased with increases in the average group experience. For these R&D groups, the best performance occurred with between two to four years of experience. Initially, performance improved as group members learned how to communicate and coordinate their activities. The decrease observed in performance at high levels of experience was attributed to the groups becoming too inwardly focused and not interacting with or learning from external sources. These results underscore both the benefits and costs of experience. Increases in experience can enhance group performance significantly by providing group members with opportunities to learn how to work together effectively. If increases with experience are also associated, however, with becoming isolated from external sources of knowledge, performance decrements can occur.

Although there is considerable evidence of individual performance improving with experience (see Chapter 1), there is also evidence that individuals may have difficulties drawing appropriate inferences from their experience (Dawes, 1988; Einhorn & Hogarth, 1986; Tversky & Kahneman, 1974). Not only does the performance of most groups improve with experience, groups may get better at interpreting their experience (e.g., see Gruenfeld & Hollingshead, 1993).

How can these conflicting viewpoints of the role of experience in individual and group performance be reconciled? One possible reconciliation would be to demonstrate that groups are somehow better than individuals at learning from experience. Comparing how individuals and groups learn from experience would extend previous comparisons of individual and group performance (Hill, 1982; Maier, 1967) in interesting ways. In their analysis of group versus individual accuracy, Gigone and Hastie (1997) concluded that: "groups tend to outperform individuals when the judgment policies of their most accurate members are both more accurate than the judgment policy of the statisticized groups and discernible by other members" (p. 163). As noted earlier in this chapter, perceptions of the expertise of other group members have been found to become more accurate as groups gain experience. This may explain an advantage groups have relative to individuals at learning from experience.

Research has been done comparing individual and group biases that is also somewhat relevant for this issue (e.g., see Argote, Seabright & Dyer, 1986; Kerr, MacCoun & Kramer, 1996; Tindale, 1993). This work examines whether groups amplify or cancel decision-making biases observed at the individual level (see Kahneman, Slovic & Tversky, 1982, for a discussion of these biases at the individual level). Most of this work has been conducted at one point in time. Hence it does not directly address questions of learning but rather provides static comparisons of group versus individual judgment.

Research comparing group and individual biases has yielded contradictory findings. Some studies have shown that groups eliminate biases observed at the individual level, whereas others have reported that groups amplify individual biases. Whether groups amplify or cancel biases depends at least in part on the nature of the bias. If the bias is not systematic, group discussion will serve to weaken the bias since members will be exposed to other points of view that are less biased or biased in a different direction (see also Gigone & Hastie, 1997). Conversely, if the bias is systematic and widely shared, group discussion is likely to amplify the bias by exposing members to others who hold the same bias and thereby, increasing confidence in its correctness. This research again suggests the importance of diversity in group membership. Exposing members to different points of view decreases the likelihood that their decisions will be systematically biased. Thus, groups may be better than individuals at learning if group members have diverse views that are utilized effectively. This, of course, does not automatically happen in groups and may account in part for the variance observed in group learning. Even when individual biases are systematic, groups may be able to outperform their best member if their discussion is facilitated to ensure that all group members participate and if members are provided feedback as a group (Reagan-Cirincione, 1994).

The context in which learning occurs within groups may help to explain why group performance improves with experience even though individuals may have difficulties interpreting their experiences. Many of the studies discussed in this monograph showing group or organizational productivity gains with experience have been conducted in production environments. Several characteristics of these environments may facilitate learning. First, the group or the organization typically makes many repetitions of the same product. For example, one truck plant we studied produced almost 1,000 trucks each day! These trucks provided many opportunities for learning since different modifications could be made on each truck and their effects assessed.

Second, feedback in these production environments is often more immediate and less forgiving than feedback in other contexts. One determines fairly quickly whether the windshield fits into its frame, whether the welding holds, or whether the lights work properly. This environment contrasts, for example, with research environments where it may take months or years to determine whether a new approach is effective.

A third reason why learning might be easier in production environments is that the factors determining organizational outcomes such as productivity and quality may be more under the organization's control than those determining more distant outcomes such as market share. Thus, it is easier to assess the effect of organizational action on outcomes and easier to determine effective responses.

Although these features of production environments can be thought of as boundary conditions that specify when an organization or group is most likely to learn from experience, the features can also be regarded as desired attributes for learning that can be emulated in other settings. That is, rather than regard the extent of repetition of production as immutable or "given," organizations can aim to increase the number of parts or processes that are repeated on their products.

The use of common "platforms" for a variety of products is consistent with this recommendation. Rather than have each product consist of unique parts and processes, products share a common base or platform of parts and processes. Since these common parts and processes are repeated on many products, the organization has a much larger experience base from which to learn.

Mass customization also has the potential to increase an organization's experience base for learning. In mass customization, a product is designed to consist of independent modules that can be assembled into different forms of the product, according to customer specifications (Feitzinger & Lee, 1997; Pine, Victor & Boynton, 1993). Manufacturing processes are also designed to consist of independent modules that can be reconfigured to produce different designs. According to Feitzinger and Lee (1997), the key to effective mass customization is to postpone differentiating the product for a specific customer as long as possible. From a learning perspective, this postponement increases the number of times a part or process is repeated since the same parts and processes will be used on many variants of the product.

Another way in which organizations can increase their ability to learn from experience is to design experiments (natural or laboratory) that have the potential to inform one about the effect of critical factors. In actual organizations, factors often covary in ways that make it hard to assess their separate effects. For example, an organization may introduce new technology at a plant that produces a diverse product mix. The performance of this plant may be lower than its three sister plants who use a better understood technology to produce a less varied product mix. How can the organization determine if it is the new technology or the more complicated product mix that is driving the first plant's lower performance? In this example, it is impossible to determine if the new technology or the complex product mix contribute to the lower productivity since the use of the new technology is perfectly correlated with the complex product mix. That is, the data from the naturally-occurring experiment described above are structured in a way that it is impossible to partial out the effect of the technology from the effect of the product mix.

In this example, the organization may have been able to structure its experience differently to enhance learning. For example, the organization could keep the product mix (and other critical factors to the extent possible) the same across the four plants and introduce the new technology at two of them. To the extent that other factors are constant or can be controlled for statistically, differences in productivity between the plants with and without the new technology can reasonably be attributed to the technology. Thus, the organization would be in a better position to learn from its experience.

More research is needed on the question of how groups (and organizations) learn from experience and the conditions under which their performance improves with experience. Determining the answer to this question will require longitudinal studies that examine groups over time. It will also require studying many groups that differ in interesting ways. This research strategy will enable us to specify more fully the conditions under which group learning occurs. Characteristics of the group, its task, structures and processes, and the environment in which it is embedded are likely to condition the extent to which group learning occurs.

4.6 Conclusion

Several key processes must occur in order for groups to learn. First, groups must acquire knowledge. They can do this by sharing knowledge members already possess or by generating new knowledge. Several important conditions increase the likelihood that knowledge will be shared by group members: having group members with different expertise, keeping groups small in size, creating the perception that some solutions to the problem are better than others, having leaders or facilitators present, refraining from overburdening the groups, and providing group members with experience or training and enough time in meetings to get past the initial tendency to focus on shared information.

Several of these conditions that increase the likelihood that group members will share information are the same conditions that increase the likelihood that new or emergent knowledge will be generated in groups. Having members with different backgrounds and views increases the likelihood that new or emergent knowledge will develop as a result of their interactions. Groups with diverse members or minority views are more likely to experience conflict than homogeneous groups or groups lacking minority dissent. The presence of this conflict coupled with an absence of pressure to conform can lead to the development of new approaches and alternatives. Thus, conflict can lead to the creation of new knowledge. Providing group members with experience working together also leads to the creation of new knowledge. Groups can also acquire knowledge by importing it from outside the group. This mechanism for knowledge acquisition is discussed in Chapter 5 on knowledge transfer.

Once information has been shared or new information generated, groups must evaluate the information they have acquired and determine its weight in the final judgment. This involves judging the expertise, status, and role of the individual providing the information as well as considering the implications of accepting it. Groups are more likely to accept information contributed by a recognized expert than by someone not perceived as having relevant expertise. With experience working together, groups learn who the experts are in various areas. Individuals are also likely to persuade the group to accept their point of view when they take a consistent—but not rigid—stance, when they are not perceived as having a personal stake in the group's decision, and when their position is supported by another group member.

Once group members have acquired information and determined (either implicitly or explicitly) the weight it receives, the various bits of information must be combined into a collective product. There are many strategies that groups can use to combine information. These strategies range on a continuum from relying on one person to make the decision to basing the decision on consensus of all group members. Several factors tip a group toward one versus the other end of the continuum. The more the task is perceived as having a demonstrably correct answer, the fewer the number of persons supporting the answer required for the group to accept that answer. By contrast, for judgmental tasks lacking a demonstrably correct answer, a majority of group members are required for a group to accept a point of view. The more member acceptance is viewed as critical for decision success, the greater the number of group members who will typically be involved in a decision.

Although there are important examples of groups making disastrous decisions, on balance, groups are generally better than individuals (at least the average individual) on a variety of tasks. Further, group performance typically improves with experience. Groups become better at sharing information. They learn who knows what and whom they can rely upon. This meta knowledge of each other's expertise improves group performance. Members know whom to go to for information or advice. Tasks are assigned to the most qualified group member. Groups develop effective strategies for coordinating their activities. Thus, as groups acquire experience, they develop effective connections for getting their work done (cf. Huberman, 1996).

Although this chapter acknowledged that heterogeneous groups composed of diverse members do not always outperform homogeneous groups, the chapter has emphasized the benefits of diversity in functional areas or members' backgrounds for acquiring new knowledge. Diverse groups are more likely to share "unshared" information and to generate new knowledge as a result of their interaction. Diversity causes group members to rethink their positions and to create new approaches and alternatives that accommodate different views. Diversity is particularly beneficial for the creation of new knowledge. Too much diversity, however, can impair the generation of new knowledge, if there is not some overlap or base of common understanding (cf. Owens & Neale, 1998). Too much diversity can also impair the transfer of knowledge across organizational units. This issue is discussed in the next chapter.

References

Aldag, R. J., & Fuller, S. R. (1993). Beyond fiasco: A reappraisal of the groupthink phenomenon and a new model of group decision processes. *Psychological Bulletin, 113*, 533-552.

Ancona, D. G., & Nadler, D. A. (1989). Top hats and executive tales: Designing the senior team. *Sloan Management Review, 31*(1), 19-28.

Argote, L. (1989). Agreement about norms and work unit effectiveness: Evidence from the field. *Basic and Applied Social Psychology, 10*, 131-140.

Argote, L., Gruenfeld, D., & Naquin, C. (in press). Group learning in organizations. In M. E. Turner (Ed.), *Groups at work: Advances in theory and research.* Mahwah, NJ: Erlbaum.

Argote, L., Insko, C. A., Yovetich, N., & Romero, A. A. (1995). Group learning curves: The effects of turnover and task complexity on group performance. *Journal of Applied Social Psychology, 25*, 512-529.

Argote, L., & McGrath, J. E. (1993). Group processes in organizations: Continuity and change. *International Review of Industrial and Organizational Psychology, 8*, 333-389.

Argote, L., Seabright, M. A., & Dyer, L. (1986). Individual versus group use of base-rate and individuating information. *Organizational Behavior and Human Decision Processes, 38*, 65-75.

Argyris, C. (1992). *On organizational learning.* Cambridge, MA: Blackwell Business.

Argyris, C., & Schon, P. (1978). *Organizational learning.* Reading, Mass: Addison-Wesley.

Bantel, K. A., & Jackson, S. E. (1989). Top management and innovations in banking: Does the composition of the top team make a difference? *Strategic Management Journal, 10*(summer special issue), 107-124.

Bettenhausen, K. L. (1991) Five years of groups research: What we have learned and what needs to be addressed. *Journal of Management, 17*, 345-381.

Burnstein, E., & Vinokur, A. (1977). Persuasive argumentation and social comparison as determinants of attitude polarization. *Journal of Experimental Social Psychology, 13*, 315-332.

Cartwright, D. (1973, March). Determinants of scientific progress: The case of research on the risky shift. *American Psychologist, 28*, 222-231.

Clark, N. K., & Stephenson, G. M. (1989). Group remembering. In P. B. Paulus (Ed.), *Psychology of group influence* (2nd ed., pp. 357-391). Hillsdale, NJ: Erlbaum.

Cohen, S. G., & Bailey, D. E. (1997). What makes teams work: Group effectiveness research from the shop floor to the executive suite. *Journal of Management, 23*, 239-290.

Cotton, J. L., Vollrath, D. A., Froggart, K. L., Lengnick-Hall, M. L., & Jennings, K. R. (1988). Employee participation: Diverse forms and different outcomes. *Academy of Management Review, 13*, 8-22.

Davis, J. H. (1973). Group decision and social interaction: A theory of social decision schemes. *Psychological Review, 80*, 97-125.

Davis, J. H. (1980). Group decision and procedural justice. In M. Fishbein (Ed.), *Progress in social psychology* (Vol. 1, pp. 157-229). Hillsdale, NJ: Erlbaum.

Davis, J. H. (1982). Social interaction as a combinatorial process in group decision. In H. Brandstätter, J. H. Davis & G. Stocker-Kreichgauer (Eds.), *Group decision making* (pp. 27-58). London: Academic Press.

Dawes, R. M. (1988). *Rational choice in an uncertain world*. San Diego, CA: Harcourt Brace Joonovich.

Dearborn, D. C., & Simon, H. A. (1958). Selective perception: A note on the departmental identification of executives. *Sociometry, 21*, 140-144.

Dion, K. L., Baron, R. S., & Miller, N. (1970). Why do groups make riskier decisions than individuals? *Advances in Experimental Social Psychology, 5*, 305-377.

Dougherty, D. (1992). Interpretive barriers to successful product innovation in large firms. *Organization Science, 3*, 179-202.

Eagly, A. H., Wood, W., & Chaiken, S. (1978). Causal inferences about communicators and their effect on opinion change. *Journal of Personality and Social Psychology, 36*, 424-435.

Einhorn, H. J., & Hogarth, R. M. (1986). Judging probable cause. *Psychological Bulletin, 99*, 3-19.

Einhorn, H. J., Hogarth, R. M., & Klempner, E. (1977). Quality of group judgment. *Psychological Bulletin, 84*, 158-172.

Eisenhardt, K. M., & Tabrizi, B. N. (1995). Accelerating adaptive processes: Product innovation in the global computer industry. *Administrative Science Quarterly, 40*, 84-110.

Feitzinger, E., & Lee, H. L. (1997). Mass customization at Hewlett-Packard: The power of postponement. *Harvard Business Review, 75*(1), 116-121.

Gigone, D., & Hastie, R. (1993). The common knowledge effect: Information sharing and group judgment. *Journal of Personality and Social Psychology, 65*, 959-974.

Gigone, D., & Hastie, R. (1997). Proper analysis of the accuracy of group judgments. *Psychological Bulletin, 121*, 149-167.

Goodman, P. S., & Leyden, D. P. (1991). Familiarity and group productivity. *Journal of Applied Psychology, 76*, 578-586.

Gruenfeld, D. H. (1995a). *Divergent thinking, accountability, and integrative complexity: Public versus private reactions to majority and minority status*. Unpublished manuscript, Kellogg Graduate School of Management, Northwestern University.

Gruenfeld, D. H. (1995b). Status, ideology and integrative complexity on the U. S. Supreme Court: Rethinking the politics of political decision making. *Journal of Personality and Social Psychology, 68*, 5-20.

Gruenfeld, D. H., & Hollingshead, A. B. (1993). Sociocognition in work groups: The evolution of group integrative complexity and its relation to task performance. *Small Group Research, 24,* 383-405.

Guetzkow, H., & Simon, H. A. (1955). The impact of certain communication nets upon organization and performance in task-oriented groups. *Management Science, 1,* 233-250.

Guzzo, R. A., & Dickson, M. W. (1996). Teams in organizations: Recent research on performance and effectiveness. *Annual Review of Psychology, 47,* 307-338.

Hambrick, D. C., Cho, T. S., & Chen, M. (1996). The influence of top management team heterogeneity on firms' competitive moves. *Administrative Science Quarterly, 41,* 659-684.

Hartwick, J., Sheppard, B. L., & Davis, J. H. (1982). Group remembering: Research and implications. In R. A. Guzzo (Ed.), *Improving group decision making in organizations: Approaches from theory and research* (pp. 41-72). London: Academic Press.

Hayes, R. H., & Wheelwright, S. C. (1984). *Restoring our competitive edge: Competing through manufacturing.* New York: Wiley.

Hayes, R. H., Wheelwright, S. C., & Clark, K. B. (1988). *Dynamic manufacturing: Creating the learning organization.* New York: Free Press

Henry, R. A. (1995). Improving group judgment accuracy: Information sharing and determining the best member. *Organizational Behavior and Human Decision Processes, 62,* 190-197.

Henry, R. A., Strickland, O. J., Yorges, S. L., & Ladd, D. (1996). Helping groups determine their most accurate member: The role of outcome feedback. *Journal of Applied Social Psychology, 26,* 1153-1170.

Hill, G. W. (1982). Group versus individual performance: Are N + 1 heads better than one? *Psychological Bulletin, 91,* 517-539.

Hinsz, V. B. (1990). Cognitive and consensus processes in group recognition memory performance. *Journal of Personality and Social Psychology, 59,* 705-718.

Hinsz, V. B., Tindale, R. S., & Vollrath, D. A. (1997). The emerging conception of groups as information processors. *Psychological Bulletin, 121,* 43-64.

Hoerr, J. (1989, July 10). The payoff from teamwork: The gains in quality are substantial—so why isn't it spreading faster? *Business Week,* pp. 56-59.

Hollenbeck, J. R., Ilgen, D. R., Sego, D. J., Hedlund, J., Major, D. A., & Philips, J. (1995). Multilevel theory of team decision making: Decision performance in teams incorporating distributed expertise. *Journal of Applied Psychology, 80,* 292-316.

Huberman, B. A. (1996). *The dynamics of organizational learning.* Working paper, Xerox Palo Alto Research Center, Palo Alto, CA.

Jackson, S. E., May, K. E., & Whitney, K. (1995). Understanding the diversity of dynamics in decision making teams. In R. A. Guzzo, E. Salas and Associates, *Team effectiveness and decision making in organizations,* (pp. 204-261). San Francisco: Jossey-Bass.

Janis, I. L. (1972). *Victims of groupthink.* Boston: Houghton Mifflin.

Kahn, R. L., Wolfe, D. M., Quinn, R. P., Snoek, J. D., & Rosenthal, R. A. (1964). *Organizational stress: Studies in role conflict and ambiguity.* New York: Wiley.

Kahneman, D., Slovic, P., & Tversky, A. (Eds.) (1982). *Judgment under uncertainty: Heuristics and biases.* Cambridge, England: Cambridge University Press.

Karau, S. J., & Williams, K. D. (1993). Social loafing: A meta-analytic review and theoretical integration. *Journal of Personality and Social Psychology, 65,* 681-706.

Katz, R. (1982). The effects of group longevity on communication and performance. *Administrative Science Quarterly, 27,* 81-104.

Kerr, N. L., MacCoun, R. J., & Kramer, G. P. (1996). Bias in judgment: Comparing individuals and groups. *Psychological Review, 103,* 687-719.

Kim, P. H. (1997). When what you know can hurt you: A study of experiential affects on group discussion and performance. *Organizational Behavior and Human Decision Processes, 69,* 165-177.

Klimoski, R., & Mohammed, S. (1994). Team mental model: Construct or metaphor? *Journal of Management, 20,* 403-437.

Kogut, B., & Zander, U. (1992). Knowledge of the firm, combinative capabilities and the replication of technology. *Organization Science, 3,* 383-397.

Larson, J. R., Jr., & Christensen, C. (1993). Groups as problem-solving units: Toward a new meaning of social cognition. *The British Psychological Society, 32,* 5-30.

Larson, J. R., Jr., Christensen, C., Abbott, A. S., & Franz, T. M. (1996). Diagnosing groups: Charting the flow of information in medical decision-making teams. *Journal of Personality and Social Psychology, 71,* 315-330.

Larson, J. R., Foster-Fishman, P. G., & Keys, C. B. (1994). The discussion of shared and unshared information in decision making groups. *Journal of Personality and Social Psychology, 67,* 446-461.

Latane, B., Williams, K., & Harkins, S. (1979). Many hands make light the work: The causes and consequences of social loafing. *Journal of Personality and Social Psychology, 37,* 822-832.

Laughlin, P. R. (1988). Collective induction: Group performance, social combination processes, and mutual majority and minority influence. *Journal of Personality and Social Psychology, 54,* 254-267.

Laughlin, P. R., & Adamopoulos, J. (1980). Social combination processes and individual learning for six-person cooperative groups on an intellective task. *Journal of Personality and Social Psychology, 38,* 941-947.

Laughlin, P. R., & Ellis, A. L. (1986). Demonstrability and social combination processes on mathematical intellective tasks. *Journal of Experimental Social Psychology, 22,* 177-189.

Laughlin, P. R., & Futoran, G. C. (1985). Collective induction: Social combination and sequential transition. *Journal of Personality and Social Psychology, 48,* 608-613.

Laughlin, P. R., & Hollingshead, A. B. (1995). A theory of collective induction. *Organizational Behavior and Human Decision Processes, 61,* 94-107.

Laughlin, P. R., & Shippy, T. A. (1983). Collective induction. *Journal of Personality and Social Psychology, 45,* 94-100.

Lawrence, P. R., & Lorsch, J. W. (1967). Differentiation and integration in complex organizations. *Administrative Science Quarterly, 12,* 1-47.

Levine, J. M., & Moreland, R. L. (1991). Culture and socialization in work groups. In L. B. Resnick, J. M. Levine & S. D. Teasley (Eds.), *Perspectives on socially shared cognition* (pp. 257-279). Washington, DC: American Psychological Association.

Levine, J. M., Saxe, L., & Harris, H. J. (1976). Reaction to opinion deviance: Impact of deviate's direction and distance of movement. *Sociometry, 39,* 97-107.

Levine, J. M., & Thompson, L. (1996). Conflict in groups. In E. T. Higgins & A. W. Kruglanski (Eds.), *Social psychology: Handbook of basic principles* (pp. 745-776). New York: Guilford Press.

Liang, D. W., Moreland, R., & Argote, L. (1995). Group versus individual training and group performance: The mediating role of transactive memory. *Personality and Social Psychology Bulletin, 21,* 384-393.

Libby, R., Trotman, K. T., & Zimmer, I. (1987). Member variation, recognition of expertise, and group performance. *Journal of Applied Psychology, 72,* 81-87.

Littlepage, G., Robison, W., & Reddington, K. (1997). Effects of task experience and group experience on group performance, member ability, and recognition of expertise. *Organizational Behavior and Human Decision Processes, 69,* 133-147.

Lorge, I., & Solomon, H. (1955). Two model of group behavior in the solution of eureka-type problems. *Psychometrika, 20,* 139-148.

Maier, N. R. F. (1967). Assets and liabilities in group problem solving: The need for an integrative function. *Psychological Review, 74,* 239-249.

McGrath, J. E. (1984). *Groups: Interaction and performance.* Englewood Cliffs, NJ: Prentice-Hall.

Miner, F. C. (1984). Group versus individual decision making: An investigation of performance measures, decision strategies, and process losses/gains. *Organizational Behavior and Human Performance, 33,* 112-124.

Moorman, C., & Miner, A. S. (1997). The impact of organizational memory on new product performance and creativity. *Journal of Marketing Research, 34,* 91-106.

Moreland, R. L. (in press). Transactive memory: Learning who knows what in work groups and organizations. In L. Thompson, D. M. Messick & J. M. Levine (Eds.), *Shared knowledge in organizations.* Lawrence Erlbaum.

Moreland, R. L., Argote, L., & Krishnan, R. (1996). Socially shared cognition at work: Transactive memory and group performance. In J. L. Nye & Brower A. M. (Eds.), *What's so social about social cognition? Social cognition research in small groups* (pp. 57-84). Thousand Oaks, CA: Sage.

Moreland, R. L., Argote, L., & Krishnan, R. (1998). Training people to work in groups. In R. S. Tindale, L. Heath, J. Edwards, E. J. Posvac, F. B. Bryant, Y. Suarez-Balcazar, E. Henderson-King & J. Myers (Eds.), *Applications of theory and research on groups to social issues* (pp. 37-60). New York: Plenum Press.

Moreland, R. L., & Levine, J. M. (1992). The composition of small groups. *Advances in Group Processes, 9*, 237-280.

Moreland, R. L., & Levine, J. M. (in press). Socialization in organizations and work groups. In M. E. Turner (Ed.), *Groups at work: Advances in theory and research*. Mahwah, NJ: Erlbaum.

Morris, B. (1998, May 25). Doug is it. *Fortune*, pp. 70-74, 78, 80, 82, 84.

Moscovici, S., Lage, E., & Naffrechoux, M. (1969). Influence of a consistent minority on the responses of a majority in a color perception task. *Sociometry, 32*, 365-380.

Mugny, G. (1982). *The power of minorities*, New York: Academic Press.

Mullen, B., Johnson, C., & Salas, E. (1991). Productivity loss in brainstorming groups: A meta-analytic integration. *Basic and Applied Social Psychology, 12*, 3-23.

Murnighan, J. K., & Conlon, D. (1991). The dynamics of intense work groups: A study of British string quartets. *Administrative Science Quarterly, 36*, 165-186.

Myers, D. G., & Lamm, H. (1976). The group polarization phenomenon. *Psychological Bulletin, 83*, 602-627.

Nemeth, C. J. (1986). Differential contributions of majority and minority influence. *Psychological Review, 93*, 23-32.

Nemeth, C. J. (1992). Minority dissent as a stimulant to group performance. In S. Worchel, W. Wood & J. A. Simpson (Eds.), *Group process and productivity* (pp. 95-111). Newbury Park, CA: Sage.

Nemeth, C. J., & Kwan, J. L. (1987). Minority influence, divergent thinking and detection of correct solutions. *Journal of Applied Social Psychology, 17*, 786-797.

Nemeth, C. J., & Wachtler, J. (1983). Creative problem solving as a result of majority and minority influence. *European Journal of Social Psychology, 13*, 45-55.

Nonaka, I. (1991). The knowledge-creating company. *Harvard Business Review, 69*(6), 96-104.

Olivera, F., & Argote, L. (in press). Organizational learning and new product development: CORE processes. In L. Thompson, D. M. Messick & J. M. Levine (Eds.), *Shared knowledge in organizations*. Lawrence Erlbaum.

Ophir, R., Ingram, P., & Argote, L. (1998, October). *The impact of demographic composition on organizational learning: An empirical investigation.* Paper presented at the INFORMS National Fall Conference, Seattle, WA.

Osborn, A. F. (1957). *Applied imagination* (2nd ed.). New York: Scribner.

Owens, D., & Neale, M. (1998, June). *The dubious benefit of group heterogeneity in highly uncertain tasks: Too much of a good thing?* Paper presented at Carnegie-Wisconsin Conference on Knowledge Transfer and Levels of Learning, Carnegie Mellon University, Pittsburgh, PA.

Paulus, P. B., & Dzindolet, M. T. (1993). Social influence processes in group brainstorming. *Journal of Personality and Social Psychology, 64,* 575-586.

Penrod, S., & Hastie, R. (1979). Models of jury decision making: A critical review. *Psychological Bulletin, 86,* 462-492.

Penrod, S., & Hastie, R. (1980). A computer simulation of jury decision making. *Psychological Review, 87,* 133-159.

Pfeffer, J. (1981). *Power in organizations.* Marshfield, MA: Pitman & Sons.

Pine, B. J., II, Victor, B., Boynton, A. C. (1993). Making mass customization work. *Harvard Business Review, 71*(5), 108-119.

Reagan-Cirincione, P. (1994). Improving the accuracy of group judgment: A process intervention combining group facilitation, social judgment analysis, and information technology. *Organizational Behavior and Human Decision Processes, 58,* 246-270.

Rhodes, L. (1986, June). That's easy for you to say. *Inc., 8*(6), 63-66.

Sandelands, L. E., & Stablein, R. (1987). The concept of organization mind. *Research in the Sociology of Organizations., 5,* 135-161.

Shaw, M. E. (1981). *Group dynamics: The psychology of small group behavior* (3rd ed.). New York: McGraw-Hill.

Shure, G. H., Rogers, M. S., Larsen, I. M., & Tassone, J. (1962). Group planning and task effectiveness. *Sociometry, 25,* 263-282.

Skinner, W. (1974). The focused factory. *Harvard Business Review, 52*(3), 113-121.

Smith, C. M., Tindale, R. S., & Dugoni, B. L. (1996). Minority and majority influence on freely interacting groups: Qualitative versus quantitative differences. *British Journal of Social Psychology, 35,* 137-149.

Stasser, G. (1988). Computer simulation as a research tool: The DISCUSS model of group decision making. *Journal of Experimental Social Psychology, 24,* 393-422.

Stasser, G., & Stewart, D. D. (1992). The discovery of hidden profiles by decision making groups: Solving a problem versus making a judgment. *Journal of Personality and Social Psychology, 63,* 426-434.

Stasser, G., Stewart, D., & Wittenbaum, G. M. (1995). Expert roles and information exchange during discussion: The importance of knowing who knows what. *Journal of Experimental Social Psychology, 31,* 244-265.

Stasser, G., Taylor, L. A., & Hanna, C. (1989). Information sampling in structured and unstructured discussion of three and six person groups. *Journal of Personality and Social Psychology, 57,* 67-78.

Stasser, G., & Titus, W. (1985). Pooling of unshared information in group decision making: Biased information sampling during discussion. *Journal of Personality and Social Psychology, 48,* 1467-1478.

Stasser, G., & Titus, W. (1987). Effects of information load and percentage of shared information on the dissemination of unshared information during group discussion. *Journal of Personality and Social Psychology, 53,* 81-93.

Steiner, F. F. (1972). *Group process and productivity.* New York: Academic Press.

Stewart, D. D., & Stasser, G. (1995). Expert role assignment and information sampling during collective recall and decision making. *Journal of Personality and Social Psychology, 69,* 619-628.

Stewart, T. A. (1995a, October 30). Mapping corporate brainpower. *Fortune,* pp. 209-201, 212.

Stewart, T. A. (1995b, November 27). Getting real about brainpower. *Fortune,* pp. 201-203.

Stroebe, W., & Diehl, M. (1994). Why groups are less effective than their members: On productivity loss in idea generating groups. *European Review of Social Psychology, 5,* 271-304.

Sutton, R. I., & Hargadon, A. (1996). Brainstorming groups in context: Effectiveness in a product design firm. *Administrative Science Quarterly, 41,* 685-718.

Tindale, R. S. (1993). Decision errors made by individuals and groups. In N. Castellan, Jr. (Ed.) *Individual and group decision making: Current issues* (pp. 109-124). Hillsdale, NJ: Lawrence Erlbaum.

Turner, M. E., Pratkanis, A. R., Probasco, P., & Leve, C. (1992). Threat, cohesion, and group effectiveness: Testing a social identity maintenance perspective on groupthink. *Journal of Personality and Social Psychology, 63,* 781-796.

Tversky, A., & Kahneman, D. P. (1974, September 27). Judgment under uncertainty: Heuristics and biases. *Science, 185,* 1124-1131.

Vroom, V., & Jago, A. (1988). *The new leadership: Managing participation in organizations.* Englewood Cliffs, NJ: Prentice-Hall.

Vroom, V. H., & Yetton, P. W. (1973). *Leadership and decision making.* Pittsburgh: University of Pittsburgh Press.

Watson, W. E., Kumar, K., & Michaelson, L. K. (1993). Cultural diversity's impact on interaction process and performance: Comparing homogeneous and diverse task groups. *Academy of Management Journal, 36,* 590-602.

Wegner, D. M. (1986). Transactive memory: A contemporary analysis of the group mind. In B. Mullen & G. R. Goethals (Eds.), *Theories of Group Behavior* (pp. 185-205). New York: Springer-Verlag.

Weingart, L. R. (1992). Impact of group goals, task component complexity, effort, and planning on group performance. *Journal of Applied Psychology, 77,* 682-693.

Weldon, M. S., & Bellinger, K. D. (1997). Collective memory: Collaborative and individual processes in remembering. *Journal of Experimental Psychology: Learning, Memory and Cognition, 23,* 1160-1175.

Williams, K. Y., & O'Reilly, C. A. (1998). Demography and diversity in organizations: A review of 40 years of research. *Research in Organizational Behavior, 20,* 77-140.

Wittenbaum, G. M. (1996). *Information sampling in mixed-sex decision-making groups: The impact of diffuse status and task-relevant cues.* Unpublished doctoral dissertation, Miami University, Oxford, OH.

Wittenbaum, G. M., & Stasser, G. (1996). Management of information in small groups. In J. L. Nye & A. M. Brower, (Eds). *What's social about social cognition? Research on socially shared cognition in small groups* (pp. 3-28). Thousand Oaks, CA: Sage.

Wood, W., Lundgren, S., Ouellette, J. A., Busceme, S., & Blackstone, T. (1994). Minority influence: A meta-analytic review of social influence processes. *Psychological Bulletin, 115,* 323-345.

Wysocki, B. Jr. (1997, October 6). Why an acquisition? Often it's the people. *The Wall Street Journal,* p. A1.

Yetton, P. W., & Bottger, P. C. (1982). Individual versus group problem solving: An empirical test of a best-member strategy. *Organizational Behavior and Human Performance, 29,* 307-321.

Chapter 5

Knowledge Transfer in Organizations

5.1 Introduction

General Motors Corporation announces that it has decided to build identical plants in Argentina, Poland, China, and Thailand so that knowledge acquired at one plant will be relevant for and transferable to others (Blumenstein, 1997). An interview with John Reed, Chief Executive Officer of Citicorp, attributes a significant component of the firm's success to its ability to transfer local innovations in consumer banking around the world (Tichy & Charan, 1990). Intel uses a "copy exactly" approach to their multiple facilities in which establishments are replicated down to the color of their paint so that knowledge acquired in one establishment is relevant for others (Reinhardt, 1997). US Airways arms its employees with cameras, stopwatches, and pads of paper and sends them on other airlines to identify their competitor's best practices (Carey, 1998). These four examples illustrate the importance firms attach to transferring knowledge in organizations. General Motors, Citicorp, Intel, and US Airways expect to realize tremendous benefits by transferring knowledge acquired at one establishment to another. That is, the firms expect to realize benefits when one of their units "learns" from another unit or organization. This chapter describes research on one organization learning from another—on knowledge transfer across organizations.

The chapter begins with a case example of a firm that expects to reap large rewards from transferring knowledge from one assembly plant to another. Mechanisms for knowledge transfer are then described. A method for assessing the extent of knowledge transfer is presented. Results from a study of knowledge transfer in fast food franchises are described in depth to illustrate how the extent of knowledge transfer can be assessed empirically. Empirical results from studies of knowledge transfer are integrated and the conditions under which knowledge is most likely to transfer are described. Challenges to transferring knowledge across groups or units within organizations are developed.   Strategies for the effective transfer of knowledge are described.

5.2 A Case Example

General Motors Corporation recently announced a "four-plant strategy" in which it is building identical plants in Argentina, Poland, China, and Thailand at the same time (Blumenstein, 1997). According to an article in the *Wall Street Journal*:

> The company has designed the plants to look so much alike that engineers may mistake which country they are in. And the assembly lines are being set up so that a glitch in a robot in Thailand, rather than turning into an expensive engineering problem that requires an expert for each machine at each plant, may well be solved by a quick call to Rosario (Argentina) or to Shanghai, China (Blumenstein, 1997, p. A1).

Thus, General Motors is making the plants very similar to increase the relevance of knowledge acquired at one for another. And General Motors expects that the larger experience base at the four plants will provide many problem solutions that the plants can use. That is, General Motors expects that knowledge acquired at one plant will transfer to another so that it benefits as well.

Designing plants differently limits the potential for transferring knowledge across them since knowledge acquired at one plant may not be relevant for another with a different design. For example, a plant using a particular assembly system may discover a way to improve its performance. But, if its sister plant that manufactures the same product does not use the same system, the performance improvements may not be transferable to the second site. General Motors' four-plant strategy aims to increase the relevance of knowledge acquired at one plant for another. General Motors' strategy is similar to Toyota's strategy of designing plants so similarly that productivity improvements developed in one can quickly transfer around the world (Blumenstein, 1997).

Although the General Motors plants are designed to be very similar, local conditions dictate some differences. For example, General Motors anticipates that supplies will have to be delivered to the Shanghai plant by bicycle since the transportation system there is poor (Blumenstein, 1997). Also, the climate in Thailand is so humid that considerable effort will have to be made to protect the equipment from rust. Thus, the operation of the plants will have to be tailored somewhat to local differences. These differences notwithstanding, enormous potential exists for transferring knowledge across the four plants so that all benefit from knowledge acquired at one.

5.3 Mechanisms of Knowledge Transfer

When knowledge acquired in one organization affects another (either positively or negatively), transfer of knowledge occurs. There has been a long tradition of research in psychology that examines whether individuals are able to transfer knowledge from one situation or task to another (e.g., see Thompson, 1998). This work examines whether experience with one task affects individual performance on a subsequent task. More recently, researchers have begun to examine transfer at the group and organizational levels of analysis. Theorists have argued that not only do organizations learn from their own direct experience, they also learn from the experiences of other organizations (e.g., see Huber, 1991; Levitt & March, 1988). Empirical research is starting to accumulate on whether one organization learns from the experience of other organizations.

How might one organization learn from another organization? Many mechanisms exist for transferring knowledge from one organization to another. The mechanisms include training members of the recipient organization, allowing them to observe the performance of experts at the donor organization, and providing opportunities for communication between members of both organizations. Providing documents, blueprints, and descriptions of the organizational structure to the recipient organization as well as transferring experienced personnel there are additional mechanisms. Since some of the donor's knowledge may be embedded in its hardware, software, and products, providing those to the recipient organization also facilitates knowledge transfer. These various mechanisms map onto the previous discussion in Chapter 3 of where knowledge is embedded in a firm: its people, its technology, or its structure. Thus, in very general terms, knowledge can be transferred by moving people, technology, or structure to the recipient organization or by modifying the people (e.g., through training), technology, and structure of the recipient organization.

Organizations also acquire knowledge from external sources in the environment. Suppliers can be a very important source of productivity improvements. For example, Chrysler Corporation reported that its suppliers developed ideas that saved Chrysler $1 billion and increased its profits by $280 million in 1996 (Christian, 1997). Chrysler expects that ideas submitted by suppliers in 1997 will increase that year's profitability by $325 million. Examples of cost-saving ideas submitted by suppliers include suggestions for decreasing the weight of a car and for reducing the size of its cooling system.

Products also contain knowledge. By "reverse engineering," or tearing down a competitor's product, a firm can obtain useful information that may improve its product or reduce its costs. Mansfield (1985) argued that knowledge embedded in products transferred more readily than knowledge embedded in processes or organizational practices and routines.

Customers are also an important source of knowledge that can improve a firm's performance (von Hippel, 1988). For example, engineers from Caterpillar go to construction sites around the world to study customers using their earth-moving equipment in order to identify ways to improve it ("Survey of manufacturing," 1998).

In addition, other organizations are important sources of knowledge. The popularity of "benchmarking" and programs to transfer "best practices" or "lessons learned" from one organization to another reflects the usefulness of acquiring knowledge from other firms. Similarly, knowledge available through patent applications (Appleyard, 1996), scientific and trade publications, consultants and conferences can be useful to a firm. At a more macro level, inter-organizational arrangements, such as cooperative relationships (Shan, Walker & Kogut, 1994), strategic alliances (Hamel, 1991; Larsson, Bengtsson, Henriksson & Sparks, 1998; Mowery, Oxley & Silverman, 1996), joint ventures (Barkema, Bell & Pennings, 1996; Kogut, 1988, 1991; Makhija & Ganesh, 1997), transplants (Lewis, 1993), interlocking boards of directorates (Davis, 1991; Haunschild, 1993), consortia (Browning, Beyer & Shetler, 1995), and business groups such as Japanese Keiretsu (Cho, Kim & Rhee, 1998) are also potential mechanisms for knowledge transfer across firms.

A recent study aimed to determine the effectiveness of various knowledge transfer mechanisms. Appleyard (1996) asked respondents in the United States and Japanese semiconductor firms to rate the importance of nine sources of technical information, including colleagues in their company, colleagues at other companies, vendors, suppliers, customers, benchmarking studies, presentations at conferences, scientific publications, and patents. Respondents from both the United States and Japan rated colleagues in their own company as the most important source of technical information. Scientific publications and presentations at conferences were rated second and third in importance by respondents from both countries. Responses of representatives of U.S. and Japanese firms diverged on the source rated as fourth in importance: Japanese respondents rated patents fourth, whereas U.S. respondents rated colleagues in other companies as the fourth most important source of technical information.

Appleyard (1996) also asked respondents to rate their preferred mode of knowledge sharing with both "horizontal" (another semiconductor company) and "vertical" (vendors) sources. Japanese respondents preferred public mechanisms for knowledge sharing with other semiconductor companies such as conferences, the press, trade journals and patents. In contrast, U.S. respondents preferred a mix of public (trade journals and conferences) and private (telephone and face-to-face meetings) mechanisms. A similar pattern of results emerged for the preferred mode of knowledge sharing with vendors: Japanese respondents preferred public sources, whereas U.S. respondents preferred a mix of public and private sources.

Further work is needed to determine the conditions under which various modes of knowledge sharing will be most effective. In addition to describing patterns of knowledge sharing, it will also be important to determine how patterns of knowledge sharing affect organizational outcomes.

How can one determine if knowledge transfer has occurred? The learning curve model described in Chapter 1 can be expanded to investigate whether knowledge transfers across organizational units. We turn now to our study of fast food franchises to illustrate the approach we use to assessing the extent of knowledge transfer.

5.4 The Franchise Study

Our primary goal in the franchise study was to assess the extent to which knowledge transferred across organizations. That is, we wanted to examine whether one organization learned or benefited from experience at another. A secondary goal for the franchise study was to determine the extent to which knowledge transferred over time—the extent to which knowledge persisted. Thus, we also investigated whether knowledge depreciated (see Chapter 2). To accomplish our first goal, we required a study context in which a large number of organizations produced the same product. This would permit us to assess the extent of knowledge transfer across a reasonable sample of organizations. Fast food franchises seemed an ideal setting for this purpose since many organizations produce the same product.

Another benefit of studying knowledge transfer in fast food franchises is that it provides information about the dynamics of organizational learning and transfer in a service industry. The preponderance of previous work on organizational learning has been conducted in manufacturing settings. Extending this line of work to service organizations provides information about the extent to which their rates of learning, forgetting, and transfer compare to those found in manufacturing. Since the United States and other developed economies are increasingly service economies ("Survey of manufacturing," 1998), understanding the dynamics of productivity growth in service settings is an important undertaking.

All of the fast food stores in our study produced the same product (pizzas) and were franchised from the same parent corporation. All of the stores had opportunities to learn from the parent corporation. For example, at the time each store started, the parent corporation provided routines, blueprints, and procedures as well as training. The parent corporation also provided ongoing assistance to the stores. Franchise owners were required to attend yearly meetings of the corporation and consultants from the parent corporation visited the various stores.

Our primary focus is on knowledge transfer across the stores themselves. Several of the franchisees owned only one store, whereas others owned multiple stores. We analyzed whether stores learned from their own direct experience, whether they learned from the experience of other stores owned by the same franchisee, and whether they learned from the experience of stores owned by different franchisees. We also analyzed whether knowledge transferred over time by assessing the extent of knowledge depreciation.

5.4.1 Method and Sources of Data

We collected data from the entire set of stores in Southwestern Pennsylvania that are franchised from one of the largest pizza corporations. The sample included 10 different franchisees who owned a total of 36 stores. The largest franchisee owned 11 stores, whereas five of the franchisees owned only one store each. The oldest franchise organization had been in business for 11 years, and the youngest for just 3 months. The average age of the franchise organizations was 3.75 years.

The corporation's regional office provided data concerning pizzas sold and production costs for each store per week for a one and one half year period. Thus, we had approximately 75 observations for 36 stores, which resulted in a data set of over 2,500 observations. Structured interviews with the franchisees provided additional information about the frequency that various mechanisms were used to transfer information and also about the timeliness of service at the stores.

The franchise data have many attractive properties. The inputs to the production function (i.e., the raw materials) are homogeneous.

Therefore, input characteristics are controlled for naturally in the sample. Differences in technology across pizza stores are very small. Thus, factors that may be hard to control for statistically in production environments are controlled for naturally in the sample. The symbols used and the variables they represent are listed in Table 5.1.

Table 5.1
Variables Used in the Franchise Study

Symbol	Variable
t	Calendar time in weeks
J_n	Number of stores in franchise n
q_{nit}	Pizzas produced by franchise n in store i in week t
c_{nit}	Costs (food and labor) for store i in franchise n in week t
$Q_{nit} = \sum_{s=0}^{t} q_{nis}$	Cumulative number of pizzas produced by store i in franchise n through week t
$FQ_{nt} = \sum_{i=1}^{J_n} Q_{nit}$	Cumulative number of pizzas produced by franchise n through week t
$IQ_t = \sum_{n=1}^{10} FQ_{nt}$	Cumulative number of pizzas produced in all stores in all franchises through week t
p_{nit}	Percentage of pan pizzas produced by franchise n in store i in week t
s_{ni}	Dummy variables for each store

As noted previously in the discussion of measuring knowledge (see Chapters 1 and 2), the cumulative number of products produced at a particular organization serves as a proxy variable for knowledge acquired by the organization. In this particular study, the cumulative number of pizzas produced, Q, is a proxy for store-specific knowledge. To investigate knowledge transfer across the stores, we extended the approach to measuring knowledge by aggregating the cumulative number of units produced by all the stores in the relevant set. Thus, franchise-specific knowledge, FQ, is measured by summing the cumulative number of units produced by all stores in the franchise. Just as the cumulative number of units produced at a store is a proxy for store-specific knowledge, the cumulative number of units produced by all stores in the franchise is a proxy for franchise-specific knowledge. Similarly, inter-franchise knowledge, IQ, is measured by summing the cumulative number of units produced by all stores in all franchises.

We estimated several models in which the unit cost of production was analyzed as a function of store-specific experience, franchise experience, inter-franchise experience, and other variables. The most basic model we estimated using least-squares regression (Column 1 in Table 5.2) was:

$$\ln(c_{nit} / q_{nit}) = b_0 + b_1 \ln(Q_{nit-1}) + b_2 \ln(FQ_{nt-1})$$
$$+ b_3 \ln(IQ_{t-1}) + b_{ni} s_{ni} + u_{nit} \tag{5.1}$$

We allowed for serial correlation of the error term, u_{nit}, in all the models we estimated.   We also included dummy variables for each store in all equations. The dummy variables, s_{ni}, control for variance associated with store specifics such as management style, age, and location.

In Equation (5.1), if the coefficient on Q (b_1) is significant, store-specific learning has occurred. That is, a store's unit cost was affected by production experience at the store.   If the coefficient on FQ (b_2) is significant, transfer of learning between stores owned by a common franchisee has occurred. That is, the unit cost of production at a store was affected by production experience at other stores in the franchise. If the coefficient on IQ (b_3) is significant, transfer of learning between stores owned by different franchisees has occurred.

In these analyses, the unit of time is a week. The variables Q, FQ, and IQ are the cumulative pizza production through the end of the previous week. The lagged cumulative output is used on the right-hand side of Equation (5.1) because cumulative output serves as a proxy for experience acquired as a result of past output.

We used the same approach to investigate whether knowledge persists through time or whether it depreciates as we used in our previous studies (see Chapter 2). We replaced the conventional cumulative output measure with the following knowledge variable:

$$K_{nit} = \lambda K_{nit-1} + q_{nit} \tag{5.2}$$

Equation 5.2 allows for the possibility that knowledge depreciates over time by including the parameter λ. As in our discussion of the shipyard results, if $\lambda = 1$, the accumulated stock of knowledge is simply equal to lagged cumulative output, the conventional measure of learning, and there is no evidence of depreciation. If $\lambda < 1$, there is evidence of depreciation: recent output is a more important predictor of current productivity than past output.

We also investigated alternative explanations of our findings by estimating models with additional control variables. We controlled for economies of scale in the analysis. As noted previously, the scale of operation may expand as organizations gain experience and therefore, may be correlated with cumulative output. Some of the productivity gains apparently associated with cumulative output could actually be due to changes in the scale of operation. To avoid this problem, we controlled for economies of scale by including measures of the number of pizzas produced each week and its square.

We also controlled for product mix, measured here by the percentage of "pan" pizzas. As noted previously, some product options may be more costly to produce than others. Hence, it is appropriate to control for the percentage of these options in estimating learning rates. Furthermore, we controlled for technological progress associated with the passage of time by including a calendar time variable. This enables one to separate the extent to which productivity gains are a function of general technological changes in the environment versus changes in the particular organization. Finally, we allowed the rate of learning to change over time by including a quadratic term for the knowledge variable. This enabled us to test whether the leveling off in the rate of learning, or the "plateau" effect observed in several studies occurred here.

The model that included the full set of control variables (Column 4 in Table 5.2) was:

$$\ln(c_{nit} / q_{nit}) = b_0 + b_1 \ln K_{nit-1} + b_2 \ln FK_{nt-1}$$
$$+ b_3 \ln IK_{t-1} + b_4 t + b_5 q_{nit}$$
$$+ b_6 q^2_{nit} + b_7 (\ln K_{nit-1})^2$$
$$+ b_8 p_{nit} + b_{ni} s_{ni} + u_{nit} \qquad (5.3)$$

where FK and IK are defined the same as FQ and IQ except that K replaces Q in the summations. Thus, knowledge that transfers is also allowed to depreciate.

An issue that arose in the franchise study that may confront other researchers who study learning in multiple organizations is the absence of data from the start of operation at all of the organizations. In particular, we did not have data from the start of production for half the stores. These stores were in operation several years before the data collection began. We dealt with this limitation by treating pizza production prior to the beginning of the data collection as an unknown coefficient in the model (see Column 5 of Table 5.2) and estimating it along with the other coefficients. As will be seen shortly, the results from estimating this model were virtually the same as from the other models.

5.4.2 Results

A learning curve plotted from a single store is shown in Figure 5.1. This figure shows the characteristic learning curve pattern: the unit cost of producing pizza decreased at a decreasing rate as the cumulative number of pizzas produced increased.

5.4.2.1 Store-Specific and Franchise-Specific Learning

Results concerning the effects of store-specific learning, transfer between commonly owned stores, and transfer between differently owned stores on the unit cost of pizza production are presented in Table 5.2. This table

Figure 5.1
The Relationship Between Total Costs Per Pizza and Cumulative Output

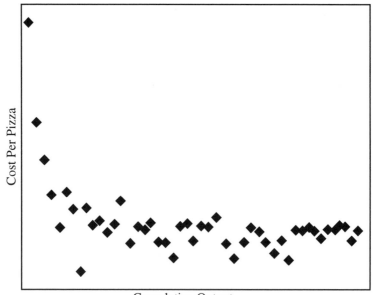

Cumulative Output

Note. Reprinted by permission from E. Darr, L. Argote and D. Epple, The acquisition, transfer and depreciation of knowledge in service organizations: Productivity in franchises, *Management Science*, Volume *41*, Number 11, (November, 1995). Copyright 1995, The Institute of Operations Research and the Management Sciences (INFORMS), 2 Charles Street, Suite 300, Providence, RI 02904 USA. These data are from a single store for a period of 1.5 years. Units were omitted to protect confidentiality of the data.

shows the results of estimating five different models of unit cost. The dependent variable in each model is the cost per unit of producing each pizza. The independent variables in each model are shown in the five columns. As can be seen from the table, we estimated increasingly complex models that included more predictor variables.

Results of estimating Equation (5.1) using a maximum-likelihood estimation algorithm allowing for first-order autocorrelation of the residuals are shown in Column 1 of Table 5.2. Analysis of the residuals from Equation (5.1) revealed first-order autocorrelation. There was no evidence of higher order autocorrelation. All of the models shown in Table 5.2 correct for first-order autocorrelation by jointly estimating the correlation coefficient with other coefficients in the models.

The coefficients of the store-specific dummy variables are not of particular interest so are not reported here. A joint test of the null hypothesis that there were no store-specific effects was rejected at a high significance level ($p < .001$), so important store-specific effects were present in the sample. Store-specific dummy variables were included in all analyses. The estimate of the constant term is not of particular interest for the research questions. The constant terms are omitted in order to preserve confidentiality of the data.

Column 1 shows the effect of the conventional measure of store-specific learning (lagged cumulative output for each store) on cost per unit. As can be seen from the table, the variable representing store-specific learning has a significant negative coefficient, supporting our expectation that the unit cost of production would decrease as the cumulative number of pizzas produced at each store increased.

Learning curves are often characterized in terms of a progress ratio, p. As noted previously, the progress ratio, p, is related to the coefficient for store-specific learning, b_1, as follows:

$$p = 2^{-b_1} \tag{5.4}$$

Based on the results shown in column 1 of Table 5.2, a progress ratio for the entire sample was calculated to be $p = 0.93$. For each doubling of cumulative output, the unit cost of producing a pizza decreased to 93% of its previous value. Thus, pizza stores in the sample demonstrated a slower learning rate than the modal "80% learning curve" found in manufacturing firms. Although it was slower in this service sector than typically observed in manufacturing, the rate of learning was significant.

The effects of transfer between commonly owned stores and transfer between differently owned stores on cost per unit are also presented in

Table 5.2
Results Concerning the Transfer of Knowledge From the Franchise Study

	(1)	(2)	(3)	(4)	(5)
Store-Specific Learning (b_1)	-.117◊ (.019)	-.098◊ (.020)	-.097◊ (.020)	-.104◊ (.019)	-.106◊ (.022)
Transfer between commonly owned stores (b_2)	-.104◊ (.016)	-.066◊ (.019)	-.064‡ (.020)	-.059‡ (.022)	-.094* (.047)
Transfer between differently owned stores (b_3)	-.015* (.007)	-.008 (.010)	-.009 (.010)	-.004 (.010)	-.001 (.011)
Calendar Time (b_4)		.003‡ (.001)	.003‡ (.001)	.004‡ (.002)	.002‡ (.0008)
Current Pizza Count (b_5)		-.0003◊ (.1E-04)	-.0003◊ (.1E-04)	-.0003◊ (.1E-04)	-.0004◊ (.9E-05)
Square of Current Pizza Count (b_6)		.6E-07◊ (.4E-08)	.5E-07◊ (.4E-08)	.5E-07◊ (.4E-08)	.9E-07◊ (.4E-08)
Square of Store-Specific Learning (b_7)			.009 (.007)	.009 (.008)	.003 (.009)
Percentage Pan Pizza (b_8)			.021 (.017)	.022 (.021)	.052 (.048)
Depreciation of Knowledge (λ)				.80◊ (.046)	.83◊ (.042)
Autocorrelation Coefficient (u)	.569◊ (.017)	.581◊ (.014)	.589◊ (.015)	.512◊ (.022)	.492◊ (.024)
R^2	.237	.557	.565	.593	.653

Note. Standard errors are shown in parentheses.

Reprinted by permission from E. Darr, L. Argote and D. Epple, The acquisition, transfer and depreciation of knowledge in service organizations: Productivity in franchises, *Management Science*, Volume *41*, Number 11, (November, 1995). Copyright 1995, The Institute of Operations Research and the Management Sciences (INFORMS), 2 Charles Street, Suite 300, Providence, RI 02904 USA.

*p<.05, ‡p<.01, and ◊p<.001

Column 1 of Table 5.2. The negative coefficients b_2 and b_3 suggest that both transfer between commonly owned stores and transfer between differently owned stores accounted for significant decreases in the unit cost of production. The latter effect, however, was not robust to alternative specifications of the model. This is discussed in the following paragraphs.

Models with more control variables were estimated to explore alternative explanations for the results. We divided the control variables into two separate sets (Columns 2 and 3) in order to understand better their incremental impact. In Column 2 of Table 5.2, calendar time was introduced to capture the possibility that technical change associated with the passage of time rather than learning associated with organizational experience was responsible for decreases in unit production costs. The positive coefficient for the time variable in Column 2 of Table 5.2 indicates that time is not a viable alternative explanation for the decrease observed in unit production cost. The coefficient on the time variable actually indicates that the cost of pizza production increased with the passage of time, perhaps reflecting increases in food and labor costs over the one and a half year period of the study.

Current pizza count and the square of current pizza count were also included in Column 2 to capture the possible effects of economies of scale on cost per unit. The negative coefficient for current pizza count and the positive coefficient for the square of current pizza count in Column 2 of Table 5.2 indicate that significant scale effects were present. Cost per unit first decreased and then increased with increases in the current volume of production.

The decrease in cost per unit as volume rises from relatively low output levels is natural since some labor and operating costs must be borne merely to keep a store open, and those costs are spread over more units as volume increases. Increasing cost per unit at higher volumes seemed to result from increased coordination costs. Coordination became difficult for high-volume production, especially since less experienced part-time employees were used to supplement regular employees during peak loads.

Comparing Column 1 and Column 2 of Table 5.2 reveals that the impact of transfer between differently owned stores was no longer significant, whereas the effects of store-specific learning and transfer between commonly owned stores on the unit cost of production were unchanged with the addition of calendar time, current pizza count, and the square of current count. This illustrates the importance of controlling for scale economies since other variables may pick up their effects if scale variables are excluded.

We conducted a specification test (Hausman, 1978) to assess whether there might be simultaneity in the determination of cost per pizza and current pizza count. Our model allows for current pizza count to affect costs through economies of scale. It is conceivable that there is also an effect in the reverse direction: stores with lower cost per pizza may charge lower prices and thereby generate a larger sales volume. Such simultaneity or endogeneity would lead to biased coefficient estimates. To test for the possibility of endogeneity of current count, the model was estimated with a two-stage least squares procedure that Fair (1970) developed. This instrumental variables procedure provides consistent estimates of models with endogenous variables and serially correlated errors. The coefficient estimates using instrumental variables were compared to the original coefficient estimates. The two sets of coefficient estimates were very similar. A test statistic of 8.16 was calculated for Hausman's specification test. The test statistic was distributed as X^2, df=44, with a critical value of 60.48 at the .05 level. Thus, there was no evidence of endogeneity of current pizza count in the model.

In Column 3 of Table 5.2 the square of the knowledge variable was introduced into the model to allow for possible changes in the learning rate. The coefficient for this variable was insignificant, indicating that there was no change in the rate of learning over the length of the study. Thus, we did not observe the "plateau" effect in this study.

The proportion of total pizza production accounted for by pan pizza was also introduced into the model at this stage to control for product mix. The estimate of pan pizza effects in Column 3 was insignificant, indicating that product mix did not affect the unit cost of production. A comparison between Column 2 and Column 3 reveals that the learning, time, and scale effects were unchanged by the inclusion of these additional variables.

The possibility that the results were driven by a few newly opened stores in the sample was investigated by removing the four new stores from the sample. The results from the reduced sample were almost identical to the results in shown in Table 5.2.

5.4.2.2 Depreciation

Results on the depreciation of learning are presented in Columns 4 and 5 of Table 5.2. Column 4 is a linear model that does not include entire production histories, whereas Column 5 is a nonlinear model including entire production histories. The maximum likelihood estimate of λ for the model shown in Column 4 was 0.80. The hypothesis of no depreciation ($\lambda = 1.0$) was very strongly rejected. The depreciation rate is very rapid for these organizations.

Learning curve analysis has traditionally proceeded from the beginning of production in an organization. The majority of stores in this sample were in operation several years prior to the beginning of data collection. Through further data collection, we obtained complete production histories for 18 of the 36 stores in our sample. The impact of including entire production histories for each store on estimated learning effects was investigated using a nonlinear model in which pizza production prior to the beginning of our sample was added to the store, intra-franchise, and inter-franchise aggregates. For each of the 18 stores for which we were unable to obtain complete data, production history was treated as an unknown coefficient.

The results of these analyses are shown in Column 5 of Table 5.2. Including complete production histories did not change our results concerning store-specific learning, time, scale effects, and product mix. The effect of transfer between commonly owned stores remained significant but became somewhat less significant than in the previous analysis. The maximum likelihood estimate of the depreciation parameter, 0.83, remained significantly less than one in this model.

These results indicate a very rapid rate of depreciation. A value of $\lambda = 0.83$ implies that roughly one half (0.83^4) of the stock of knowledge at the beginning of a month would remain at the end of the month. From a stock of knowledge available at the beginning of a year, a negligible amount (0.83^{52}) would remain one year later. In fact, without continuing production to replenish the stock of knowledge, virtually all production knowledge would be lost by mid-year.

We hypothesized that knowledge transfer between commonly owned stores should be greater than transfer between differently owned stores because of greater use of transfer mechanisms between commonly owned stores. There are many mechanisms for transferring knowledge across franchises. For example, all franchises are required to attend a yearly meeting. And a consultant from the parent corporation routinely visits each store to provide advice. These transfer mechanisms were more or less constant for all the stores in the sample. Other mechanisms, however, varied across stores. For example, there seemed to be more communication and interaction between some stores than others. We measured the frequencies of phone calls, personal acquaintances, and meetings between the various stores. We found that the frequencies of these communication mechanisms for transferring knowledge were significantly greater between commonly owned stores than between differently owned stores. Further research is needed to determine if these (and other mechanisms) contributed to the knowledge transfer observed.

5.4.2.3 Timeliness

We also investigated whether a different but also important outcome, service timeliness, evidenced learning (Argote & Darr, in press). Service timeliness was measured as the percentage of "late" pizzas. We adopted the corporation's metric for coding a pizza as late: if a prespecified amount of time elapsed from when an order arrived to when the pizza was completely prepared, it was listed as late.

The dependent measure in our analysis of service timeliness was the number of late pizzas per unit of pizzas produced each week. The predictor variables paralleled those previously described for our analysis of cost per unit. Thus, we examined whether service timeliness improved as a function of a store's direct experience, of the experience of other stores owned by the same franchisee, and of the experience of stores owned by different franchisees. As in the analysis just described of cost per unit, dummy variables for each store and key control variables were also included in the models. In the service timeliness model, we also controlled for labor costs at each store. Finally, we allowed for the possibility that service knowledge depreciated by replacing the conventional cumulative output measure with the specification of knowledge shown in Equation (5.2).

Results indicated that stores benefited from their own direct experience and from the experience of other stores owned by the same franchisee. Service timeliness was not affected by the experience of stores owned by different franchisees. These results paralleled those reported earlier for cost per unit. Knowledge transferred across stores owned by the same franchisee but not across stores owned by different franchisees. Results also indicated that service knowledge depreciated. Recent output was found to be a more important predictor of service timeliness than cumulative output.

5.4.3 Discussion

The fast food stores in our study evidenced firm-specific learning: as they gained experience, the unit cost of production decreased at a decreasing rate. The results on firm-specific learning are robust: firm-specific learning effects contributed to reductions in production cost independent of calendar time, scale effects, and product mix. Additionally, store-specific learning was evident when we added complete production histories and allowed for knowledge depreciation.

This is one of the first studies to focus on learning in service organizations. Although the modal progress ratio in the fast food franchises we studied was less than the modal figure found in manufacturing, learning effects were significant contributors to the productivity of the stores. Further research is needed to determine whether the slower rate of learning is characteristic of most service organizations and if so, why the rate is slower than that typically observed in manufacturing. To accomplish this, we believe that it will be more fruitful to move beyond the diffuse characterization of "service" versus "manufacturing" organizations and focus on the specific variables that differentiate the two environments.

Indeed the line between manufacturing and service is blurring. An automotive company recently looked to a fast food firm for ideas about improving performance. Alex Trotman, Ford's Chairman, sent a task force to McDonald's to learn how McDonald's produces the same hamburgers all around the world ("Survey of manufacturing," 1998). Just as McDonald's delivers the same hamburger around the world, Ford wanted to be able to produce the same car on a global basis. This example of a manufacturing firm seeking to imitate a service firm suggests that the underlying business processes at each firm have much in common.

There are also points on which manufacturing and service firms generally differ. For example, there was much less opportunity to match tasks to the expertise and interests of individual workers in the pizza stores we studied than in the manufacturing plants. Thus, an important source of productivity gains was not available to the fast food stores. Similarly, many manufacturing organizations are able to sequence their products in a way that maximizes productivity. This option may not be available to service organizations who produce on demand. For example, the truck plants we studied sequenced their products such that trucks with options that required significantly more steps to include such as air conditioning were never sequenced back-to-back in the production line. By contrast, the pizza franchises produced on demand to satisfy customers and had less opportunity to sequence their pizzas so as to maximize their productivity. Future research is needed to determine if these factors are the underlying variables that explain differences between rates of learning in service and manufacturing sectors.

The results on transfer of learning extend our current understanding of the conditions under which transfer occurs. The results suggest that knowledge transfer between affiliated organizations is greater than transfer between independent organizations. Future research is needed to determine why knowledge transfer is greater between stores in the same franchise than between stores in different franchises. For example, is the pattern of differential transfer largely a function of differences in motivation, differences in opportunities to communicate, or otherwise? Competition was minimized in the franchise organizations by corporate policies that, for example, limited how close the stores could locate to each other. Also, the stores cooperated on marketing and promotions. Although there was little competition between the stores and some cooperation, there were more incentives to share information with stores owned by the same franchisee that with stores owned by different franchisees. Thus, differences in motivation could have contributed to differences in the degree of knowledge transfer.

There were also more personal relationships and opportunities to communicate among stores owned by the same franchisee than among stores owned by different franchisees. These results are consistent with past work demonstrating that social networks are denser within related than between independent organizations (e.g., see Tichy, Tushman & Fromburn, 1979; Tushman, 1977). In the current study, opportunities to share information were greater within than between franchises. Differences in opportunities to communicate and share information could also have contributed to differences observed in the degree of knowledge transfer. Further research is needed to determine why knowledge transfer is greater between affiliated than independent organizations.

The finding that being embedded in a superordinate relationship such as a franchise increased the degree of knowledge transfer has important practical implications. It suggests that embedding organizations in a network that gives them a larger experience base to draw on is a powerful way for improving the performance of a focal firm. This suggestion is consistent with the trend noted on the part of many franchise organizations to move away from single store owners to owners who own very large numbers of stores. A recent *Wall Street Journal* article argued that most franchise systems are moving away from "mom-and-pop" franchises to franchises where the same individual owns many stores:

> Franchising specialists say such high-flying franchisees are becoming more numerous—and vastly more important. Most franchise systems have a growing number of "big boys" with 20 or more stores. For example, Grand Metropolitan PLC's Burger King Corporation unit in Miami says five U.S. franchisees top the 50 store mark, compared with only two in 1985 (Tannenbaum, 1996, p. A1).

Our results suggest that the ability to learn from a larger experience base and to transfer knowledge from one store to another contributes to the greater productivity of multi-store franchises.

Recent results of a study by McEvily and Zaheer (1998) are consistent with the recommendation that being embedded in a network improves organizational performance. The researchers examined whether participating in regional institutions, Manufacturing Extension Partnership (MEP) centers, improved the capabilities of small manufacturers. The MEP centers provide training courses, workshops, equipment demonstrations, supplier certification and the like to small manufacturers. Based on an analysis of data from 227 small manufacturers in the metal-working sector located in the Midwestern area of the United States, McEvily and Zaheer (1998) concluded that participation in a regional network was generally associated with enhanced competitive capabilities.

The transfer results from the franchise study are generally consistent with our previous results on the extent to which transfer of learning occurs (Argote, Beckman & Epple, 1990; Epple, Argote & Murphy, 1996). The previous studies found that intra-plant transfer across shifts within a production facility was greater than transfer across geographically separated production facilities, such as the shipyards. Groups within a single plant such as two shifts are more related than geographically separated groups. Previous results concerning transfer of learning are, therefore, consistent with the results presented here.

Events that occurred in the food franchises after we completed data collection provided additional validation for our finding about the importance of being embedded in a multi-store network. Three of the stores in the sample closed or changed owners due to productivity problems. All three stores that closed or changed owners were single-store franchises. These stores were not able to benefit from production experience at other stores. Consistent with our results, these stores were less productive than their counterparts in multi-store franchises.

5.5 Levels of Knowledge Transfer

Knowledge transfer in organizations has been studied at different levels of analysis. This section provides an overview of whether knowledge has been found to transfer at these different levels. Subsequent sections identify the conditions under which knowledge transfer is most likely to occur. Some researchers have examined whether knowledge transfer occurs across products or models of the same product within an organizational context (e.g., Udayajiri & Balakrishnan, 1993). Others have studied whether knowledge transfers between units of the same organization, such as shifts within a manufacturing plant (Epple, Argote & Murphy, 1996) or Product Development and Marketing departments (Adler, 1990). Others have examined whether knowledge transfers across organizations embedded in a superordinate relationship, such as a franchise or chain (e.g., Baum &

Ingram, 1998; Darr, Argote & Epple, 1995). Still others have examined whether knowledge transfers or "spills over" across competitors (e.g., Henderson & Cockburn, 1996; Irwin & Klenow, 1994). The extent of knowledge transfer found to occur at each of these levels will now be reviewed: across products, across units of the same organization, across organizations embedded in a superordinate relationship, and across independent organizations.

Knowledge transfer from one model to another or from one product to another can contribute significantly to a firm's performance. Ghemawat (1985) described a dramatic example of knowledge transfer across products in the motorcycle industry. British motorcycle manufacturers apparently did not understand that achieving a viable cost position on one product depended on their manufacture of other products, since different products shared parts and manufacturing processes. British manufacturers stopped producing small motor bikes when they were threatened with competition from the Japanese on that end of the market. Although getting out of the small bike market improved their performance initially, it destroyed their performance in the long run. The small bikes shared many parts and processes with their larger counterparts. When the British stopped production of the small bikes, they dramatically reduced their experience base for learning about the parts and processes shared with the large bikes. According to Ghemawat (1985), the British share of their own home market fell from 34% in 1968 to only 3% in 1974.

The Lockheed case previously described in Chapter 2 also suggests the importance of the ability to transfer knowledge across products for firm performance and survival. A competitor of Lockheed, McDonnell Douglas, produced a military KC-10 tanker that was very similar to its commercial DC-10 counterpart. The ability to transfer knowledge across the KC-10 and the DC-10 may have contributed to the more favorable cost position McDonnell Douglas enjoyed relative to Lockheed.

Several studies have empirically examined the extent of knowledge transfer across models or products. These studies have generally found that knowledge transfer occurs—but to an incomplete degree. In his detailed analysis of the Lockheed L-1011 production program, Benkard (1997) found that transfer of knowledge occurred from one model of the L-1011 to another. The transfer, however, was incomplete: not all of the knowledge acquired on the production of the first model transferred to the second. Lockheed began producing one model and produced it with minor variations throughout the entire production program. Several years into the production program, Lockheed began producing a different model with a shorter fuselage and different cargo and galley configurations. Benkard (1997) found considerable—but incomplete—transfer from the first to the second model. Benkard estimated that the first unit of the second model required approximately 25% more labor than another unit of the original model would have required.

Henderson and Cockburn (1996) also found considerable knowledge transfer across products. In their analysis of the determinants of research productivity in drug discovery, Henderson and Cockburn (1996) found evidence of internal spillovers of knowledge between related research programs within the same firm.

Irwin and Klenow (1994) found weak evidence for learning spillovers across different generations of products in the semiconductor industry. Irwin and Klenow (1994) did not have access to firm-level data on production cost but rather used price as a proxy for unit cost data. Using firm-level price data, Irwin and Klenow (1994) concluded that knowledge transferred or spilled over only in two of the seven product generations. By contrast, using industry-level price data, Udayagiri and Balakrishnan (1993) presented evidence that knowledge transferred over generations for the five semiconductor products they analyzed. Further, the researchers found that experience producing Dynamic Random Access Memory (DRAM) chips benefited the production of other memory products. The difference in findings across these two studies of knowledge transfer in the semiconductor industry may be due to their differing focus on firm- versus industry-level data.

Both studies used price as a proxy variable for unit costs. It is hard to disentangle the price effects that arise as a consequence of market dynamics from the effects that derive from knowledge transfer. Clearly more work is needed on knowledge transfer effects in the semiconductor industry.

More generally, further research is needed to understand the conditions under which knowledge transfers across products or generations of products. The similarity of products and the extent to which they build on a common knowledge base are key factors conditioning the ease of transferring knowledge across them. The role of similarity will be addressed in a subsequent section of this chapter.

Researchers have also studied knowledge transfer across the components of an organization. For example, as described in Chapter 3, my colleagues and I studied the amount of knowledge transfer that occurred from the first shift to the second shift when the new shift was introduced at a truck assembly plant (Epple, Argote & Murphy, 1996). We found that the transfer from the period of one-shift operation to the period of two-shift operation was rapid and almost complete. Within two weeks, the second shift achieved a level of productivity that it had taken the first shift almost two years to achieve. We suggested that the rapid and complete transfer was due to much of the organization's knowledge being embedded in its technology (cf. Mishina, 1992).

A significant amount of knowledge has also been found to transfer across organizations that are embedded in a superordinate relationship. My colleagues and I examined transfer of knowledge across 13 World War II shipyards that went into production at different points in time (Argote, Beckman & Epple, 1990). Mechanisms for transferring knowledge across the shipyards existed (Lane, 1951). The organizations produced the same product with a standardized design. A central agency was responsible for purchasing, designing each yard's layout, approving the technology it used, and supervising its construction. The central agency also stationed engineers, inspectors, and auditors at each site to share information about "best practices." Shipyards that began production later were found to be more productive initially than those with earlier start dates. Once shipyards began production, however, they did not benefit further from production experience at other yards. Thus, transfer of knowledge occurred across the shipyards at the start of production but not thereafter.

The results of our franchise study described earlier in this chapter indicated that fast food stores benefited from the experience of other stores in the same franchise (Darr, Argote & Epple, 1995). Similarly, Baum and Ingram (1998) found that Manhattan hotels benefited from the experience of other hotels in the same chain. Ingram and Simons (1997) found that kibbutzim benefited from the experience of other kibbutzim in the same federation but not from the experience of kibbutzim in different federations.

Several studies have examined whether knowledge transfers or spills over across firms in an industry. Although there is evidence of knowledge transfer from other firms in the industry, firms typically learn more from their own direct experience than from the experience of their competitors. For example, Zimmerman (1982) studied transfer of knowledge in nuclear reactors built between 1953 and 1963. The unit cost of construction was analyzed as a function of a firm's direct experience constructing power plants and the cumulative experience in the industry constructing power plants. Both types of experience were found to be significant predictors of the unit cost of construction. The effect of firm-specific experience, however, was more significant than the effect of industry experience.

Joskow and Rose (1985) took a more refined approach to measuring experience in their study of 411 coal-burning steam-electric generating units built between 1960 and 1980. Joskow and Rose (1985) analyzed the unit cost of construction as a function of firm-specific experience, architect-engineer experience, and industry experience. An architect-engineer team typically designed plants for more than one firm. Joskow and Rose (1985) found that firm-specific and architect-engineer experience were significant predictors of the unit cost of construction, whereas industry experience was not significant. Thus, firms learned from their own direct experience and the experience of architect-engineer teams. Transfer of knowledge occurred across firms that employed the same architect-engineer team but not across other firms in the industry.

Irwin and Klenow (1994) also studied knowledge transfer across competitors. Although knowledge transfer was found to occur, firms learned three times as much from an additional unit of their own direct experience as from an additional unit of experience at another firm. Further, knowledge appeared to spill over as much between firms in different countries as between firms within a country. In contrast to popular notions about learning in Japanese firms, Japanese semiconductor firms were not found to differ from firms in other countries in their rate of learning.

Henderson and Cockburn (1996) also analyzed knowledge transfer across competitors. In their study of factors affecting research productivity in drug discovery, Henderson and Cockburn (1996) found that firms benefited from their own direct experience and from the experience of their competitors. Although the effect of the experience of competitors was considerably smaller than the effect of a firm's own experience, the benefits of the experience of others accounted for a significant amount of the total variance in productivity. Thus, the Henderson and Cockburn results are similar to those of Irwin and Klenow as well as Zimmerman. Firms generally learn from their own direct experience and from the experience of their competitors. Although they do not learn as much from their competitors as from their own experience, the transfer of knowledge from other firms contributes significantly to a focal firm's productivity.

Thus, knowledge transfer has been found (to varying degrees) at all levels of analysis. Related research will now be discussed and the conditions under which knowledge is most likely to transfer across organizations will be developed. The focus is primarily on knowledge transfer across organizations or units of organizations. Related work that helps illuminate these processes will be included.

5.6 Related Research

Although interest in how one organization transfers knowledge to another is relatively new, considerable work has been done in the past on related topics. For example, work has been done on "transfer of training." This work examines how to design training programs to increase the likelihood that participants transfer skills acquired in the training program to on-the-job performance (e.g., see Baldwin & Ford, 1988, for a review). Work has also been done in psychology on how individuals transfer knowledge learned on one task to another (e.g., see Singley & Anderson, 1989, for a review). This research might examine, for example, how experience with one programming task affects performance on another. In a somewhat different vein, work has been done on the transfer or diffusion of innovation (e.g., see Rogers, 1995). This work might examine, for example, how a new farming practice diffused across farmers. These different lines of work focus primarily on individual (rather than organizational) outcomes and hence are beyond the scope of this monograph. These lines of work will be drawn upon when they have implications for the transfer of knowledge across organizations.

Some work has been done at the organizational level on the diffusion of practices across organizations (e.g., DiMaggio & Powell, 1983; Tolbert & Zucker, 1983). For example, Tolbert and Zucker (1983) examined the diffusion of civil service reforms across cities in the United States. Much of this work has emphasized that organizations often adopt practices to achieve legitimacy rather than to improve their efficiency (see Scott, 1987, for a review of this perspective). Research has also been done on factors affecting the adoption or transfer of practices or technology within organizations (e.g., see Allen, 1977; Attewell, 1992; Cool, Dierickx & Szulanski, 1997; Keller & Chinta, 1990; Leonard-Barton, 1988; Ouinjian & Carne, 1987). For example, Cool, Dierickx and Szulanski (1997) examined factors explaining the diffusion of electronic switching technology within the operating companies of the Bell System.

Our focus is somewhat different than past work on the adoption of organizational practices or technology. We do not examine whether or not an organization adopts a practice. Instead we examine whether an organization learns from the experience of other organizations. Because their experience may be embedded in practices or technology, research on the adoption of practices may be relevant for understanding how one organization learns from the experience of another. Past work on the adoption of practices will be drawn upon when it illuminates how the adoption of practices affects the performance of the recipient unit.

Our work on knowledge transfer at the organizational level of analysis is most analogous to research on knowledge transfer at the individual level of analysis. Just as researchers of individual knowledge transfer examine how experience on one task affects performance on another, we examine how experience at one organization affects performance at another. Factors such as similarity that are important predictors of the extent of knowledge transfer at the individual level turn out to be important at the organizational level as well. Additional factors, however, come into play in understanding knowledge transfer at the organizational level of analysis. These factors will now be discussed.

5.7 Conditions Under Which Knowledge Transfers

This section identifies the conditions under which knowledge transfers across organizational units. That is, the section identifies the conditions under which experience in one organization affects the performance of another. The section is organized into examining how knowledge transfer is affected by characteristics of the relationship among the organizations, characteristics of the organizations involved in the transfer, features of the knowledge being transferred, and dimensions of the transfer process.

5.7.1 Characteristics of the Relationship Among Organizations

As noted previously, one very important factor affecting transfer of knowledge across organizations is whether the organizations are embedded in a superordinate relationship. My colleagues and I found that being embedded in a superordinate relationship, such as a franchise, increased the likelihood of knowledge transfer (Darr, Argote & Epple, 1995). Similarly, Baum and Ingram (1998) found that Manhattan hotels benefited from their own direct experience and the experience of hotels that were related to them through belonging to the same chain. Along similar lines, Ingram and Simons (1997) found that kibbutzim benefited from the experience of other kibbutzim that belonged to the same federation, whereas they did not benefit from the experience of those in different federations.

Powell, Koput and Smith-Doerr (1996) found that biotechnology firms that were linked together in a Research and Development alliance were more likely to have access to critical information and resource flows that facilitated their growth than firms not engaged in such collaborative relationships. McEvily and Zaheer (1998) found that participation in regional institutions, Manufacturing Extension Partnership centers, improved the competitive capabilities of small manufacturers. Uzzi (1996) found that clothing apparel firms that were embedded in networks had a greater chance of survival than firms connected to other firms only through "arms-length" ties. Uzzi suggested that learning from one another contributed to the superior performance of firms in the network. Burns and Wholey (1993) found that regional and local hospital networks influenced the diffusion of an administrative innovation, matrix management. Thus, being embedded in a franchise, chain, or network relationship facilitates the transfer of knowledge.

Being embedded in a superordinate relationship may affect both the motivation and communication of participants in ways that facilitate knowledge transfer. Incentives of firms involved in superordinate relationships are typically more favorable to knowledge transfer than incentives at independent firms. For example, competition is usually minimized among organizations that belong to franchises, chains, or networks. These organizations cooperate in certain arenas. The organizations generally trust each other to a greater degree than those not embedded in a network or superordinate relationship (Granovetter, 1985; Uzzi, 1996).

Being embedded in a franchise, chain, or network also provides more opportunities to communicate than are afforded independent organizations (who may even be proscribed from direct communication with each other). Meetings, informal interactions, and opportunities to observe each other's organizations are all more likely to occur among organizations embedded in such a relationship than among independent organizations. Personnel movement may also be encouraged among the organizations and they may have access to each others' documents and databases. These communication opportunities provide mechanisms for transferring both explicit and tacit knowledge across organizations. For example, Uzzi (1996) noted that more tacit knowledge flowed across the firms embedded in a network than across independent organizations. Thus, organizations embedded in superordinate relationships have more opportunities to share information and learn from one another.

Being close geographically has also been found to facilitate knowledge transfer. Galbraith (1990) analyzed 32 different attempts to transfer manufacturing technology from one facility of an organization to another. He examined the amount of time it took to increase productivity at the recipient facility to the level achieved at the donor site prior to transfer. Galbraith found that the time it took for productivity to recover was slower when the organizations were geographically far apart.

The results of our research on intershift transfer of knowledge also suggest that geographic proximity facilitates knowledge transfer. Results from our study of transfer of knowledge across shifts in a manufacturing facility indicated that knowledge acquired during the period of one-shift operation carried forward quite rapidly to the period of two-shift operation (Epple, Argote & Murphy, 1996). The carry-forward of knowledge was almost complete within two weeks of the second shift's start-up. We found a more rapid and more complete degree of knowledge transfer in this study of inter-shift transfer than in studies of knowledge transfer across geographically dispersed organizations. It seems likely that the greater proximity of the two shifts facilitated knowledge transfer between them.

Research on transfer of knowledge in nuclear power plant operation also underscores the importance of proximity for knowledge transfer. Lester and McCabe (1993) examined how the performance of nuclear reactors in the United States and France varied as a function of industry structure. The researchers found that transfer of knowledge across reactors was greatest when the reactors were located at the same site. This finding explained much of the performance advantage of France, which typically builds four reactors at the same site, relative to the United States, where the preponderance of units are built at sites where there is at most one other reactor.

By contrast, Darr (1994) found that geographical proximity was not a predictor of knowledge transfer in pizza stores in Great Britain, once similarity of store strategy was taken into account (cf. Burt, 1987). Darr (1994) found that stores were more likely to learn from other stores following a similar than a dissimilar strategy. Geographic similarity and customer similarity were insignificant predictors of knowledge transfer when strategic similarity was taken into account.

Other studies have found similarity to be an important predictor of the extent to which firms monitor and imitate each other. For example, Porac and Thomas (1994) found that similar retail organizations were more likely to monitor each other than dissimilar organizations. In a longitudinal simulation of student groups, Baum and Berta (1998) found that groups were more likely to imitate other student groups that occupied a similar market position.

Further research is needed on the role of geographic proximity and similarity in knowledge transfer. This research would benefit from specifying (and testing) the underlying processes through which the factors affect knowledge transfer. For example, does proximity facilitate communication and, thereby, improve knowledge transfer? Alternatively, are proximate organizations more likely to be similar and thus, have more relevant knowledge to share? A greater understanding of the processes that mediate the relationship between proximity and knowledge transfer is needed.

The quality of the relationship among organizations also affects knowledge transfer. Szulanski (1996) examined barriers to the transfer of best practices within organizations. One of the factors found to contribute to the degree of knowledge transfer was the quality of the relationship between the donor and the recipient. A poor relationship made it more difficult to transfer best practices. The relationship between organizational subunits or work groups will be discussed more fully later in this chapter.

5.7.2 Characteristics of the Organizations

Characteristics of an organization, such as its size or success, also affect the likelihood that it will be imitated by other organizations. In a study of imitation among firms in their choice of investment banker, Haunschild and Miner (1997) found that organizations were more likely to imitate firms with exceptional performance than to imitate firms with average performance. Somewhat surprisingly, firms imitated both the best and the worst performers. The latter effect was particularly pronounced for deals completed during the most recent year, when publicity might have the greatest impact (cf. Haunschild & Miner, 1997). Thus, imitation of firms with the high premiums (i.e., the worst deals) may reflect the salience of these investment bankers rather than the quality of their deals. Haunschild and Miner (1997) also found that firms were more likely to imitate large firms and to follow a particular strategy when it was used by many other firms in the industry (see also Burns & Wholey, 1993). Baum and Berta (1998) found that student groups were more likely to copy successful than unsuccessful groups.

Further research is needed to determine the conditions under which imitating other firms with particular characteristics affects the performance of the imitator. Several of the characteristics found to increase imitation in the Haunschild and Miner study may be proxy variables for the use of practices that enhance firm performance. For example, large firms or firms with exceptionally high performance may primarily use practices that enhance performance (cf. Haunschild & Miner, 1997). Thus, imitating firms with these characteristics may enhance the performance of the imitator. Imitating firms with other characteristics, such as the use of popular strategies, may confer legitimacy on the imitator and thereby enhance performance. Imitating firms with still other characteristics such as exceptionally low performance seems unlikely to improve the performance of the imitator. Research is needed on the conditions which imitation improves the performance of the imitating firm. It seems likely, for example, that imitating practices at another firm will improve the performance of a focal firm when the contribution of the practice to performance is well understood.

Characteristics of the recipient organization can also affect the extent of knowledge transfer. Cohen and Levinthal (1990) introduced the important concept of "absorptive capacity," which they defined as the ability of a firm to recognize the value of external information, assimilate it, and apply it. Cohen and Levinthal argued that absorptive capacity, which is largely a function of the firm's level of prior related knowledge, is critical to innovation. In an empirical study of the transfer of best practices within a firm, Szulanski (1996) found that high absorptive capacity on the part of recipients facilitated the transfer of best practices.

In a related vein, Rothwell (1978) described the many problems that develop when the technology to be transferred is beyond the understanding of the recipient organization. Similarly, Galbraith (1990) found that previous experience with technology transfers minimized the initial productivity loss associated with transfer of manufacturing technology to new establishments. Furthermore, Hamel (1991) reported that a wide gap in skills between partners in a strategic alliance impaired transfer of knowledge between them. In order to replicate a partner's skills, a firm must understand the steps between its current capability and that of its partner.

Allen's (1977) work on technology transfer also underscores the importance of absorptive capacity on the part of recipients and suggests a structure for facilitating it. Allen found that for applied research problems whose solution could not be completely codified in scientific principles, having a "gatekeeper" at the boundary of a group who could communicate with internal and external constituencies facilitated performance. The gatekeeper absorbed knowledge from outside and interpreted it for internal constituencies.

Ancona and Caldwell (1992) also examined the activities groups use to manage relationships with other groups. Based on interviews and questionnaires from managers of new product teams, the researchers identified strategies groups took vis-à-vis external constituencies. Ambassadorial activities, which involved protecting the team and garnering resources and support for it, initially had a positive effect on meeting deadlines and budgets but the effect dissipated over time. Although activities aimed at coordinating technical and design issues did not affect team performance initially, these activities had a positive effect on innovation over the long run. Prolonged scouting activities that involved gathering information and scanning the environment were negatively associated with team performance—both initially and over the long run. These results suggest that task-coordinator activities, which are intimately connected to the organization's workflow, may be more important over the long run than ambassadorial or scouting activities.

Motivation also matters in knowledge transfer across groups. Szulanski (1996) found that the higher the motivation of the recipient organization, the greater the knowledge transfer. Similarly, Zander and Kogut (1995) found that the more competitors were perceived as engaging in developing a similar product, the faster the speed of internal technology transfer. Thus, the fear of being surpassed by competitors enhanced the transfer of capabilities within the firm.

Interestingly enough, Szulanski (1996) concluded that although motivation mattered, it mattered less than cognitive or knowledge-related factors in explaining the transfer of best practices within an organization. According to Szulanski (1996), characteristics of the practice and opportunities to acquire a deep understanding of it were more important than motivational issues in determining whether transfer occurred.

5.7.3 Characteristics of the Knowledge Transferred

Characteristics of the information being transferred also affect the ease and success of knowledge transfer. Tacit knowledge or knowledge that is not well understood is more difficult to transfer than explicit knowledge. In their study of factors affecting the speed of transfer of manufacturing capabilities, Zander and Kogut (1995) found that knowledge that was codified in documents and software and that could be readily taught to new workers transferred more easily than capabilities not codified or easily taught. Similarly, Szulanski (1996) found that knowledge that was high in "causal ambiguity" was harder to transfer than well-understood knowledge. Our work on intershift transfer of knowledge suggests that embedding knowledge in technology is a very powerful and effective way to transfer knowledge (Epple, Argote & Murphy, 1996). Much of the knowledge embedded in technology was explicit and well-understood.

The complexity of the information being transferred is also likely to influence the success of the transfer. Galbraith (1990) found that attempts to transfer complex manufacturing technology were associated with higher initial losses in productivity at the recipient organization than attempts to transfer simpler technology. Similarly, Ounjian and Carne (1987) and Rothwell (1978) found that increased complexity reduced the rate of diffusion of innovation. By contrast, Meyer and Goes (1988) found that an innovation was more likely to be assimilated into hospitals when it was complex.

The observability of knowledge also affects its ease of transfer. Meyer and Goes (1988) found that the ease of observing an innovation and seeing its effect influenced its rate of assimilation. Observable innovations were assembled more easily than ones that were more difficult to observe.

The information features of the innovation from our study of fast food franchises that transferred most widely are consistent with these features found to facilitate knowledge transfer. As described in Chapter 3, an innovative method for placing pepperoni was developed at one of the stores in Southwestern Pennsylvania. The method of distributing pepperoni evenly on a pizza before it was cooked that had worked well for regular pizza did not work well for deep dish pizza. When the method was used on deep dish pizza, distributing pepperoni evenly before cooking resulted in a cooked pie with a clump of pepperoni at the center. A store in Southwestern Pennsylvania discovered an effective method for achieving an even distribution of pepperoni on deep dish pizza after it was cooked. The pepperoni was placed on the pie in a pattern that resembled spokes on a wheel. As the pizza cooked and the cheese flowed, the pepperoni would distribute themselves (more or less) evenly on the pizza. This method for distributing pepperoni was not complex. It was observable and codified in a routine that could be easily taught to new employees. Thus, the method scored high on features of information found to facilitate knowledge transfer. The pepperoni placement method transferred initially to other stores in the same franchise. A consultant from the parent corporation recognized the effectiveness of the method and promoted it in visits to other franchises and at national meetings. The method is now used by almost every store in the corporation. This example illustrates that knowledge that is observable, explicit, and not overly complex transfers readily to other organizations.

Interestingly enough, in their study of assimilation of innovations in hospitals, Meyer and Goes (1988) found that characteristics of the innovation itself, such as its observability, were more important predictors of the innovation's assimilation than characteristics of the organization, its leadership or the environment in which the organization was embedded (see also Szulanski, 1996). Organizational leaders, structures, and environments mattered less than attributes of the innovation in determining assimilation. Thus, characteristics of the knowledge being transferred may be particularly important in determining the degree of transfer.

Although some features of knowledge may be immutable, others may be amenable to change. In our study of pizza franchises, some tacit knowledge seemed inherently tacit. Knowledge about how to hand toss pizza, for example, was a kind of tacit knowledge not easily made explicit. By contrast, other knowledge that was tacit could have been codified in more explicit terms that would enable the knowledge to transfer more readily. For example, one order taker at a store developed heuristics for sequencing pizza preparation in a way that took advantage of differences in cooking times for different types and sizes of pizza. The heuristic enabled the ovens to be used more efficiently and the pizzas to be prepared more quickly. Although the heuristic remained in the mind of one employee, it could have been codified in a procedure that others could use.

5.7.4 Characteristics of the Transfer Process

Characteristics of the transfer process itself, such as its timing, also affect the extent of knowledge transfer. Organizations seem particularly open to learning from the experience of others early in their life cycle. Thus, there may be "windows of opportunity" (Tyre & Orlikowski, 1994) for transferring knowledge from others.

The results of our shipyard study are consistent with the prediction that organizations are more likely to learn from others at the start of their operation (Argote, Beckman & Epple, 1990). We examined transfer of knowledge across 13 World War II shipyards that went into production at different points in time. Shipyards that began production later were found to be more productive initially than those with earlier start dates. Once shipyards began production, however, they did not benefit further from production experience at other yards. Thus, transfer of knowledge occurred at the start of production but not thereafter.

The results of Baum and Ingram's work on hotel chains are also consistent with the prediction that organizations are more open to learning at the start of operation. Baum and Ingram (1998) found that Manhattan hotels benefited from the experience of hotels in different chains in the industry up to the time of the focal hotel's founding but not thereafter. Similarly, in their study of the adoption of farming practices, Foster and Rosenzweig (1995) found that framers learned from the experience of other farmers and that their learning from others diminished over time. In a study of success rates at angioplasty surgery, Kelsey et al. (1984) found that organizations were most likely to learn from the experience of others when they first began to perform the new surgical procedure.

By contrast, in a study of imitation of which investment banker to use on an acquisition, Haunschild and Miner (1997) found that firms learned from each other on a continuing basis. Along similar lines, we found that pizza stores learned from other stores in the same franchise on an ongoing basis (Darr, Argote & Epple, 1995). The different results regarding whether learning is confined to the start of operation or occurs on a continuing basis may be due to differences in prevailing knowledge repositories across the settings. For both the shipyards and the hotels, a significant component of the knowledge was embedded in the physical equipment, layout and technology of the establishments. By contrast, less knowledge regarding the investment banker decision or pizza production was embedded in "hard" form. Changing physical equipment, layout and technology may be more costly and disruptive than changing softer forms of knowledge. Future research is needed to examine factors affecting when firms are most open to learn from other firms. The extent to which knowledge is embedded in technology versus softer forms is likely to be a key factor.

The learning mechanism also affects the extent of knowledge transfer. Rulke, Zaheer and Anderson (1998) contrasted the extent to which three learning channels affected an organization's knowledge of its own capabilities as well as the capabilities of other firms. Three types of learning channels were identified empirically and supported by factor analysis: purposive (learning through deliberate attempts to transfer knowledge through company newsletters, formal training programs and the like), relational (learning from personal contacts both inside and outside the firm), and external arm's length (learning from trade association publications and newsletters). Rulke, Zaheer and Anderson (1998) found that purposive and relational (but not external) channels contributed to greater self-knowledge of an organization's own capabilities. Somewhat surprisingly, an organization's knowledge of the capabilities of other organizations was not affected by any of these learning channels.

Additional aspects of the transfer process affect its success. In his study of attempts to transfer manufacturing technology from one facility to another within a firm, Galbraith (1990) found that the time it took for productivity to recover was faster when co-production continued at the donor site and when the engineering team from the donor organization was relocated for at least one month to the recipient organization. Continuing production at the donor site may facilitate the transfer of tacit knowledge that is not written down or embedded in documents and plans. Since production continues at the donor site, the recipient site would be able to access the donor's store of tacit knowledge through observation. Once production is discontinued at the donor site much of the tacit knowledge would be lost.

Moving engineering personnel to the recipient organization is a powerful way to transfer tacit as well as explicit knowledge. Many other studies have found that moving personnel is a very powerful way to facilitate knowledge transfer. Allen (1977) argued that individuals are the most effective carriers of information because they are able to restructure information so that it applies to new contexts. Similarly, based on results from a study of technology transfer in the textile machinery sector, Rothwell (1978) concluded that the most effective way to transfer technology was to move people.

Research on tacit knowledge provides insights into why moving personnel is a powerful way to transfer knowledge. Berry and Broadbent (1987) found that although experienced individuals were not able to articulate their knowledge, they were able to transfer their knowledge to a similar task. That is, experience on one task improved performance on another task even though individuals were not able to articulate why their performance had improved on the first task. Individuals were thus able to transfer tacit knowledge from one task to another. This ability to transfer tacit knowledge across different contexts makes personnel movement a powerful transfer mechanism.

This richness of information transferred may explain the effectiveness of personal meetings and conferences relative to correspondence, papers, and publications in transferring technology (cf. Daft & Lengel, 1984). In a study of the diffusion of computer simulation technology, Dutton and Starbuck (1979) found that face-to-face meetings and conferences were more effective in diffusing the technology than written media such as papers, proceedings, and correspondence. Face-to-face meetings and conferences provide opportunities to transfer a richer set of information, including some tacit knowledge, than written media. The richness afforded by face-to-face communication conferences was especially important early in the diffusion of technology, when common understandings were being developed.

Future research is needed to understand more fully the conditions under which knowledge transfers and to determine the effectiveness of various transfer mechanisms. Are certain mechanisms more effective knowledge conduits than others? Does the effectiveness of a particular mechanism vary as a function of the type of knowledge being transferred or the stage of the transfer process? More generally, a greater understanding of the micro processes underlying the transfer of knowledge is needed.

5.8 Challenges to Knowledge Transfer Across Units Within Organizations

Although there are many benefits to knowledge transfer across organizations, it can be difficult to achieve. This section focuses on barriers to transferring knowledge across units of the same organization. While firms usually want to minimize or at least circumscribe knowledge transfer to other firms, they typically desire to foster knowledge transfer across their own departments or units. Even when knowledge transfer is desired, however, it can be difficult to achieve.

There are many reasons why it is difficult to transfer knowledge across units in the same organization. For example, the knowledge organizations acquire may be tacit and not easily articulated. As discussed previously, if knowledge cannot be articulated, it poses particular challenges for transfer since it is not easily communicated through verbal or written media. Transferring knowledge across organizational subunits or departments (rather than across individuals) poses particular challenges. Two factors make it particularly hard to transfer knowledge across subunits or work groups: competition between units and differences in context. These two factors are the focus of this section.

The first factor that impedes knowledge transfer across organizational subunits or work groups is competition between them (see Messick and Mackie, 1989, for a review). Competition between groups or units is a barrier to transferring knowledge since members of one group may not be motivated to share information with another (cf. Szulanski, 1994). Drawing on social identity theory (e.g., see Tajfel, 1981; Turner, Hogg, Oakes, Reicher & Wetherell, 1987), Ashforth and Mael (1989) argued that much of the conflict that occurs between groups in organizations derives from the very existence of different groups. According to social identity theory, individuals' desires for positive self-evaluation lead them to differentiate between social groups by perceiving one's own group more favorably than other groups (Abrams & Hogg, 1990). Thus, the desire to enhance one's social identity leads to more positive perceptions of the "in group" and more negative perceptions of the "out group." While there is disagreement as to the precise mechanism through which in-group biases occur, the in-group bias is very robust (see Brewer, 1979, for a review).

Building on social identity theory, Kramer (1991) argued that categorizing individuals into distinctive groups produces intergroup competition in organizations. Thus, attempts to promote group identity in organizations may also produce intergroup competition. Giving groups distinct names, providing opportunities for members to interact, publicizing the performance of different groups, providing rewards based on the performance of different groups, and other techniques designed to increase group identity are also likely to increase intergroup competition. Intergroup competition, in turn, impairs sharing of information and transfer of knowledge across groups.

There is debate about the minimal conditions necessary to produce in-group favoritism and intergroup competition (e.g., see Insko & Schopler, 1987). Is merely being categorized into groups sufficient to produce in-group biases or do other factors such as differences in interaction and rewards have to be present? Since other factors, such as more interaction within than between groups, typically exist in organizations, it seems likely that in-group favoritism would develop there.

Kramer (1991) noted that organizational settings may be particularly conducive to the development of competition between groups. In organizational settings, it is often difficult or impossible to assess performance in absolute terms. Instead, organizations rely on relative comparisons. Is Department A more or less productive than Department B?

Being perceived as a high-performing department thus means being perceived as performing better than some other department. This emphasis on relative performance exacerbates competition between units, because often the only way a unit can be perceived as high-performing and thereby enhance members' social identity is to be seen as being better than other units. The increased competition between groups thereby limits knowledge sharing across them.

The second factor that affects transfer of knowledge across groups in organizations is the degree of similarity of group contexts. Transfer of knowledge from one situation to another requires some degree of similarity between the two situations for transfer to occur. Much research has been done on transfer at the individual level of analysis. A recurring theme in this research is how difficult it is for an individual to transfer knowledge acquired in one situation to another (Singley & Anderson, 1989). Singley and Anderson (1989) proposed a model of transfer built on Thorndike's earlier identical elements theory of transfer. According to these models, transfer is based upon the elements shared between tasks. The more elements that are shared, the greater the transfer will be.

When one moves from the individual to the group or subunit level of analysis, the likelihood of finding identical elements diminishes. Groups typically develop their own idiosyncratic ways of doing work (Levine & Moreland, 1991). Groups may divide tasks in different ways, use technologies somewhat differently, develop different ways of coordinating and communicating, and develop their own unique cultures. Differences across groups are likely to be accentuated by providing groups autonomy in deciding how to accomplish their work and by encouraging them to develop their own culture and task-performance strategies. Differences in how groups accomplish their tasks make it hard to transfer knowledge from one group to another since knowledge acquired in one group may not be applicable to another.

We saw examples of differences developing in how work was done in our study of truck assembly plants (Argote & Epple, 1990). Two of the plants started out with the identical technology. Over time, one of the plants drastically changed how it used the technology to override key features. After these changes were made, managers at the other plant argued that much of the knowledge acquired at the first plant was not relevant for their operation because the technologies of the two plants were so different.

Research on situated cognition also implies that knowledge may be difficult to transfer across work groups. In this tradition, knowledge is seen as situated—highly dependent upon the particular constellation of people, machines, and conditions that exist at the work site (e.g., see Hutchins, 1991; Lave, 1991; Suchman, 1987). Individuals learn through intensive apprenticeships that expose them to the idiosyncratic conditions that exist in their work settings. Brown and Duquid (1991) provided compelling examples of situated cognition in their study of service technicians. Training manuals were not very helpful for these technicians. Instead they learned their jobs through interacting with other service technicians, customers, and the machines. Stories that other technicians told were often more helpful in diagnosing what was wrong with a machine than the machine's error code because the stories captured idiosyncratic local conditions while the error codes did not. Idiosyncratic local conditions make it very difficult to transfer knowledge across groups.

We have seen instances where local conditions limited the potential of knowledge transfer in our research. For example, one of the organizations we studied was fortunate to have a particularly gifted manager. Over time, the manager assumed more and more responsibilities. Micro changes in the distribution of responsibilities at the organization accumulated to the point where its macro structure started to differ from its sister organizations. These differences in expertise and in the division of labor at the two organizations decreased the relevance of some of the knowledge acquired in one organization for another.

5.9 Promoting Knowledge Transfer Across Organizational Units

It is difficult to transfer knowledge across organizational units. Several reasons why it is difficult for one unit to benefit from the experience of others have to do with the nature of experience. A unit's own experience is likely to be more relevant than the experience of other units. As noted previously, differences in member capabilities, culture, structure, or technology may make knowledge acquired at a different organizational unit less relevant than a unit's own knowledge. Further, a unit's own direct experience may be easier to interpret than the experience of another unit. Causal connections may be clearer and the link between actions and outcomes easier to understand. Thus, there may be inherent differences in the structure of experience that make it easier for an organization to learn from its own experience than from the experience of others.

These inherent differences in experience notwithstanding, organizations seemingly do not fully exploit their opportunities to learn from other organizations or even other parts of their own organization. There are obvious reasons why it is difficult to learn from a competitor, yet even when organizational units are part of the same firm or involved in a cooperative relationship with other firms, knowledge transfer is difficult to achieve (Szulanski, 1996).

The differences documented in the performance of plants that are part of the same firm and produce the same product with similar technology illustrate the difficulty of transferring knowledge across organizational units (Argote & Epple, 1990; Hayes & Clark, 1986). Although it could be argued that some of the knowledge acquired at one plant is not relevant for another, it is hard to explain the dramatic productivity differences between plants on the order of 2:1 by such an argument (Chew, Bresnahan & Clark, 1990). It could also be argued that these plants do learn from one another—and that the learning results in one plant being superior at one point in time and another plant superior at a different point in time. This argument, however, is inconsistent with the data, which generally show that the same relative ranking in productivity may persist across plants for years (e.g., see Argote & Epple, 1990). Thus, the pattern of results suggests that organizations do not take full advantage of the opportunity to transfer knowledge from one part of their operations to another.

How can organizations promote knowledge transfer across their units? Adler and Cole (1993) described how Nummi, the General Motors-Toyota joint venture in Fremont, California, transferred knowledge through minute standardization and documentation of activities. The standardization increased the relevance of knowledge acquired in one part of the establishment for another and the documentation served as a conduit for knowledge to flow from one part of the organization to another. This approach was highly successful in the Nummi environment where a high volume of a homogeneous product was manufactured.

Benefits of knowledge transfer can be achieved, however, even in more decentralized organizations which face more heterogeneous environments. For these units, a balance between standardization and local adaptation is key. Rather than regiment what the units should do, providing them opportunities to interact with each other, to learn "best" practices, and to adapt them to local conditions will be more effective.

Strategies for improving relationships between groups will be helpful in facilitating knowledge sharing among them (see Kramer, 1991). For example, providing incentives for group members to interact by introducing "superordinate goals" (Sherif, 1958) that require the cooperation of different units will increase knowledge sharing. Increasing the salience of higher-level organizational boundaries and emphasizing the need to compete effectively against other firms can also contribute to knowledge sharing within the organization. These approaches are likely to reduce strong in-group favoritism and induce a higher level categorization of belonging to the same organization.

Providing opportunities to interact through conferences and meetings will also foster knowledge sharing. Interaction with members of other groups is likely to reduce in-group favoritism and provide opportunities for group members to see that knowledge acquired by another group may have some relevance to their operation as well. These face-to-face interactions provide opportunities to acquire deep understandings of how and why "best practices" work. Thus, members of organizational units can acquire a deep understanding of the practices of their counterparts that enables them to tailor the practices to local conditions by keeping key features and eliminating superficial ones. These opportunities to interact also contribute to the development of transactive memory systems or meta knowledge of who knows what in the organization that enhance organizational performance (see Chapter 3). Providing opportunities to interact and learn about best practices rather than legislating the adoption of them has the further advantage of providing employees control over their work. In addition to allowing employees to adapt practices to their contexts, the control also has psychological benefits for employees (Tannenbaum, 1968).

Face-to-face methods of communication such as meetings and conferences can be fruitfully supplemented by electronic means once a relationship is established. Electronic means of communication are generally more effective at augmenting existing relationships than establishing new means (Kraut, Egido & Galegher, 1990). Electronic means can be effective at transferring knowledge across organizational units, especially when participants already have some familiarity with each other.

Personnel movement, where feasible, is also an effective means of transferring knowledge across organizational units. As noted previously, people are capable of transferring tacit as well as explicit knowledge. Thus, moving personnel is a particularly potent mechanism for transferring knowledge.

In short, a multiplex approach to knowledge transfer is likely to be most effective. Personal contacts and face-to-face communication are rich communication media (cf. Daft & Lengel, 1984) that are particularly well-suited for identifying information to be transferred and acquiring a deep understanding of it. Personal interactions are likely to be most effective early in the transfer process (cf. Dutton & Starbuck, 1979). Once information has been identified and adapted to the new context, less personal means of communication such as documents, routines, and technology can be very effective. Indeed, if information is to be transferred on a large and consistent scale, it is important that it eventually be embedded in less personal means such as routines and technology. If there is little need to adapt the information to local conditions, an organization can rely less heavily on personal means of communication from the start and rely more heavily on impersonal means such as documents, blueprints, routines, and technology.

At a more macro level, embedding an organizational unit in a superordinate relationship such as a community of practice or a consortia is likely to facilitate knowledge transfer. These relationships lower motivational barriers to knowledge transfer. They also foster communication among members and thereby facilitate the flow of information across groups or departments.

5.10 Conclusion

Transferring knowledge from other groups or organizations is an important source of productivity gains. Although organizations learn more from their own direct experience than from the experience of others, learning from others contributes significantly to a firm's productivity and survival prospects. The ability to transfer knowledge from other groups or organizations and learn from their experience has been found to affect important organizational outcomes, including productivity, timeliness, and survival.

Several factors have been found to increase the likelihood of knowledge transfer across organizational boundaries. Organizations seem particularly open to benefiting from knowledge acquired by other organizations at certain points in their development, such as when they begin operation. Embedding organizations in a superordinate relationship such as a franchise, chain, or network increases the likelihood that knowledge will transfer across the organizations. Proximity and similarity also facilitate knowledge transfer. Codifying knowledge in observable artifacts such as routines also facilitates knowledge transfer. Rich communication mechanisms such as face-to-face interactions and personnel movement are particularly powerful mechanisms for knowledge transfer. These media permit the transfer of tacit as well as explicit knowledge and allow for the acquisition of a deep understanding of the information being transferred. Thus, these mechanisms are particularly well-suited for identifying knowledge to be transferred and adapting it to local conditions. Once the information has been adapted to local conditions, less personal transfer mechanisms such as routines and technology will be particularly useful since they permit the consistent transfer of knowledge on a large scale.

References

Abrams, D., & Hogg, M. A. (Eds.) (1990). *Social identity theory: Constructive and critical advances.* New York: Springer-Verlag.

Adler, P. S. (1990). Shared Learning. *Management Science, 36,* 938-957.

Adler, P. S., & Cole, R. E. (1993). Designed for learning: A tale of two auto plants. *Sloan Management Review, 34*(3), 85-94.

Allen, T. J. (1977). *Managing the flow of technology: Technology transfer and the dissemination of technological information within the R&D organization.* Cambridge, MA: MIT Press.

Ancona, D. G., & Caldwell, D. F. (1992). Bridging the boundary: External activity and performance in organizational teams. *Administrative Science Quarterly, 37,* 634-665.

Appleyard, M. M. (1996). How does knowledge flow? Interfirm patterns in the semiconductor industry. *Strategic Management Journal, 17,* 137-154.

Argote, L., Beckman, S. L., & Epple, D. (1990). The persistence and transfer of learning in industrial settings. *Management Science, 36,* 140-154.

Argote, L., & Darr, E. D. (in press). Repositories of knowledge in franchise organizations: Individual, structural and technological. In G. Dosi, R. Nelson & S. Winter (Eds.), *Nature and dynamics of organizational capabilities.*

Argote, L., & Epple, D. (1990, February 23). Learning curves in manufacturing. *Science, 247,* 920-924.

Ashforth, B. E., & Mael, F. (1989). Social identify theory and the organization. *Academy of Management Review, 14,* 20-39.

Attewell, P (1992). Technology diffusion and organizational learning: The case of business computing. *Organization Science, 3,* 1-19.

Baldwin, T. T., & Ford, J. K. (1988). Transfer of training: A review and direction for future research. *Personnel Psychology, 41,* 63-105.

Barkema, H. G., Bell, J. H. J., & Pennings, J. M. (1996). Foreign entry, cultural barriers, and learning. *Strategic Management Journal, 17,* 151-166.

Baum, J. A. C., & Berta, W. B. (1998, June). *Sources, timing, and speed: Population-level learning by organizations in a longitudinal behavioral simulation.* Paper presented at Carnegie-Wisconsin Conference on Knowledge Transfer and Levels of Learning, Carnegie Mellon University, Pittsburgh, PA.

Baum, J. A. C., & Ingram, P. (1998). Survival-enhancing learning in the Manhattan hotel industry, 1898-1980. *Management Science, 44,* 996-1016.

Benkard, C. L. (1997). *Learning and forgetting: The dynamics of aircraft production.* Working paper, Yale University

Berry, D. C., & Broadbent, D. E. (1987). The combination of explicit and implicit learning processes in task control. *Psychological Research, 49,* 7-15.

Blumenstein, R. (1997, August 4). GM is building plants in developing nations to woo new markets. *The Wall Street Journal,* pp. A1, A4.

Brewer, M. B. (1979). In-group bias in the minimal intergroup situation: A cognitive-motivational analysis. *Psychological Bulletin, 86,* 307-324.

Brown, J. S., & Duguid, P. (1991). Organizational learning and communities of practice: Toward a unified view of working, learning and innovation. *Organization Science, 2*, 40-57.

Browning, L. D., Beyer, J. M., & Shetler, J. C. (1995). Building cooperation in a competitive industry: SEMATECH and the semiconductor industry. *Academy of Management Journal, 38*, 113-151.

Burns, L. R., & Wholey, D. R. (1993). Adoption and abandonment of matrix management programs: Effects of organizational characteristics and interorganizational networks. *Academy of Management Journal, 36*, 106-138.

Burt, R. S. (1987). Social contagion and innovation, cohesion versus structural equivalence. *American Journal of Sociology, 92*, 1287-1335.

Carey, S. (1998, March 24). Management: US Air 'peon' team pilots start-up of low-fare airline. *The Wall Street Journal*, p. B1

Chew, W. B., Bresnahan, T. F., & Clark, K. B. (1990). Measurement, coordination and learning in a multi-plant network. In R. S. Kaplan (Ed.), *Measures for manufacturing excellence* (pp. 129-162). Boston: Harvard Business Press.

Cho, D., Kim, D., & Rhee, D. (1998). Latecomer strategies: Evidence from the semiconductor industry in Japan and Korea. *Organization Science, 9*, 489-505.

Christian, N. M. (1997, June 5). Chrysler suppliers' cost-saving ideas likely to add $325 million to its '97 net. *The Wall Street Journal*, p. A6.

Cohen, W. M., & Levinthal, D. (1990). Absorptive capacity: A new perspective on learning and innovation. *Administrative Science Quarterly, 35*, 128-152.

Cool, K. D., Dierickx, I., & Szulanski, G. (1997). Diffusion of innovations within organizations: Electronic switching in the Bell System, 1971-1982. *Organization Science, 8*, 543-559.

Daft, R. L., & Lengel, R. H. (1984). Information richness: A new approach to managerial behavior and organization design. *Research in Organizational Behavior, 6*, 191-223.

Darr, E. (1994, May 4). *Partner Similarity and Knowledge Transfer in English Franchise Organizations*. Unpublished doctoral dissertation, Carnegie Mellon University.

Darr, E., Argote, L., & Epple, D. (1995). The acquisition, transfer and depreciation of knowledge in service organizations: Productivity in franchises. *Management Science, 41*, 1750-1762.

Davis, G. (1991). Agents without principles? The spread of the poison pill through the intercorporate network. *Administrative Science Quarterly, 36*, 583-613.

DiMaggio, P. J., & Powell, W. W. (1983). The iron cage revisited: Institutional isomorphism and collective rationality in organizational fields. *American Sociological Review, 48*, 147-160.

Dutton, J. M., & Starbuck, W. H. (1979). Diffusion of an intellectual technology. In K. Krippendorff (Ed.), *Communication and control in society* (pp. 489-511). New York: Gordon & Breach Science.

Epple, D., Argote, L., & Devadas, R. (1991). Organizational learning curves: A method for investigating intra-plant transfer of knowledge acquired through learning by doing. *Organization Science, 2*, 58-70.

Epple, D., Argote, L., & Murphy, K. (1996). An empirical investigation of the micro structure of knowledge acquisition and transfer through learning by doing. *Operations Research, 44*, 77-86.

Fair, R. C. (1970). The estimation of simultaneous equation models with lagged endogenous variables and first order serially correlated errors. *Econometrica, 38*, 507-516.

Foster, A. D., & Rosenzweig, M. R. (1995). Learning by doing and learning from others: Human capital and technical change in agriculture. *Journal of Political Economy, 103*, 1176-1209.

Galbraith, C. S. (1990). Transferring core manufacturing technologies in high technology firms. *California Management Review, 32*(4), 56-70.

Ghemawat, P. (1985). Building strategy on the experience curve. *Harvard Business Review, 63*(2), 143-149.

Granovetter, M. (1985). Economic action and social structure: The problem of embeddedness. *American Journal of Sociology, 91*, 481-510.

Hamel, G. (1991). Competition for competence and inter-partner learning within international strategic alliances. *Strategic Management Journal, 12*, 83-103.

Haunschild, P. (1993). Interorganizational imitation: The impact of interlocks on corporate acquisition activity. *Administrative Science Quarterly, 38*, 564-592.

Haunschild, P. R., & Miner, A. S. (1997). Modes of interorganizational imitation: The effects of outcome salience and uncertainty. *Administrative Science Quarterly, 42*, 472-500.

Hausman, J. A. (1978). Specification tests in econometrics. *ECTRA, 46*, 1251-1271.

Hayes, R. H., & Clark, K. B. (1986). Why some factories are more productive than others. *Harvard Business Review, 64*(5), 66-73.

Henderson, R., & Cockburn, I. (1996). Scale, scope and spillovers: The determinants of research productivity in drug discovery. The *Rand Journal of Economics, 27*, 32-59.

Huber, G. P. (1991). Organizational learning: The contributing processes and the literatures. *Organization Science, 2*, 88-115.

Hutchins, E., (1991). Organizing work by adaptation. *Organization Science, 2*, 14-39.

Ingram, P., & Simons, T. (1997). *Interorganizational relations and the performance outcomes of experience.* Working paper, Graduate School of Industrial Administration, Carnegie Mellon University.

Insko, C. A., & Schopler, J. (1987). Categorization, competition and collectivity. In C. Hendrick (Ed.), *Group process* (pp. 213-251). Newbury Park, CA: Sage.

Irwin, D. A., & Klenow, P. J. (1994). Learning-by-doing spillovers in the semiconductor industry. *Journal of Political Economy, 102*, 1200-1227.

Joskow, P. L., & Rose, N. L. (1985). The effects of technological change, experience, and environmental regulation on the construction cost of coal-burning generating units. *The Rand Journal of Economics, 16,* 1-27.

Keller, R. T. & Chinta, R. R. (1990). International technology transfer: Strategies for success. *Academy of Management Executive, 4*(2), 33-43.

Kelsey, S. F., Mullin, S. M., Detre, K. M., Mitchell, H., Cowley, M. J., Gruentzig, A. R., & Kent, K. M. (1984). Effect of investigator experience on percutaneous transluminal coronary angioplasty. *American Journal of Cardiology, 53,* 56C-64C.

Kogut, B. (1988). A study of the life cycles of joint ventures. *Management International Review, 28,* 39-52.

Kogut, B. (1991). Joint ventures and the option to expand and acquire. *Management Science, 37,* 19-33.

Kramer, R. M. (1991). Intergroup relations and organizational dilemmas: The role of categorization processes. *Research in Organizational Behavior, 13,* 191-228.

Kraut, R. E., Egido, C., & Galegher, J. (1990). Patterns of contact and communication in scientific research collaboration. In J. Galegher, R. E. Kraut & C. Egido (Eds.), *Intellectual teamwork: Social and technological foundations of cooperative work* (pp. 149-172). Hillsdale, NJ: Lawwrence Erlbaum.

Lane, F. C. (1951). *Ships for victory: A history of shipbuilding under the U.S. Maritime Commission in World War II.* Baltimore: The Johns Hopkins Press.

Larsson, R., Bengtsson, L., Henriksson, K., & Sparks, J. (1998). The interorganizational learning dilemma: Collective knowledge development in strategic alliances. *Organization Science, 9,* 285-305.

Lave, J. (1991). Situating learning in communities of practice. In L. B. Resnick, J. M. Levine & S. D. Teasley (Eds.), *Perspectives on socially shared cognition* (pp. 63-82). Washington, DC: American Psychological Association

Leonard-Barton, D. (1988). Implementation as mutual adaptation of technology and organization. *Research Policy, 17,* 251-267.

Lester, R. K., & McCabe, M. J. (1993). The effect of industrial structure on learning by doing in nuclear power plant operation. *The Rand Journal of Economics, 24,* 418-438.

Levine, J. M., & Moreland, R. L. (1991). Culture and socialization in work groups. In L. B. Resnick, J. M. Levine & S. D. Teasley (Eds.), *Perspectives on socially shared cognition* (pp. 257-279). Washington, DC: American Psychological Association.

Levitt, B., & March, J. G. (1988). Organizational learning. *Annual Review of Sociology, 14,* 319-340.

Lewis, W. (1993, October 22). The secret to competitiveness. *The Wall Street Journal,* p. A14.

Makhija, M. V., & Ganesh, U. (1997). The relationship between control and partner learning in learning-related joint ventures. *Organization Science, 8*, 508-527.

Mansfield, E. (1985). How rapidly does industrial technology leak out? *The Journal of Industrial Economics, 34*, 217-224.

McEvily, B., & Zaheer, A. (1998). *Bridging ties: A source of firm heterogeneity in competitive capabilities.* Working paper, Graduate School of Industrial Administration, Carnegie Mellon University.

Messick, D. M., & Mackie, D. M. (1989). Intergroup relations. *Annual Review of Psychology, 40*, 45-81.

Meyer, A. D., & Goes, J. B. (1988). Organizational assimilation of innovations: A multilevel contextual analysis. *Academy of Management Journal, 31*, 897-923.

Mishina, K., (1992). *Learning by new experiences.* Working Paper, Harvard Business School.

Mowery, D. C., Oxley, J. E., & Silverman, B. (1996). Strategic alliances and interfirm knowledge transfer. *Strategic Management Journal, 17*, 77-91.

Ounjian, M. L., & Carne, E. B. (1987). A study of the factors which affect technology transfer in a multilocation multibusiness unit corporation. *IEEE Transactions on Engineering Management, EM-34*, 194-201.

Porac, J. F., & Thomas, H. (1994). Cognitive categorization and subjective rivalry among retailers in a small city. *Journal of Applied Psychology, 79*, 54-66.

Powell, W. W., Koput, K. W., & Smith-Doerr, L., (1996). Interorganziational collaboration and the locus of innovation: Networks of learning in biotechnology. *Administrative Science Quarterly, 41*, 116-145.

Reinhardt, A. (1997, May 26). Intel's dreamers make room for a details man. *Business Week*, pp. 125-128.

Rogers, E. (1995). *Diffusion of innovations* (4th ed.). New York: Free Press.

Rothwell, R. (1978). Some problems of technology transfer into industry: Examples from the textile machinery sector. *IEEE Transactions on Engineering Management, EM-25*, 15-20.

Rulke, D., Zaheer, S., & Anderson, M. (1998, June). *Transactive knowledge and performance in the retail food industry.* Paper presented at Carnegie-Wisconsin Conference on Knowledge Transfer and Levels of Learning, Carnegie Mellon University, Pittsburgh, PA.

Scott, W. R. (1987). The adolescence of institutional theory. *Administrative Science Quarterly, 32*, 493-511.

Shan, W., Walker, G., & Kogut, B. (1994). Interfirm cooperation and startup innovation in the biotechnology industry. *Strategic Management Journal, 15*, 387-394.

Sherif, M. (1958). Superordinate goals in the reduction of intergroup conflict. *American Journal of Sociology, 63*, 349-356.

Singley, M. K., & Anderson, J. R. (1989). *The transfer of cognitive skill.* Cambridge, MA: Harvard University Press.

Suchman, L. (1987). *Plans and situated actions: The problem of human-machine communication.* New York: Cambridge University Press.

A survey of manufacturing: Meet the global factory (1998, June 20). *The Economist*, pp. M1-M18.

Szulanski, G. (1994). *Unpacking stickiness: An empirical investigation of the barriers to transfer best practice inside the firm.* Working paper, INSEAD, France.

Szulanski, G. (1996). Exploring internal stickiness: Impediments to the transfer of best practice within the firm. *Strategic Management Journal, 17*, 27-43.

Tajfel, H. (1981). *Human groups and social categories: Studies in social psychology.* Cambridge, England: Cambridge University Press.

Tannenbaum, A. S. (1968). *Control in organizations.* New York: McGraw-Hill.

Tannenbaum, J. A. (1996, May 21). Chicken and burgers create hot new class: Powerful franchisees. *The Wall Street Journal*, pp. A1, A8.

Thompson, L. (1998, June). *Analogical Reasoning in the Transfer of Managerial Knowledge.* Paper presented at Carnegie-Wisconsin Conference on Knowledge Transfer and Levels of Learning, Carnegie Mellon University, Pittsburgh, PA.

Tichy, N., & Charan, R. (1990). Citicorp faces the world: An interview with John Reed. *Harvard Business Review, 68*(6), 135-144.

Tichy, N. M., Tushman, M. L., & Frombrun, C. (1979). Social network analysis for organizations. *Academy of Management Review, 4*, 507-519.

Tolbert, P. S., & Zucker, L. G. (1983). Institutional sources of change in the formal structure of organizations: The diffusion of civil service reform, 1880-1935. *Administrative Science Quarterly, 28*, 22-39.

Turner, J. C., Hogg, M. A., Oakes, P. J., Reicher, S. D., & Wetherell, M. S. (1987). *Rediscovering the social group: A self-categorization theory.* Oxford, England: Basil Blackwell.

Tushman, M. L. (1977). Special boundary roles in the innovation process. *Administrative Science Quarterly, 22*, 587-605.

Tyre, M. J., & Orlikowski, W. J. (1994). Windows of opportunity: Temporal patterns of technological adaptation in organizations. *Organization Science, 5*, 98-118.

Udayajiri, N. D., & Balakrishnan, S. (1993, May). *Learning curves and knowledge spillovers: The case of semiconductor memories.* Paper presented at the TIMS/ORSA Meeting, Chicago.

Uzzi, B. (1996). Sources and consequences of embeddedness for the economic performance of organizations. *American Sociological Review, 61*, 674-698.

von Hippel, E., (1988). *The sources of innovation.* New York: Oxford University Press.

Zander, U., & Kogut, B. (1995). Knowledge and the speed of the transfer and imitation of organizational capabilities: An empirical test. *Organization Science, 6*, 76-92.

Zimmerman, M. B. (1982). Learning effects and the commercialization of new energy technologies: The case of nuclear power. *Bell Journal of Economics, 13*, 297-310.

Chapter 6

Tensions in the Learning Process
and Future Directions

6.1 Introduction

The business press contains many examples of firms exerting effort to reduce their labor costs. For example, a recent report announced that General Motors (GM) Corporation spends over one third more in labor costs per vehicle than Ford (White, 1998). A GM executive was quoted as saying: "We're the high-cost producer. We have a gap that has to be closed (White, 1998, p. A4)."

This example illustrates the importance of differences in labor costs for firm performance. Although low labor costs are only part of the equation for firm success, they are an important contributor to an organization's performance and competitiveness. Further, studies of unit labor costs provide a gauge of the overall learning potential at a firm as well as provide information about an important performance outcome. A firm whose labor costs do not decline with experience may not be adept at interpreting its experience or identifying how to make improvements. An unusually slow decline in labor costs can be an indicator of performance problems along other dimensions at a firm.

As noted in the introductory chapter, recent work on organizational learning is examining a wider set of outcomes than unit labor costs. For example, recent work has been done on the important performance outcomes of quality, timeliness, and survival. Putting these results together with findings about unit labor costs provides a more complete picture of the factors affecting firm success.

Findings presented in previous chapters of this monograph suggest important tensions or trade-offs in the learning process within organizations. This chapter identifies those trade-offs. The chapter also discusses where future research is most needed to arrive at a deeper understanding of organizational learning.

6.2 Tensions or Trade-Offs in Organizational Learning

The work reviewed in this monograph indicates four important tensions or trade-offs in the learning process. The first tension is between *group* and *organizational* learning. Is it better to foster learning at the level of the work group or learning at the level of the organization? The second (and related) tension is between *heterogeneity* and *standardization*: is *heterogeneity* or *standardization* most conducive to organizational learning? The third tension is between *learning by planning* and *learning by doing*. When will planning in advance improve an organization's performance and when will learning through performing be more effective? Finally, the fourth tension is between *fast* and *slow* learning. When is it better to learn quickly and when is it better to learn at a more measured pace? Each of these tensions will now be discussed.

6.2.1 Group Versus Organizational Learning

This section explores the tension between fostering local learning at the level of the work group or organizational subunit versus fostering learning at the level of the organization or larger system in which subunits are embedded. When are benefits of promoting learning at the level of the work group or subunit particularly strong? When can benefits be realized by transferring knowledge across groups and thus promoting learning at the level of the organization? Can organizations simultaneously promote group learning as well as organizational learning or does a focus on one form of learning preclude the other? The section begins with an example that illustrates the tension between group and organizational learning. The conditions under which it will be especially advantageous to foster local learning and those under which it will be advantageous to foster organization-wide learning are then developed.

Adler and Cole (1993) described the tension between learning at different levels of analysis in their comparison of the "democratic Taylorism" approach to production used at the Toyota-GM Nummi plant in California versus the autonomous work group approach once used at Volvo's Uddevalla plant. Adler and Cole presented data suggesting that the Nummi plant was more effective than the Uddevalla plant and argued that the difference in performance was due to an emphasis on organizational (rather than local) learning at Nummi. At Nummi, there is much emphasis on standardization and transferring knowledge across groups and departments so that productivity gains made in one area of the plant can benefit another. By contrast, the Uddevalla plant was viewed by Adler and

Cole as fostering individual or group learning at the expense of organizational learning. Work groups were given a great deal of autonomy; little effort was made at transferring knowledge across them. Thus, a productivity improvement made in one group did not benefit another. As evidence in support of this point, Adler and Cole (1994) noted the unevenness in performance of teams at Uddevalla.

In a rejoinder to the Adler and Cole article, Berggen (1994) argued that the autonomous work groups used at Uddevalla were effective and that a major benefit of those systems was their adaptability and flexibility. There has been considerable discussion in the literature of the conditions under which autonomous work groups improve organizational performance (e.g., see Goodman, Devadas & Hughson, 1988). For the purpose of this monograph, the question is: under what conditions is it most beneficial to promote learning at the group level versus at the organizational level?

In answering this question, this section specifically addresses how the nature of the environment in which groups and organizations operate and the tasks they perform affect the most appropriate balance between group and organizational learning. Although dimensions of the organization's environment and its task are socially determined to some extent, these factors are more "given" or exogenous than dimensions of an organization's structure. Environmental and task factors are more critical in determining the appropriate balance between group and organizational learning than structural factors since structural factors are more under the control of the organization. Structural factors can be designed by the organization to promote or retard group or organizational learning. These issues were discussed in Chapter 5 in the section on promoting knowledge transfer across groups.

The similarity of customer preferences affects the relative balance between group and organizational learning. Do the groups or organizational subunits face environments with customers with very different needs and preferences or are their preferences similar? John Reed, the Chief Executive Officer of Citicorp, discussed this issue in an interview with Noel Tichy and Ram Charan (Tichy & Charan, 1990). Reed argued that there are "more similarities than differences among customers around the world" (Tichy & Charan, 1990, p. 138). Reed emphasized the importance of transferring innovations made in one organizational unit to other units throughout the rest of the world as a source of competitive advantage.

To the extent that customer preferences are similar across groups and organizational units, there are great benefits of transferring knowledge because an innovation made in one group will be relevant for another. Thus, when groups face environments with similar customer preferences, organizational learning and its emphasis on transfer of knowledge across groups or establishments is favored. As customer preferences diverge, local learning at the level of the work group is preferable since these groups are better positioned to adapt to local conditions.

Similarity in customer preferences translates into a more uniform product. Building on the Nummi versus Uddevalla example, discussions of when autonomous work groups will be most effective emphasize that the extent to which the product is uniform is a determining factor. For example, Williams (1994) argued that although autonomous work groups have many benefits, these groups may not be suitable for the production of large numbers of uniform products, such as the final assembly of automobiles.

Thus, when groups face similar customers or produce similar products, there are many advantages to transferring knowledge across groups. Under these conditions, organizational learning is favored. Conversely, when groups face customers with different needs and preferences and/or produce a non-uniform product, there are benefits to providing groups with much autonomy and flexibility so that they can adapt to local conditions. Under these conditions, group learning is favored.

Another major factor indicating the relative balance between group versus organizational learning is the degree of interdependence of the tasks involved. If groups perform tasks that are highly interdependent, organizational learning is favored. Conversely, if groups perform tasks that are low in interdependence and require little interaction, group learning is favored. In systems high in interdependence, the output of one group greatly affects another, whereas in systems low in interdependence, the output of one group is decoupled from that of another (e.g., see Thompson, 1967).

To return to the Nummi versus Uddevalla discussion, car manufacturing is typically characterized by high degrees of interdependence: what happens in one part of the plant (e.g., the body shop) affects what happens in other areas (e.g., the paint shop or final assembly). Tolerances are tight; there is little room for error. Coordination is necessary even in automobile assembly systems organized into autonomous work groups because one group assembles only part of the automobile and that group's sub-assembly has to be integrated with other groups' sub-assemblies. In systems such as these where interdependence across groups is high and coordination needs are correspondingly great, an emphasis on transferring information across groups will have large payoffs.

Levinthal and March (1993) discussed a task factor closely related to interdependence: decomposability. According to Levinthal and March (1993), when the problems an organization faces can be broken down into decomposable or autonomous units, "local" learning is effective since little interaction is required across units. Decomposability is, in part, a function of the scale and complexity of the operation. Some of the operations where productivity has been boosted dramatically by organizing into autonomous work groups or "manufacturing cells" have this property of decomposability (e.g., see Levin, 1994, discussion of assembly of personal computers): all of the work to assemble the product can be accomplished by one group.

Thus, if tasks can be broken down into decomposable units, group or local learning is favored. Conversely, if tasks are highly interdependent, there is a need to transfer knowledge across groups to insure that one group's activities are coordinated with another's. Under those conditions, organizational learning is favored.

This discussion of when to emphasize group learning and when to emphasize organizational learning is somewhat reminiscent of earlier discussions of when to organize along product lines and when to organize along functional lines (e.g., see Duncan, 1979). A lesson learned from analyzing organizational structures is that they are not static. For example, some organizations are centralizing after being decentralized (e.g., see Stata's, 1989, discussion of Analog Devices), while others, such as Xerox, are decentralizing formerly centralized structures.

These structural changes may, in part, be due to changes in environmental or task characteristics that indicate the appropriateness of a different structure. The changes, however, may also be due to an organization's need to coordinate across both functions and products. An organization's primary grouping along product or functional lines facilitates one form of coordination; the other form of coordination is achieved by lateral relations, personal relationships, and the like. Over time, it may become more difficult to coordinate across the non-primary grouping. Personal relationships may atrophy or dissolve through turnover. Proximity, organizational incentives, and the social psychological factors of in-group favoritism discussed in the last chapter increasingly favor interacting more with one's own group and less with other groups. Thus, over time, a product-based organization may find that it is increasingly difficult to coordinate across the different products. An organization may then centralize to transfer knowledge across the different products. Conversely, a functional organization may find that it becomes increasingly difficult to coordinate across the different functions for each product. If problems associated with this lack of coordination are severe, the organization may decentralize into a product organization.

Thus, for some organizations, a product form of organization is appropriate and likely to remain so for a reasonable time period. For other organizations, a functional form of organization is appropriate and likely to remain so. But for many organizations, the forces favoring one form of organization are only slightly stronger than the forces favoring another.

Matrix organizations are one solution to this dilemma. They are challenging to manage, however, and have a somewhat mixed record of success (Davis & Lawrence, 1977). Another solution to the dilemma is to alternate over time between different forms of organizing as a way of achieving the benefits of both product and functional organizations.

The same may be true of group versus organizational learning. Some organizations may be well-served by emphasizing group learning while others may be better served by placing relatively more emphasis on organizational learning. The similarity of environmental and task conditions and the interdependence of groups or subunits are important factors that affect the relative balance between group and organizational learning. For some organizations, however, these factors may not clearly favor one form of learning over another. These organizations will need to achieve learning at both levels.

Achieving learning at both organizational and group levels is difficult. Basing his arguments on evolutionary theory, March (1991) argued that strategies that improve the survival of a system's components may not be the same as strategies that improve the survival of the system as a whole. The social psychological arguments developed in Chapter 5 also suggest that it may be difficult to promote group and organizational learning simultaneously. Providing groups with considerable autonomy and allowing them to develop their own unique task performance strategies undermines an organization's ability to transfer knowledge across groups. Conversely, transferring knowledge across groups requires some degree of standardization which can conflict with the emphasis on group autonomy. For these organizations where both group and organizational learning are favored, one may see an alteration of focus on one form of learning versus the other over time.

6.2.2 Heterogeneity Versus Standardization

The second (and related) tension is between *heterogeneity* and *standardization*. When is it better to foster heterogeneity of experience in an organization and when is it better to encourage standardization? An organization can foster heterogeneity of experience by employing individuals with different backgrounds, using different technologies, experimenting with different structures, encouraging different strategies, and so on. Alternatively, an organization can foster standardization by hiring similar members, socializing them intensely, using similar procedures and technologies, and discouraging experimentation. The fundamental tension is that some heterogeneity of experience is needed to generate new combinations and create new knowledge while some standardization is needed to develop common understandings and transfer knowledge throughout the enterprise.

This tension is related to the previously described tension between group and organizational learning. An organization that fosters learning at the level of the group is more likely to have a diverse experience base than one that fosters learning at the level of the organization. Thus, factors that lead an organization to promote learning at one level over another also lead an organization to favor heterogeneity of experience over standardization. For example, a similar customer base would favor standardization while dissimilar customers would require heterogeneity to meet their different needs. A tightly coupled organization where components are highly interdependent requires standardization because one component's actions directly affect another's. By contrast, an organization where components are less dependent on each other would not require standardization and may benefit from heterogeneity. In addition, organizations performing creative tasks (cf. Jackson, May & Whitney, 1995) or facing turbulent environments (cf. Moorman & Miner, 1997) are more likely to benefit from heterogeneity than their counterparts who perform less creative tasks in less turbulent environments.

Although the tension between heterogeneity and standardization has much in common with the tension between group and organizational learning, the heterogeneity versus standardization trade-off highlights different aspects of the learning process. The trade-off between heterogeneity and standardization highlights that different factors may be more important in the creation of knowledge than in the transfer of knowledge. Heterogeneity fosters the development of new knowledge. For example, groups composed of diverse members have been found to be better at generating new or emergent knowledge and developing more sophisticated solutions than groups composed of similar members (see Chapter 4). By contrast, standardization promotes knowledge transfer (see the Nummi example, as described by Adler and Cole, 1993). Standardization increases the relevance of knowledge acquired in one unit for another. Standardization (and the accompanying documentation and routines) also provides mechanisms for knowledge to transfer from one unit to another.

Organizations can handle the tension between heterogeneity and standardization to some extent by encouraging units engaged primarily in knowledge creation, such as Research and Development departments, to have a more diverse experience base (e.g., by promoting diversity of members' backgrounds and encouraging experimentation) than units such as production where knowledge creation is not the primary goal. The approach should be used with appreciation that too much diversity can be harmful even for knowledge-creation tasks such as research if the diversity results in a lack of shared values or goals (cf. Owens & Neale, 1998). Further, some degree of diversity may be beneficial—even for groups such as production not explicitly charged with knowledge creation—because innovation and learning occur in these groups as well (cf. Brown & Duguid, 1991). Indeed, in our studies of production facilities, we saw many instances of new knowledge being created (see also von Hippel & Trye, 1995).

Another approach to dealing with the tension between heterogeneity and standardization is to foster heterogeneity during certain phases of the product's life cycle and standardization during others. This approach is related to the first since different organizational departments tend to specialize somewhat in different phases of a product's life cycle. Diversity is most likely to be beneficial in the development, design and initial launching of a product while standardization is most beneficial during its production. This approach is consistent with the finding that diversity fosters creativity (Jackson, May & Whitney, 1995) as well as with the finding that too much diversity (as measured by engineering change orders) can harm productivity (Hayes & Clark, 1986). The approach has merit but should be used with appreciation that some diversity may still be beneficial even after an organization goes into the production phase and some standardization is needed even in the research and development stage. The approach should also be used with acknowledgement that there is feedback and recycling across the phases of a product's life cycle and some of them occur concurrently.

The tension between heterogeneity and standardization is related to the tension between exploiting old competencies and exploring new possibilities eloquently described by March (1991). According to March, maintaining the right balance between exploitation and exploration is key to organizational survival and prosperity. Too much emphasis on exploitation can lead an organization to fall into a "competency trap" (Lant & Mezias, 1990; Levitt & March, 1988) whereby it persists in a strategy it perfected that may no longer be optimal. Too much emphasis on exploration can lead to a lack of depth or distinctive competence for a firm.

The right balance between exploration and exploitation is difficult to achieve or maintain. Since the rewards to exploitation are more immediate and certain, exploitation often drives out exploration in organizations (March, 1991). Ford's production of the Model T Ford is a classic example of the costs incurred by a firm when exploitation drove out exploration (Abernathy & Wayne, 1974). Ford became so proficient at producing the Model T that it neglected exploring other options that turned out to be more attractive to customers (see Leonard-Barton, 1992, for further discussion of "rigidities" that impair organizational performance).

Although the balance between exploration and exploitation is difficult to achieve, some organizations are adept at both. Tushman and Anderson (1986) examined whether competence-enhancing or competence-destroying innovations were most likely to come from incumbent firms or new entrants to an industry. Competence-enhancing innovations build on the existing knowledge base and are therefore related to exploitation. By contrast, competence-destroying innovations depart form the existing knowledge base and involve experimentation and exploration. Results indicated that competence-enhancing innovations generally came from incumbent firms in an industry. Although competence-destroying innovations came primarily from new entrants in the cement industry, they came about equally from both incumbent firms and new entrants in the computer industry (Tushman & Anderson, 1986). Thus, some incumbent firms in the computer industry were able to make both competence-enhancing and competence-destroying innovations (cf. Dahlin & Casciaro, 1998). That is, some organizations were able to benefit from both exploitation and exploration. How these organizations exploit existing competencies while exploring new ones is an important topic that would benefit from future research.

6.2.3 Learning by Planning Versus Learning by Doing

The third tension in the learning process is between *learning by planning* versus *learning by doing*. When will planning in advance result in desirable outcomes for the organization? When is learning by doing the best way to proceed?

A few studies have explicitly addressed whether learning by planning or learning by doing is the preferred mode of knowledge acquisition for firms. Pisano (1994) contrasted how an emphasis on laboratory experimentation (learning *before* doing or planning) affected process development lead times in traditional chemical-based pharmaceuticals and newer biotechnology-based pharmaceuticals. Results indicated that the extent to which the underlying scientific knowledge base was well-understood determined the effectiveness of learning *before* doing (planning in our terminology). For chemical-based pharmaceuticals, where the underlying knowledge base was well-understood, an emphasis on laboratory experimentation and learning *before* doing was associated with more rapid development. In contrast, for biotechnology-based pharmaceuticals where the underlying knowledge base was not well-understood, hours invested in laboratory research did not shorten project lead times. Pisano concluded that the nature of a firm's knowledge base influenced the effectiveness of learning strategies. Deep knowledge of the effect of specific variables and their interactions or higher "stages" of knowledge (cf. Bohn, 1994) increased the effectiveness of planning and learning *before* doing. By contrast, learning *by* doing is indicated when organizations do not have the underlying knowledge base needed to simulate effects in advance. Under these conditions, it is only through learning *by* doing that an organization acquires an understanding of how variables interact to affect performance. Von Hippel and Tyre (1995) made a similar argument in their analysis of problem identification on the factory floor.

Similarly, Eisenhardt and Tabrizi (1995) concluded that learning by doing was more effective than planning for launching uncertain new products in the computer industry. Planning slowed the pace of product development while learning by doing (measured by design iterations and testing) accelerated the pace. Eisenhardt and Tabrizi (1995) argued that in uncertain settings improvisational approaches that combine real-time learning and testing are more effective than planning. Similarly, Argote (1982) found that relying on nonprogrammed means of coordination that involved mutual adjustment on the part of hospital staff were more effective than relying on programmed means when the uncertainty characterizing inputs was high.

The extent to which knowledge is dependent on the context also affects the relative effectiveness of planning and learning by doing. An example of knowledge that is not very dependent on the context is how to calculate net present value or other financial measures. The methods for calculations do not vary as a function of features of a particular organizational context. When knowledge is not dependent on the specific people, machines, cultures, or structures in place at a firm, planning in advance is very effective.

By contrast, when knowledge is dependent on the context, learning by doing is key. When knowledge is dependent on people, structures, and technologies in place at a firm, it is difficult to predict in advance the effects of these variables and their interactions. Under these conditions, the best way to learn is by doing. An example of such context-dependent knowledge is the best allocation of individuals to tasks. The best allocation is difficult to predict with confidence without experience with the particular people, machines, structures, and culture in place at an organization. Through actually performing a task, individuals learn about their own skills, the skills of their colleagues, the capabilities of the equipment, the limits of the structure, and so on. Thus, when knowledge is context-dependent, learning by doing is critical to successful performance.

Recent studies of the effects of individual versus group training on performance also support the effectiveness of learning by doing as a method of knowledge acquisition. In the prototypical study, some participants are given training and opportunities to practice as a group; other participants are given training and practice as individuals. When participants subsequently perform as a group, the performance of those who already practiced the task as a group is superior to the performance of those who practiced initially as individuals (e.g., see Hollingshead, 1998; Liang, Moreland & Argote, 1995). Practice as a group provides participants with opportunities to acquire context-dependent knowledge, (e.g., such as knowledge of other's skills) which improves their performance (Liang, Moreland & Argote, 1995).

In short, several factors have been found to affect the relative effectiveness of learning by planning and learning by doing. Planning will be more effective when the knowledge base is well-understood, when the knowledge is less dependent on the context, and when the task is more certain. Conversely, learning by doing is the preferred learning mode when the knowledge is uncertain, not well-understood, and highly dependent on the organizational context.

6.2.4 Fast Versus Slow Learning

A tension related to the tension between learning by planning and learning by doing is the tension between *fast* and *slow* learning.[1] Some scholars have advocated the benefits of fast learning. For example, Eisenhardt and Tabrizi (1995) advocated fast learning for uncertain tasks where it is difficult to predict in advance how best to proceed. According to Eisenhardt and Tabrizi (1995), for uncertain tasks, moving quickly to the stage where one is actually producing a product and learning through successive iterations and testing is the most effective way to launch a new product. Similarly, Boehm, Gray and Seewaldt (1984) argued that rapid prototyping approaches, in which software designs go back and forth between the designer and the user, are better at creating a good fit between the design and the users' needs and require less effort than methods that rely upon users' specifying their needs in advance.

Other scholars have advocated the consideration of slow learning. Based on simulation results, March and his colleagues concluded that fast learning can lead to premature specialization in a suboptimal strategy and thus to poorer performance over the long run (e.g., see Herriott, Levinthal & March, 1985; Levinthal and March, 1981; March, 1991). By contrast, slower learning leads to the exploration of a wider set of strategies that can enhance long-term performance. Thus, it may not be advantageous to be a fast learner if being a fast learner forecloses options prematurely.

In manufacturing organizations, striking a balance between being fast to start production but producing a small number of units initially may be the best strategy. Being fast to start production provides a firm with opportunities to learn how a design and prototype translates into an actual product and how production depends on the technology, people, culture, and procedures in place at the firm. Ramping up production slowly provides a firm with opportunities to identify and correct problems while they apply to a small rather than to a large number of units.

The tension between fast and slow learning relates to the advantages and disadvantages of being a "first mover," the first organization to launch a new product. Researchers have examined the conditions under which it is better to be a first mover and when it is better to be a follower. Lieberman and Montgomery (1988), for example, concluded that several mechanisms created advantages for first movers: learning benefits associated with accumulating a large stock of cumulative output, benefits associated with patents, benefits associated with preempting scarce resources such as desirable locations, and reputational benefits or costs associated with changing products that bind customers to early movers.

Similarly, Cho, Kim and Rhee (1998) grouped sources of early mover advantage into three categories: the market, the competition, and the firm itself. Market factors include reputational or loyalty effects as well as costs customers bear when they switch to a different product that favor early movers. Competitive effects include the ability of early movers to preempt limited opportunities in areas such as natural resources, location, suppliers, and employees. Firm-level factors include the benefits of learning how to develop, produce and market a product sooner than others. Conversely, sources of early mover disadvantage include "free-rider" effects through which a follower benefits from knowledge acquired by an early entrant, shifts in customer preferences or technology, and inertial forces that may make it hard for an incumbent to change (Cho, Kim & Rhee, 1998; Lieberman & Montgomery, 1988).

New results on organizational learning suggest an additional factor that should be considered in calculating the advantages of being a first mover: the extent of knowledge depreciation. If knowledge depreciates, the benefits of being a first mover are less than if knowledge is cumulative and persists through time. If knowledge depreciates, a follower would not be at a competitive disadvantage relative to a first mover if the recent output of the follower is comparable to that of the first mover. Knowledge depreciation may explain why late entrants to some industries have been so successful.

New results on knowledge transfer underscore the importance of the extent of knowledge transfer as a key factor affecting the success of early movers. As noted previously, knowledge can transfer across firms in an industry through a variety of mechanisms, including personnel movement, suppliers, consultants, trade associations, and the like. If knowledge transfer occurs, the benefits of being a first mover are less than when knowledge can be kept proprietary (see also Lieberman, 1987). When knowledge transfers, a follower can appropriate knowledge acquired by a first mover.

Korean firms provide examples of late entrants who competed successfully with early movers in the semiconductor industry, especially in the production of Dynamic Random Access Memory (DRAM) chips (Cho, Kim & Rhee, 1998). Although Korean firms did not enter the semiconductor market until the 1980s, a Korean firm, Samsung, achieved the seventh position in total world-wide semiconductor production and the first position in DRAM production by the 1990s (Cho, Kim & Rhee, 1998). Two other Korean firms ranked in the world's top ten producers of DRAM chips by the 19990s.

According to Cho, Kim and Rhee (1998), knowledge transfer figured prominently in the success of Korean firms. Korean chip makers transferred knowledge from universities and firms in the United States by hiring Korean scientists who were trained and had worked there. Korean firms also transferred knowledge from Japanese firms, particularly Toshiba. In addition, Korean firms learned from suppliers and contractors who had worked with early entrants to the industry. Further, Korean firms may have transferred knowledge from previous products they manufactured in related industries. Thus, when knowledge transfers across firms in an industry, the benefits of being an early mover are considerably less than when knowledge does not transfer. Under conditions of knowledge transfer, a new entrant may be able to compete effectively against incumbent firms.

6.3 Future Directions

Four new trends in research on organizational learning curves were noted in Chapter 1: examining a wider set of outcome measures, understanding why some firms are more productive than others, analyzing the dynamics of knowledge acquisition and loss by firms, and understanding the conditions under which knowledge transfers across organizations. I expect and encourage research to continue on all four fronts—with some modifications.

Examining a wider set of outcome measures and also different organizational contexts, including more service settings, should continue. This will help us understand the boundary conditions under which the learning results described here hold. More importantly, since different outcomes may be generated by different processes, studying different outcomes will provide a deeper understanding of the learning process. For example, factors that contribute to quality improvements in service interactions may overlap only partially with those contributing to productivity gains in manufacturing. Factors that affect the survival prospects of a firm are likely to differ somewhat from those determining its efficiency. Investigating different dependent variables requires investigating different independent variables and thereby leads to a more complete picture of factors affecting organizational learning.

Understanding why some firms are more productive than others or why some firms are better at learning than others should continue to be an overarching question that motivates research. Rather than design studies to address such a general question, however, it will be more fruitful to design studies that analyze the contribution of specific factors to organizational learning in depth. Studies, for example, that compare the effects of different types of training or different methods of communication will be more productive at this point than studies that aim to assess whether training or communication (or some other variable) matters. Specifying (and testing) the conditions under which key variables affect organizational learning will be most fruitful. Thus, a "conditions-seeking" approach that identifies the conditions under which particular variables have desired effects on organizational learning outcomes is needed (Greenwald, Pratkanis, Leippe & Baumgardner, 1986).

Additional analyses of the dynamics of knowledge acquisition and depreciation in firms are needed. Identifying the conditions under which knowledge depreciation occurs would be a major contribution. A greater understanding of how both firm-level and industry-level factors affect knowledge depreciation is needed. Studies that examine the micro processes through which knowledge is retained in firms and the implications of where and how knowledge is retained for firm performance are likely to be fruitful. More macro analyses that examine, for example, the implications of knowledge depreciation for the structure of industries and strategic behavior of firms (e.g., see Benkard, 1997) would also provide significant information. Thus, analyses that increase our understanding of the conditions under which depreciation occurs and the implications of depreciation for firm performance are needed.

A greater understanding of the dynamics of knowledge transfer is also needed. Developing the conditions under which knowledge transfers and the implications of knowledge transfer for firm and industry performance would be major contributions. Studies that examine the micro processes through which knowledge transfers within and across firms are likely to be fruitful. More macro analyses of knowledge transfer across populations (e.g., see Mezias & Lant, 1994; Miner & Haunschild, 1995) will also provide significant information. Additional studies that examine knowledge transfer in an international context would also make important contributions. These international knowledge transfer studies provide information about a phenomenon that is important in its own right as well as provide more interesting variation on independent variables, such as culture, that may explain differences in knowledge transfer patterns across organizations. Understanding the dynamics of knowledge transfer will also shed light on the dynamics of knowledge retention in firms since an organization has to retain knowledge in order to transfer it.

In addition to further research on the four themes already described, research that explicitly examines the tensions or trade-offs in the learning process will also be fruitful. This research will help crystallize the conditions under which a particular learning strategy will be most effective for a firm.

We know relatively more about knowledge retention and transfer than we know about knowledge creation in organizations. Entrepreneurial firms may provide important opportunities for examining how knowledge is created in organizations. Most entrepreneurial firms are small enough that researchers can more readily observe learning processes in them than in large established organizations. In addition, entrepreneurial firms are new enough that one can study organizational learning from the beginning of a firm's operation. Thus, researchers could observe the building of connections and establishment of relationships that are central to organizational learning models (cf. Huberman, 1996). Thus, entrepreneurial firms seem to be especially promising sites for studying knowledge creation.

This monograph has presented evidence that organizations vary tremendously in the rates at which they learn. The monograph has argued that differences in patterns of knowledge creation, retention, and transfer contribute to differences in the rates at which organizations learn. The monograph has synthesized the significant set of findings we already know about knowledge creation, retention, and transfer. A greater understanding of these factors would further our understanding of organizational learning and provide additional insights about how to improve firm performance.

Note

1.   The discussion of fast and slow learning here differs somewhat from the discussion of fast and slow rates of learning in the learning-curve framework (see Chapter 1). The discussion of fast and slow learning here refers to how quickly a firm begins production and its attempted rate of output. By contrast, the learning rate in the learning-curve framework refers to the rate at which productivity (or some other outcome) improves with experience. A firm that adopts a fast learning strategy in the sense described here would quickly start to produce a reasonable volume of output. This firm may or may not have a fast rate of learning in the learning-curve framework. In order for the firm to have a fast rate of learning in the learning-curve framework, the cost of producing each unit of output would have to decline rapidly with experience.

References

Abernathy, W. J., & Wayne, K. (1974). Limits of the learning curve. *Harvard Business Review, 52*(5), 109-119.

Adler, P. S., & Cole, R. E. (1993). Designed for learning: A tale of two auto plants. *Sloan Management Review, 34*(3), 85-94.

Adler, P. S., & Cole, R. E. (1994). Rejoinder, *Sloan Management Review, 35*(2), 45-49.

Argote, L. (1982). Input uncertainty and organizational coordination in hospital emergency units. *Administrative Science Quarterly, 27*, 420-434.

Benkard, C. L. (1997). *Dynamic equilibrium in the commercial aircraft market.* Working paper, Department of Economics, Yale University.

Berggen, C. (1994). Nummi vs. Uddevalla. *Sloan Management Review, 35*(2), 37-45.

Boehm, B. W., Gray, T. E., & Seewaldt, T. (1984). Prototyping versus specifying: A multiproject experiment. *IEEE Transactions on Software Engineering, SE-10*(3), 290-303.

Bohn, R. E. (1994). Measuring and managing technological knowledge. *Sloan Management Review, 36*(1), 61-73.

Brown, J. S., & Duguid, P. (1991). Organizational learning and communities of practice: Toward a unified view of working, learning and innovation. *Organization Science, 2*, 40-57.

Cho, D., Kim, D., & Rhee, D. (1998). Latecomer strategies: Evidence from the semiconductor industry in Japan and Korea. *Organization Science, 9*, 489-505.

Dahlin, K., & Casciaro, T. (1998, August). *Radical or incremental? A new measure of novelty value in innovations.* Paper presented at the Academy of Management meetings, San Diego, CA.

Davis, S. M., & Lawrence, P. R. (1977). *Matrix.* Reading, MA: Addison-Wesley.

Duncan, R. (1979). What is the right organizational structure? Decision tree analysis provides the answer. *Organizational Dynamics, 7*(winter), 59-79.

Eisenhardt, K. M., & Tabrizi, B. N. (1995). Accelerating adaptive processes: Product innovation in the global computer industry. *Administrative Science Quarterly, 40,* 84-110.

Goodman, P. S., Devadas, R., & Hughson, T. (1988). Groups and productivity: Analyzing the effectiveness of self-managing teams. In J. P. Campebell, R. S. Campbell & Associates Eds.), *Productivity in organizations* (pp. 295-327). San Francisco: Jossey Bass

Granovetter, M. (1985). Economic action and social structure: The problem of embeddedness. *American Journal of Sociology, 91,* 481-510.

Greenwald, A. G., Pratkanis, A. R., Leippe, M. R., & Baumgardner, M. H. (1986). Under what conditions does theory obstruct research progress? *Psychological Review, 93,* 216-229.

Hayes, R. H., & Clark, K. B. (1986). Why some factories are more productive than others. *Harvard Business Review, 64*(5), 66-73.

Herriott, S. R., Levinthal, D., & March, J. G. (1985). Learning from experience in organizations. *American Economic Review, 75,* 298-302.

Huberman, B. A. (1996). *The dynamics of organizational learning.* Working paper, Xerox Palo Alto Research Center, Palo Alto, CA.

Jackson, S. E., May, K. E., & Whitney, K. (1995). Understanding the diversity of dynamics in decision making teams. In R. A. Guzzo, E. Salas and Associates, *Team effectiveness and decision making in organizations,* (pp. 204-261). San Francisco: Jossey-Bass.

Lant, T. K., & Mezias, S. J. (1990). Managing discontinuous change: A simulation study of organizational learning and entrepreneurship. *Strategic Management Journal, 11*(summer special issue), 147-179.

Leonard-Barton, D. (1992). Core capabilities and core rigidities: A paradox in managing new product development. *Strategic Management Journal, 13,* 111-125.

Levin, D. P. (1994, November 13). Compaq storms the PC heights from its factory floor. *The New York Times,* p. F5.

Levinthal, D. A., & March, J. G. (1981). A model of adaptive organizational search. *Journal of Economic Behavior in Organizations, 2,* 307-333.

Levinthal, D. A., & March, J. G. (1993). The myopia of learning. *Strategic Management Journal, 1*(winter special issue), 95-112.

Levitt, B., & March, J. G. (1988). Organizational learning. *Annual Review of Sociology, 14,* 319-340.

Lieberman, M. B. (1987). The learning curve, diffusion, and competitive strategy. *Strategic Management Journal, 8,* 441-452.

Lieberman, M. B., & Montgomery, D. B. (1988). First-mover advantages. *Strategic Management Journal, 9,* 41-58.

March, J. G. (1991). Exploration and exploitation in organizational learning. *Organization Science, 2,* 71-87.

Mezias, S. J., & Lant, T. K. (1994). Mimetic learning and the evolution of organizational populations. In J. A. C. Baum & J. V. Singh (Eds.), *Evolutionary Dynamics of Organizations* (pp. 179-198). New York: Oxford University Press.

Miner, A. S., & Haunschild, P. R. (1995). Population level learning. *Research in Organizational Behavior, 17*, 115-166.

Owens, D., & Neale, M. (1998, June). *The dubious benefit of group heterogeneity in highly uncertain tasks: Too much of a good thing?* Paper presented at Carnegie-Wisconsin Conference on Knowledge Transfer and Levels of Learning, Carnegie Mellon University, Pittsburgh, PA.

Pisano, G. P. (1994). Knowledge, integration, and the locus of learning: An empirical analysis of process development. *Strategic Management Journal, 15*, 85-100.

Stata, R. (1989). Organizational learning: The key to management innovation. *Sloan Management Review, 30*(3), 63-74.

Thompson, J. D. (1967). *Organizations in action.* New York: McGraw-Hill.

Tichy, N., & Charan, R. (1990). Citicorp faces the world: An interview with John Reed. *Harvard Business Review, 68*(6), 135-144.

Tushman, M. L., & Anderson, P. (1986). Technological discontinuities and organizational environments. *Administrative Science Quarterly, 31*, 439-465.

von Hippel, E., & Tyre, M. J. (1995). How learning by doing is done: Problem identification in novel process equipment, *Research Policy, 24*, 1-12.

White, J. B. (1998, July 16). Wide gap exists between GM, rivals in labor productivity, report says. *The Wall Street Journal*, p. A4.

Williams, M. (1994, October 24). Some plants tear out long assembly lines, switch to craft work. *The Wall Street Journal*, pp. A1, A6.

Index